The Definitive California
Bed & Breakfast

CW01521234

by Stephen P. Gittings
& John R.H. Walker

Published by Travel Print International, Inc.
Berkeley & San Francisco, California

Printed by Quebecor

The Definitive California Bed & Breakfast Touring Guide 1994

Authors
Stephen Gittings
John R.H. Walker

Art Direction/Design
Stephen Gittings

Production Manager
John Vegher

Photography
Frank S. Balthis
Stephen Gittings
Leroy Radanovich
Odin Riedel
John R.H. Walker
Gordon Wiltsie
Photographic contributions
from innkeepers

Director of Marketing
John R.H. Walker

Production Assistants/Writers
Mary Bunnett
Terri Walker
Melissa Greenblatt

Editors
Melissa Greenblatt
Jessie Wood

© 1994 by Travel Print International
Published by Travel Print International

Film and color seperations
by COLORIP. Oakland CA.

For further information contact
Travel Print International, Inc. at
1-800-CAL-TOUR.

Library of Congress Catalog Card
Number 92-091041

ISBN 1-882641-00-0

PREFACE

It's never been done before—"Lifestyles of the Rich and Famous" meets "Bay Area Back Roads"—or rather, "California Back Roads." And it's done in color and style. We decided to produce this book after looking closely at the other bed and breakfast guides available. We felt that black-and-white artistic impressions of inns were inadequate and often misleading. We wanted our readers to get a *real* look at California's incredible variety of bed and breakfast inns, and believed that it was time to bring the traditional bed and breakfast guidebooks into the twentieth century by replacing the simple black-and-white drawings and lengthy text with glowing full-color photographs, concise descriptions, and our highly informative symbol guide. We also wanted to list each inn without favor or criticism.

What we came up with is a large amount of easily digestible information that allows *you* to choose the inn that suits your own priorities of style, location, price, facilities, and general ambiance. All of the inns featured in **The Definitive California Bed and Breakfast Touring Guide** meet our exacting standards. The restaurants we list were recommended by the innkeepers we interviewed, as well as by local editors and cognoscenti. They cover a range of prices and culinary styles, from roadhouses to exotic Thai and Indian restaurants. We have also included listings of wineries in each of the nine wine-producing regions of California.

As far as we can tell, our book is the only comprehensive bed and breakfast touring guide available for all of California. Our survey maps clearly show the locations of inns throughout the state. With this touring guide, we hope that even the places you don't have time to visit will come alive through our photographs and descriptions.

Bon Voyage!

Contents

Introduction

At last—the first full-color, full-listing, and full-of-information touring guide to the bed and breakfast inns of California, the most exciting state in America. The luxurious mansions, rustic cabins, and antique-filled hideaways presented here are as much a part of the California experience as surfing, Yosemite, Disneyland, the Golden Gate Bridge, and Hollywood. We believe that we have created a perfect match by placing this bed and breakfast publication in its rightful setting, a touring guide.

As a transplanted European, I was thrilled to discover the existence of these beautiful inns. Since I moved to California, I have made it a habit to get away at every opportunity to enjoy this unique style of living, if only for a weekend. The hospitality and knowledge that all innkeepers pride themselves on have saved me time and money. In addition, they have kept me informed about the wonders that I might have missed by staying in an impersonal and expensive hotels.

The Definitive California Bed and Breakfast Touring Guide grew out of my fascination with this unique aspect of California life. The guide includes a comprehensive listing of California bed and breakfast inns, many of which subscribe to our toll-free reservation service. Each listing is accompanied by a color photograph and a description that, along with an exclusive symbol guide, gives total information at a glance. In addition, the book includes a list of restaurants recommended by the innkeepers, which represents the best in American and international cuisine. Finally, we have included a winery guide for the thirsty traveller who would like to sample one of California's finest products. A list of wineries appears at the end of each wine-growing section in this book. I feel that this book offers more information, in a more compact form, than any other guide I have seen.

The wide variety of bed and breakfast accommodations offers the traveller a pleasant alternative to the modern, impersonal hotel or motel. You might stay in a private residence, sharing the owner's home, or in a large, luxurious mansion. There are also historic lodges, quaint cottages, farmhouses, vineyards, elegant small inns, and charming bed and breakfast hotels. The one thing that all of the accommodations listed in this book have in common is warm, personal service that is designed to make you feel at home.

You will often be greeted with flowers and chocolates in your room and wine, cheese, and fruit for refreshment. All of the accommodations we list provide a secure and comfortable environment where one can relax and enjoy American home-cooking and hospitality. These inns offer a high standard of comfort and cleanliness, and the price includes a delicious breakfast.

In addition to personal service and attention to detail, you will enjoy a sense of peace and tranquillity that is difficult to find in larger hotels, and the feeling of safety and security that comes from being a guest in someone's home. Apart from the home-away-from-home atmosphere that these accommodations provide, there is also the pleasure of meeting new people in a relaxed and informal setting. Many lifelong friendships have begun across the breakfast table or around the fireplace. Of course, if you prefer privacy, there are numerous secluded, romantic cottages and suites with complete kitchens and well-stocked refrigerators.

Your hosts will prove a valuable source of inside knowledge about what the surrounding area has to offer. You may obtain historical and cultural information as well as advice on the best walks, local attractions, restaurants, and shops. You actually feel that you have joined a small community for a brief moment and experienced its lifestyle. Although California's history is fairly short by European and Asian standards, it has many colorful and fascinating industries and communities. Los Angeles has the film industry. San Francisco offers international flair and sophistication. Carmel and Mendocino have their artistic centers. You can enjoy a stay at a fishing resort or a historical gold or silver mining area. The ski resorts are adjacent to gambling casinos. The farming communities of the Central Valley descend into the deserts of Southern California that are rich with the history of American Indians. In addition to these familiar and populated areas, there are also fascinating out-of-the-way regions of California that may not have fancy hotels, but that often boast exceptionally warm and welcoming bed and breakfast inns.

This guidebook is designed for the traveller who wishes to explore one area thoroughly, as well as for the adventurer who wants to rent a car and enjoy all that the state of California has to offer. We begin our journey in San Francisco and travel north along the Pacific coast to the Oregon border, where we head inland to explore the mountains. From there we descend to the deserts and then to the coastal cities of Southern California. We return north along the spectacular coast highway, back to San Francisco. Throughout our journey several writers have contributed unique introductory descriptions for each region, together with the historical aspects of each point of interest. Whether you decide to visit one small part or all of California, with this guidebook in hand you will be prepared to experience California to the fullest. We hope that wherever you go in California, your vacation will be full of happy memories—and of course, great photographs.

Stephen Gittings

Berkeley, California
January 1993

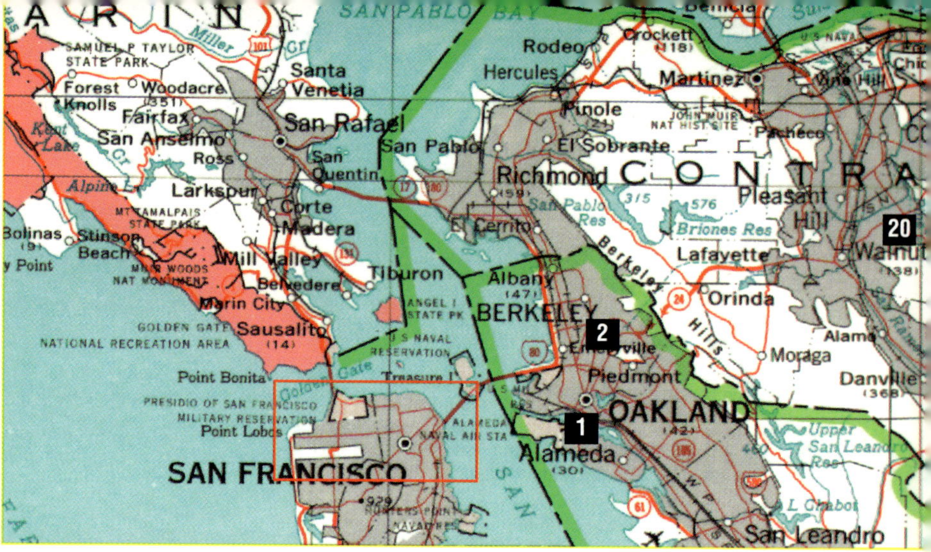

Map 1 — Bay Area (top)

M A R I N

SAN PABLO BAY

SAMUEL P TAYLOR STATE PARK
Forest Knolls
Woodacre
Santa Venetia
San Anselmo
Fairfax
Ross
Larkspur
San Rafael
San Quentin
Corte Madera
Mill Valley
Tiburon
Belvedere
Marin City
Sausalito
GOLDEN GATE NATIONAL RECREATION AREA
MT TAMALPAIS STATE PARK
MUIR WOODS NAT MONUMENT
Stinson Beach
Bolinas
Duxbury Point
Point Bonita
Point Lobos
PRESIDIO OF SAN FRANCISCO MILITARY RESERVATION

SAN FRANCISCO

Rodeo
Hercules
Crockett
Martinez
Pinole
El Sobrante
Richmond
San Pablo
El Cerrito
Albany
BERKELEY
Emeryville
Piedmont
OAKLAND
Alameda
ALAMEDA NAVAL AIR STA
San Leandro

CONTRA
Pleasant Hill
Lafayette
Orinda
Moraga
Danville
Walnut
BRIONES RES
SAN PABLO RES
Upper San Leandro Res
L. Chabot

U S NAVAL RESERVATION
Treasure I.
Angel I. STATE PK
U S NAVAL RESERVATION

2 **1** **20**

Map 2 — San Francisco (middle)

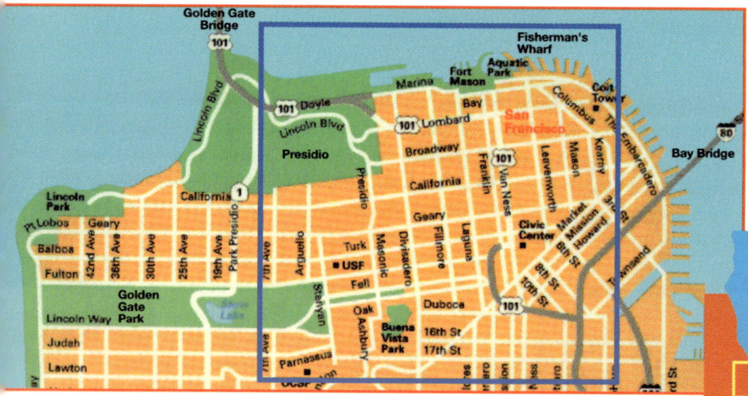

Golden Gate Bridge
Fisherman's Wharf
Aquatic Park
Fort Mason
Coit Tower
San Francisco
Bay Bridge
Presidio
Lincoln Blvd
Doyle
Marina
Bay
Lombard
Broadway
California
Franklin
Leavenworth
Mason
Kearny
Van Ness
Columbus
The Embarcadero
Lincoln Park Presidio
California
Lincoln Park
Pt Lobos
Geary
42nd Ave
36th Ave
30th Ave
25th Ave
19th Ave
Balboa
Fulton
Golden Gate Park
Lincoln Way
Judah
Lawton
Masonic
Turk
USF
Fell
Oak
Stanyan
Arguello
Geary
Fillmore
Divisadero
Laguna
Civic Center
Market
Mission
Howard
8th St
Duboce
Buena Vista Park
16th St
17th St
Parnassus
Ocean

Map 3 — San Francisco detail (bottom)

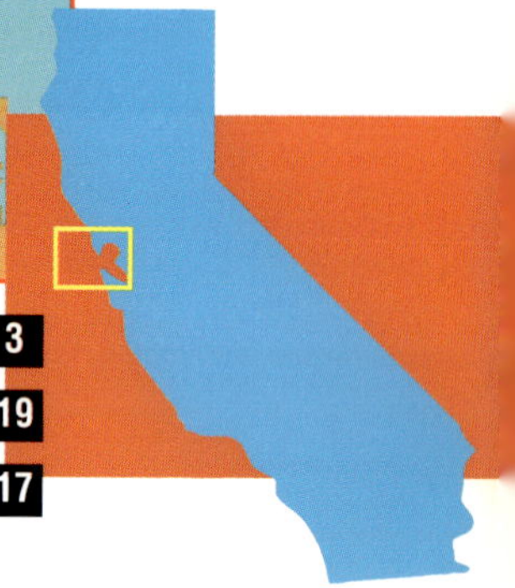

Fisherman's Wharf
Aquatic Park
Fort Mason
Coit Tower
Marina
Doyle
Lincoln Blvd
Presidio
Bay
Lombard
Broadway
California
Franklin
Van Ness
Leavenworth
Mason
Kearny
Columbus
The Embarcadero
Geary
Arguello
7th Ave
Turk
Masonic
Fillmore
Divisadero
Laguna
USF
Stanyan
Fell
Oak
Duboce
Civic Center
Market
Mission
Howard
3rd St
6th St
8th St
10th St
Townsend
Haight-Ashbury
Buena Vista Park
16th St
17th St
Parnassus
UCSF
Clarendon
Twins Peaks
Castro
Clipper
24th St
Dolores
Guerrero
Mission
S Van Ness
Potrero
DeHaro

3 19 17 6 13 12 14 15 10
11 8 9 5 4 18 16 7

SAN FRANCISCO
& EAST BAY COUNTIES

7:30 A.M. A cool white fog cuts through the Golden Gate Bridge, engulfing everything except for the rust-red towers propping up the blue California sky. Across the bay, the pyramid building rises above the downtown sky scrapers, a dramatic symbol of "The City." A red and white ferry skips over the white caps of the bay, drawn toward the distant pyramid as if by an underwater cable. The world's most spectacular morning commute is underway. Another day in paradise, also known as San Francisco, begins.

Like a modern Acropolis, San Francisco is perched on the edge of the New World, peering over the crashing Pacific surf, inspiring visitors and residents alike. Nicknamed "the city that knows how" (the citizens love this place so much they think it has its own intelligence), San Francisco has been voted the most popular vacation destination in the world. More than London, Paris, Bangkok, New York, or any of the other "heavy hitters" around the globe, San Francisco offers the greatest diversity of entertainment. Blessed with a site of immense beauty, the city offers amazing views on almost every corner and at the crest of each hill. The photo opportunities alone will keep Kodak rich and put your friends to sleep upon your return home!

With its many diverse neighborhoods, "Baghdad by the Bay" has earned its reputation as a true party town. Its restaurants, bars, and clubs are among the best, and the selection is second to none. Also, within the 46 square miles (121 sq km) of the city are housed fifty museums, the Exploratorium, the zoo, the beautiful and "acoustically improved" Davies Symphony Hall, the opera, a ballet company, numerous theaters, a spectacular park, and a thriving private gallery network.

The bay on one side of town provides many activities that are rare in large cities. Yacht clubs abound, and "wanabee" sailors can find some spectacular wind surfing. The Pacific Ocean on the other side of town is the Northern California urban surfers' paradise.

HISTORY

The thick fog that blankets the Northern California coast hid San Francisco's spectacular harbor from European explorers for over two centuries. Spanish explorers sent from Mexico colonized the territory in 1776 and named it after Saint Francis of Assisi. The Presidio was founded immediately, along with the sixth of California's twenty-one missions, Mission Dolores (Mission San Francisco de Assisi), established by the Franciscans.

In 1848 a New York Mormon by the name of Sam Brannan made an exciting discovery: gold. The population of the sleepy village of San Francisco increased from 900 inhabitants to 40,000 fortune seekers almost overnight. Thanks to its natural deep-water harbor, San Francisco became the convenient gateway to the Gold Country. By the end of the Gold Rush the main port was permanently established, and by 1900 over 300,000 people called San Francisco home.

The earthquake and fire of 1906 left much of the city in ruins, but it was soon rebuilt to emerge better than before. The Golden Gate and Bay bridges were built in the 1930s, and the port became a major embarkation point for men and materials during World War II. The post-World War II era marked a boom for construction and cultural innovation.

Despite another brush with nature in the much-publicized Loma Prieta earthquake of 1989, the city continues to thrive, and has used the earthquake as reason to remove ugly freeways and open up views to the waterfront.

THE PEOPLE

San Francisco has everything—natural beauty, sunshine, fabulous architecture, museums—but most of all it has one of the most diverse populations to be found anywhere in the world. Its mix of east and west, north and south, includes natives from all over the globe. This diversity becomes especially apparent when you look at the selection of cuisine in the city: Chinese from every region, Ethiopian, Indian, Moroccan, Korean, Thai, Japanese, Mexican, Latin American—the list goes on. You can even find California cuisine!

San Francisco is very popular with Europeans, who find it the perfect place to settle down. It is said that over 30,000 French people live in the Bay Area, and Scandinavian, German, and

British accents are frequently heard throughout the city. This cosmopolitan atmosphere makes it simply impossible to get bored.

THE NEIGHBORHOODS

San Francisco has many distinct neighborhoods, each offering the visitor something unique. Let's start in the northeast corner with one of the oldest and most popular parts of the city, **North Beach.**

This district is in the north, but it's not exactly a beach. Its northern portion does, however, overlook the bay. Its fame dates back to the Prohibition era, when the "speakeasies" were located here. It remains the center of nightlife, with bars, restaurants, and a unique club scene. Two of the most popular clubs are **Finochios** (506 Broadway, 415/982-9388), with its transvestite cabaret acts, and the extravagant costumed satirical cabaret, **Beach Blanket Babylon** (470 Columbus Ave., 415/421-4222). North Beach is also the Italian district of San Francisco and has an excellent selection of authentic Italian restaurants, delicatessens, and cafes, with the finest espresso and cappuccino outside of Italy. North Beach is home to some very funky stores, and Grant Avenue is a must. Many people like to climb **Coit Tower,** erected by Lillie Coit in honor of San Francisco's firemen. The tower offers some extraordinary panoramic views of the bay and the city.

For another dose of cultural diversity, visit North Beaches' next door neighbor, **Chinatown.** The scene of many kung fu movies, this densely populated district bustles with shops and restaurants. A stroll through Chinatown is probably the closest thing to a real Chinese experience you can have without actually setting foot in China. Souvenirs abound in this

area, where you can buy anything from authentic Chinese chopping knives and elegant jade jewelry to fake brand-name watches. The afternoon is the least crowded time to explore Chinatown, but for a real taste of this area, check out **Stockton Street** around 11:00 P.M., when the term "crowded" takes on new meaning.

The **Downtown /Financial district** is full of interesting historic buildings and skyscrapers, crowned by the famous **Transamerica Pyramid.** The waterfront area around the Embarcadero offers stunning views of the **Bay Bridge,** the less famous "big brother" of the Golden Gate Bridge. This mixture of cantilever and suspension bridge is 8 miles (13 km) long, linking San Francisco with Oakland and the East Bay. The Rincon Center and the Hills Brothers Plaza are architecturally interesting shopping malls

that are definitely worth visiting. They are located just south of the Embarcadero on the waterfront.

The **South of Market (SOMA)** district extends west from the waterfront south of Market Street. Historically the warehouse district, it is now one of the centers of hip night-life, with many trendy restaurants, bars, and nightclubs. In the last two years this area has also become a popular place for young people to shop for fashionable, reasonably priced clothes at the many boutiques that seem to sprout up each month. Combine this with the **Flower Mart** (fresh cut flowers at super low prices), the **Moscone Exhibition Hall and Conference Center,** and a variety of designer outlets, both retail and wholesale, and you have one of the most unusual neighborhoods any city could offer.

The **Castro district,** west of SOMA, is a predominantly gay neighborhood that is one of the friendliest, safest, and most creative in the city. Many unique shopping opportunities exist, as well as restaurants and outdoor cafes, like the **Cafe Flore** (2298 Market St.), a San Francisco landmark that caters to a very hip crowd. The laid-back yet vital atmosphere of this district exemplifies an energy and love of life that seem to inspire a kind of "feel-good" vigor, despite the tragedy that has beset this district in recent times.

Head north of Market from the Castro to the **Haight-Ashbury**. This district became famous in the late 1960s as the center of the hippie movement. With the beautiful Golden Gate Park at the end of the street, what better place to start a hippie revolution? "If you're going to San Francisco, be sure to wear a flower in your hair" sang the Flower Pot Men in 1967 on their worldwide chart-topping record. The Haight-Ashbury was San Francisco in the summer of love. It remains a mecca for the young, catering to the current trend. These days the neighborhood has a kind of late sixties, early seventies flared trouser Birkenstock meets punk/grunge/thrash feel about it. This youthful influence is the foundation for the excellent selection of shops that line both sides of Haight Street. It's definitely a street for the nostalgia seeker and the under-forty crowd.

Haight Street is also the gateway to **Golden Gate Park.** This large, exquisite open space stretches all the way from the Haight to the Pacific. With its huge variety of flowers and trees, an arboretum and greenhouse, lakes, roller skating/blading paths, and athletic fields, not to mention museums and even a Japanese tea garden, one can only conclude that other parks just don't cut it. Don't miss the **M.H. de Young Memorial Museum,** which exhibits American and European paintings, sculptures, textiles, and decorative arts. Tribal art from Oceania, Africa, and the Americas, in addition to travelling exhibits, are also featured. The **Asian Art Museum** displays an interesting collection of over 10,000 paintings, scrolls, sculptures, and ceramics that represent the major periods of Asian art. If you're a science enthusiast, the **California Academy of Sciences,** opposite the de Young Museum, will keep you occupied for hours. It houses both the Steinhart Aquarium and the Morrison Planetarium, and has exhibits that will fascinate people of all ages. Golden Gate Park is also host to many concerts, benefits, and open-air theater shows. It should be noted that the **Lower Haight,** at the eastern end of Haight Street, adjacent to the park, is up and coming, and has an increasing number of very trendy bars, ethnic restaurants, and small clubs as well as some eclectic stores.

In stark contrast to the lower Haight, about twenty blocks north is the Pacific Heights and Union Street area. **Pacific Heights** is the Bel Air of San Francisco with a view—across the bay, past Alcatraz, and on over the Golden Gate Bridge! With a view like this, you just have to have the mansions to go with it, and certainly Pacific Heights does not disappoint. Most of the residences here are valued in the high seven figures, and if you have the funds, why live anywhere else? A short downhill walk brings you to **Union Street** and shopping. This elegant up-market retail street has something for everyone. There are clothing boutiques, antique showrooms, hair dressers, ice-cream parlors, restaurants—over two hundred stores to choose from in a very pleasant yuppie neighborhood. Union street is just a breath away from the **Marina**, with its

extensive green (full of the stereotypical California joggers) and of course some rather nice yachts. Just around the corner you will find one of the city's finest structures, the **Palace of Fine Arts,** the last architectural remnant of the fabulous 1915 Pan-Pacific Exposition and currently home of the renowned hands-on science Exploratorium.

At the eastern end of the Union Street retail area is **Van Ness Avenue,** a major thoroughfare that runs north to south and divides the city. Go south on this street and you will find the **Hard Rock Cafe,** passé but still popular. Farther south are the **Veterans' Memorial Opera House, Davies Symphony Hall, the Museum of Modern Art, the site of a new art museum, and City Hall,** all of which are splendid structures well worth visiting.

To the east of Van Ness is the "Retail Central" of San Francisco: **Union Square.** This small park is surrounded by large department stores and hotels so that weary shoppers have somewhere to crash. Macy's, Neiman-Marcus, I. Magnin, and Sax Fifth Avenue are on the square. A five-minute walk takes you to Nordstrom and the San Francisco Shopping Center at Powell and Market Streets, where you can catch a cable car for a trip to the bay. **Fisherman's Wharf,** with the world's best clam chowder, and **Pier 39** with its many attractions, are easily accessible by cab and cable car. From Fisherman's Wharf you can catch a boat to **Alcatraz** for a tour of the notorious prison, now closed.

THE EAST BAY

When you are ready for something different, head across the Bay Bridge to **Berkeley,** a town where political activism, university pursuits, crystals, burning incense, and retrospective persuasion are the components of daily life. In Berkeley, preppie conservatives, counterculturalists, liberal do-gooders, religious zealots, Deadheads, intellectuals, skate punks, thrashers, anarchist tie-dye toters, bohemians, hip hoppers, and everyone in between are as much the common denominators as are the unfortunate homeless who walk the streets. This thriving college town, for better or for worse, boasts an unrivaled eclecticism that has made it world famous.

Telegraph Avenue, the main artery that feeds into campus, is home to colorful street vendors selling everything from tie-dyed underwear and hand-crafted jewelry to tarot card readings and political bumper stickers. In this area you will find a multitude of specialty shops, cafes, bars, restaurants, a pizza joint that insists on making pizza, not war—and street performers to entertain you while you eat. You will also notice that there are more coffee houses in Berkeley per square block than perhaps anywhere else in the world. The international ambiance of the cafe scene is unique and coffee, like the talk, is cheap. Keep the culture alive with a healthy shot of caffeine and enjoy an inconspicuous earful about anarchy, pet snakes, and the latest applications of fuzzy logic. Two popular (lucrative) spots are **Milano** on Bancroft Avenue off of Telegraph, and the outdoor **Caffé Strada** on the corner of Bancroft and College Avenues.

One center of activity is **People's Park.** Located between Haste Street and Dwight Way off Telegraph, this park is a university-owned political hotbed that has been the site of both tumultuous and peaceful rallies since the sixties, when it was a violent battlefield for the National Guard and demonstrators against the war in Vietnam. More recently the park became a haven for the homeless, which prompted university officials to refurbish it for more student-oriented activity. The park now sports volleyball and basketball courts, but still reflects its turbulent past.

The heart of town is the **University of California at Berkeley,** the first public university in California. Inaugurated in 1873, classes began with 191 enrolled students. Today, with over 30,000 students, a hearty handful of Nobel Laureates among its 1,600-member faculty, and a powerful scientific research background, "Cal" is regarded as one of the nation's top intellectual centers.

The 178-acre (72 ha) campus features wooded groves, twenty-three libraries, Sather Gate and the Campanile, the Paleontology Museum, the Lowie Museum of Anthropology, the University Art Museum, the Hearst Greek Theater, the Lawrence Hall of Science, and a 30-acre (12 ha) botanical garden. Check out the Visitors Center for tours and more information about the campus. You may also visit the information desk inside the Associated Students of the University of California (ASUC) building, located at the corner of Telegraph and Bancroft. Directly across from the ASUC building, Sproul Plaza serves as a forum for political and social expression.

Away from the bustle of the city, explore the East Bay's regional Parks including beautiful Tilden Park with acres of lawn and trees. Enjoy a picnic in the sun near Lake Anza and hike or mountain bike in the nearby hills. Take Marin Avenue to Grizzly Peak and follow the signs to the park.

If you enjoy theater, plan to attend a performance at the nationally acclaimed Berkeley Repertory Theater, located at Addison and Shattuck Avenues.

Just south of Berkeley is **Oakland,** the largest city in the East Bay. Attractions include the **Oakland Museum, Lake Merritt,** a bustling **Chinatown, Jack London Square,** and one of the country's largest container shipping ports.

West of Oakland, the island of **Alameda** has a naval base and some beautiful Victorian homes.

East of Oakland lie the suburbs of **Concord, Walnut Creek,** and **Danville,** which have many elegant, upscale shopping areas.

Vallejo, 25 miles (40 km) north of Oakland, is the home of **Marine World/Africa USA.** Featuring a zoo, animal theater, and elaborate playground, the 165-acre (67 ha) park provides entertainment, with a variety of shows starring killer whales, dolphins, sea lions, tigers, and other wildlife.

TRANSPORTATION

Bay Area Rapid Transit (BART) provides excellent light-rail transportation throughout San Francisco to Daly City and across the bay to Oakland, Berkeley, Concord, Richmond, and Fremont. Trains run Monday through Saturday from 6 A.M. until midnight and on Sunday from 9 A.M. until midnight. Fares range from $.85 to $3.00. For more information, call (415) 788-BART.

The San Francisco Municipal Railway System (MUNI) offers extensive service by bus, trolley, surface and underground streetcar, and cable car. Some buses and streetcars run Monday through Saturday from 6 A.M. until midnight and Sunday from 9 A.M. until midnight; others run twenty-four hours a day. The fare is $1 for adults and $.25 for senior citizens and children 5 through 17. Cable cars run Monday through Saturday, 6 A.M. until midnight, and Sunday from 9 A.M. until midnight. Fare is $2 for adults and $1 for children 5 through 17. Exact change is required. For more information, call (415) 673-MUNI.

Driving in San Francisco is a challenge. Parking is expensive, one-way streets are perplexing, steep hills may make you gasp (especially if you drive a five-speed), and the traffic is often stop-and-go. Take advantage of the city's wonderful public transportation whenever possible.

SAN FRANCISCO

Asian Art Museum, in Golden Gate Park, (415) 668-8921, admission collected when entering the de Young Museum. **California Academy of Sciences,** in Golden Gate Park, open daily 10-5, $6 adults, $3 seniors and students, $1 children 6-11. **Exploratorium,** in the Palace of Fine Arts, near Baker and Beach Street, (415) 563-7337, $6 adults, $2 children under 17. **Louise M. Davies Symphony Hall,** Grove St. and Van Ness Ave., (415) 552-8338, $3 adults, $2 children and senior citizens. **M.H. de Young Memorial Museum,** in Golden Gate Park, (415) 863-3330 for 24-hour information, open Wed.-Sun. 10-5, $4 adults, $2 senior citizens and children 12-17, under 12 free, free first Wed. and Sun. of the month. **Museum of Modern Art,** McAllister St. and Van Ness Ave., (415) 863-8800, $4 adults, $2 senior citizens and students 13 and over with ID, free first Tues. of the month, open Tues.,Wed., Fri., 10-5, Thurs. 10-9, Sat., Sun. 11-5. **San Francisco Convention and Visitors Bureau,** lower level at Hallidie Plaza at Powell and Market Streets, at Powell Street entrance to Bart, (415) 974-6900, or (415) 391-2001 for a 24-hour recorded message, open weekdays 9-5, Sat. 9-3, Sun. 10-2.

BERKELEY

Lawrence Hall of Science, Centennial Dr. on the hill above UC Berkeley campus, (510) 642-5132, open Mon.-Sat. 10-4:30, Sun. 12-5, nominal admission. **The Lowie Museum of Anthropology,** across from University Art Museum on Bancroft in Kroeber Hall, (510) 642-3681, open Tues.-Fri. 10-4:30, weekends 12-4:30. **The University Art Museum,** 2626 Bancroft Way, (510) 642-0808, open Wed.-Sun. 11-5, nominal admission. **University of California at Berkeley,** General Information (510) 642-6000

OAKLAND

Oakland Museum, 1000 Oak St. at 10th St., (510) 834-2413, open Wed.-Sat. 10-5, free admission. **Oakland Convention and Visitors Bureau,** 1000 Broadway, Suite 200, (510) 839-9000.

VALLEJO

Marine World/Africa USA, Marine World Pkwy., (707) 643-6722, open daily 9:30-6 in summer, Wed.-Sun. 9:30-5 Sept.-May, $19.95 adults, $14.95 ages 4-12, $16.95 seniors.

BERKELEY

Caffe Venezia
1799 University Ave.
(510) 848-4681
Italian cuisine $-$$

Cha-am
1543 Shattuck Ave.
(415) 848-9664
Thai cuisine$$

Chez Panisse
1517 Shattuck Ave.
(510) 548-5525
California cuisine $$$

Metropole
2271 Shattuck Ave.
(510) 848-3080
French cuisine $$-$$$

Skates on the Bay
100 Seawall Dr.
(510) 549-1900
Seafood $$

OAKLAND

Yoshi's Restaurant and Nitespot
6030 Claremont Ave.
(310) 652-9200
Japanese cuisine/jazz club $$-$$$

SAN FRANCISCO

Ace Café
1539 Folsom St.
(415) 621-4752
California cuisine $

Aqua
252 California St.
(415) 956-9662
French-Mediterranean seafood $$$

Asta
101 Spear St.
(415) 495-2782
American cuisine $$

Benkay
222 Mason St.
(415) 394-1105
Japanese cuisine $$$

Bix
56 Gold St.
(415) 433-6300
Classic American cuisine $$

Brandy Ho's On-Broadway
450 Broadway
(415) 362-6268
Hunan cuisine $-$$

Cafe Kati
1963 Sutter St.
(415) 775-7313
Eclectic California cuisine $$

Caffé Sport
574 Green St.
(415) 981-1251
Sicilian seafood $$

Cha Cha Cha
1805 Haight St.
(415) 386-5758
Cuban cuisine $-$$

Fog City Diner
1300 Battery St.
(415) 982-2000
California-American cuisine $$

Gaylord India Restaurant
Ghiradelli Square
(415) 771-8822
Indian cuisine $$-$$$

La Folie
2316 Polk St.
(415) 776-5577
California-French cuisine $$$

Lou Lou's
816 Folsom St.
(415) 495-5775
Southern Italian cuisine $-$$

Manora's
1600 Folsom St.
(415) 861-6224
Thai cuisine $-$$

Masa's
648 Bush St.
(415) 989-7154
French cuisine $$$

Ma Tante Sumi
4243 18th St.
(415) 626-7864
California-Asian cuisine $-$$

Moose's
1652 Stockton St. (Washington Sq.)
(415) 989-7800
California-Italian cuisine $-$$

North Beach Pizza
1499 Grant Ave.
(415) 433-2444
Italian cuisine$

Pasha
1516 Broadway
(415) 885-4477
Moroccan cuisine/entertainment
$$-$$$

Postrio
545 Post Ave.
(415) 776-7825
Contemporary Asian/Mediterranean
cuisine $$-$$$

**The Restaurant at the Ritz
Carlton Hotel**
600 Stockton St.
(415) 296-7465
California-French cuisine $$-$$$

South Park Cafe
108 South Park
(415) 495-7275
French cuisine $$

Stars
150 Redwood Alley
(415) 861-7827
Contemporary American cuisine $$$

The Stinking Rose
325 Columbus Ave.
(415) 781-7673
Garlic specialties $$-$$$

Tane E Vino
3011 Steiner St.
(415) 346-2111
Italian cuisine $$

Chouinard Vineyards & Winery
33853 Palomares Road
Castro Valley, CA 94552
(510) 582-9900
Open: Sat.+Sun. 1-5
Closed Mon. thru Fri.

Fenestra Winery
83 E. Vallecitos Road
Livermore, CA 94550
(510) 447-5246
Open: Sat.+Sun. 12-5
Closed Mon. thru Fri.

Rosenblum Cellars †
2900 Main St.
Alameda, CA 94501
(510) 865-7007
Open: Mon. thru Sat 12-5
Closed Sun.

Wente Bros. Estate Winery
5565 Tesla Road
Livermore, CA 94550
(510) 447-3603
Open: Mon. thru Sat. 10-5
Sun. 11-5

Wente Bros. Sparkling Wine Cellars
5050 Arroyo Road
Livermore, CA 94550
(510) 447-3023
Open: Mon. thru Sat. 10-5
Sun. 11-5

WEBSTER HOUSE

ALAMEDA 1

1238 Versailles Ave.
Alameda, CA 94501
Tel:1-510-523-9697

R

Step back in time in this lovingly restored 1854 Gothic Revival cottage, the oldest house on the island of Alameda. Tea is served every afternoon in true English fashion. Enjoy breakfast on the sun porch. Walk to shops and restaurants. *Northern California Best Places Award 93/94*

2 ROOMS, 1 pb   1 SUITE, pb   1 COTTAGE, pb

$75-125   OPEN: ALL YEAR   HOSTS: Susan & Andrew McCormack

GRAMMA'S ROSE GARDEN INN

BERKELEY 2

2740 Telegraph Ave.
Berkeley, CA 94705
Tel:1-510-549-2145

R

Gramma's Inn is a turn-of-the-century Tudor mansion surrounded by extensive English rose gardens—an unexpected oasis in urban Berkeley. Guest rooms are beautifully decorated, and many have fireplaces, decks, and views. Enjoy a delicious breakfast on the patio.

40 ROOMS, 40 pb

$85-150   OPEN: ALL YEAR   HOSTS: Barry Cleveland & Lori Solomon

ART CENTER

SAN FRANCISCO 3

1902 Filbert St.
San Francisco, CA 94123
Tel:1-800-821-3877
or 1-415-567-1526

R

This historic building is situated between downtown and the ocean, the Union Street boutiques and the bay. The Art Center, built in 1857, stands on the site of a Gold Rush campground. The house contains an art gallery and library. All suites have private entrances.

5 SUITES, 5 pb

$85-115   SPA   OPEN: ALL YEAR   HOSTS: Helvi & George Wamsley

4 SAN FRANCISCO

HOSTS: Wayne Corn & Klaus May

ALAMO SQUARE INN
719 Scott St.
San Francisco, CA 94117
Tel:1-415-922-2055
1-800-345-9888

These Victorian mansions, an 1895 Queen Anne and an 1896 Tudor revival, capture the grand elegance of turn-of-the century San Francisco. Located in a historic district, they overlook Alamo Square's hilltop park and other spectacular views. The private gardens feature wooden decks and brick paths among the ferns and flowers. Admire the European furnishings, oriental rugs, exquisite wall coverings, and stately staircase illuminated by a stained-glass skylight. Free parking, full American breakfast.

11 ROOMS, 11 pb   3 SUITES, 3 pb

OPEN: ALL YEAR   **$85-250**

5 SAN FRANCISCO

HOST: Kathleen Austin

ARCHBISHOP'S MANSION INN
1000 Fulton St.
San Francisco, CA 94117
Tel:1-800-543-5820

Built in 1904 for San Francisco's Catholic archbishop, this mansion is one of The City's premier inns—and one of its best-kept secrets. Of the fifteen guest rooms, most have a fireplace or a whirlpool-spa for two, and a view of the famous Victorian postcard row. Breakfast is delivered to your room in a French picnic basket. Complimentary wine is served in the parlor. Friendly, savvy concierge service.

10 ROOMS, 10 pb   5 SUITES, 5 pb

OPEN: ALL YEAR   **$115-285**

ALBION HOUSE INN
135 Gough St.
San Francisco, CA 94102
Tel:1-415-621-0896

This inn is a great place to unwind. Guests are surrounded by unique antique furnishings in the spacious living room, complete with marble fireplace and grand piano. For the adventurous, San Francisco offers many nearby delights.

9 ROOMS, 7 pb

$75-150

OPEN: ALL YEAR   HOSTS: Regina & Aziz Bouagou

CASITA BLANCA
330 Edgehill Way
San Francisco, CA 94127
Tel:1-415-564-9339

R

This delightful hilltop cottage nestled in the trees gives you a view of the bay and the San Francisco skyline. If you tire of shopping and sightseeing, just curl up by the fireplace with a complimentary glass of wine.

1 COTTAGE, pb

$90

OPEN: ALL YEAR   HOST: Joan Bard

CASA ARGUELLO
225 Arguello St.
San Francisco, CA 94118
Tel:1-415-752-9482

R

Casa Arguello is a family-run, tastefully decorated apartment. It is located in a delightful neighborhood within walking distance of restaurants and shops, five blocks north of Golden Gate Park. Convenient to the Golden Gate Bridge and public transportation.

3 ROOMS, 3 pb   1 SUITE, pb

$50-85

OPEN: ALL YEAR   HOSTS: Emma Baires & Marina McKenzie

9   SAN FRANCISCO

HOST: Rodney Karr and Bill Gersbach

CHATEAU TIVOLI
1057 Steiner St.
San Francisco, CA 94115
Tel:1-800-228-1647

R

This fabulous Landmark Mansion built in 1892 is located in the historic Alamo Square district near the center of San Francisco. Opulent rooms and suites feature canopied beds, balconies, fireplaces, antiques, stained glass, and frescoed ceilings.

5 ROOMS, 3 pb   2 SUITES, 2 pb

OPEN: ALL YEAR   **$80-200**

10   SAN FRANCISCO

HOSTS: Jane Bertorelli & Marty Neely

INN SAN FRANCISCO
943 South Van Ness
San Francisco, CA 94110
Tel:1-415-641-0188
Res:1-800-359-0913

R

Classical music, candlelight, and roses set the mood in this gracious 1872 Victorian mansion. Antiques, fresh flowers, fireplaces, private spas, hot tub, sun deck, and patio garden add to your enjoyment. Located near the Civic Center.

22 ROOMS, 17 pb

OPEN: ALL YEAR   **SPA**   **$75-175**

11   SAN FRANCISCO

JACKSON COURT
2198 Jackson St.
San Francisco, CA 94115
Tel:1-415-929-7670

R

This brownstone mansion, built in the early 1900s, is right at home in the residential neighborhood of Pacific Heights. The inn's blend of tasteful antiques and contemporary furnishings brings to mind the simple elegance that was the essence of old San Francisco.

10 ROOMS, 10 pb

HOST: Pat Cremer

OPEN: ALL YEAR   **$108-150**

LOWER GATE
198 Haight St.
San Francisco, CA 94102
Tel:1-415-863-8696

Did you ever think you would find the charm and privacy of a cottage in the middle of San Francisco? Enjoy the best of both worlds in this 1883 Victorian, which features a sitting room and three garden-level guest rooms furnished with country antiques. Whether you stay in an individual room or rent the entire apartment, you will be within easy walking distance of public transportation, restaurants, and galleries.

R

HOSTS: Joan & John Phillips

3 ROOMS, 0 pb

$75

OPEN: ALL YEAR

NOLAN HOUSE
1071 Page St.
San Francisco, CA 94117
Tel:1-800-SF-NOLAN
or 1-415-863-0384

Built in 1889, this Queen Anne Victorian inn offers old-world tranquility near the Haight-Ashbury and Golden Gate Park. Enjoy a refreshment at check-in time and evening cordials in the subtropical garden and sun deck, or by the grand piano in the parlor. Bedrooms feature marble fireplaces, antiques, featherbeds, and down comforters trimmed with lace. Hearty American breakfasts with gourmet egg dishes and Belgian waffles are served in an elegant dining room.

HOST: Tim Sockett

4 ROOMS, 1 pb

$85-135

OPEN: ALL YEAR

14 SAN FRANCISCO

THE PARSONAGE
198 Haight St.
San Francisco, CA 94102
Tel:1-415-863-8696

Enjoy an afternoon sherry beside one of six marble fireplaces, curl up with a book in the cozy library, or retire to the privacy of your sun-filled room in this 1883 Victorian landmark. Whatever your choice, all the charm and elegance of Victorian San Francisco are yours. Centrally located in historic Hayes Valley; walk to restaurants, galleries, the opera, and the symphony. Ideal for weddings and other celebrations.

HOSTS: Joan & John Phillips

4 ROOMS, 3 pb

OPEN: ALL YEAR   **$125**

15 SAN FRANCISCO

SPENCER HOUSE
1080 Haight St.
San Francisco, CA 94117
Tel:1-415-626-9205

The owners of this splendid Queen Anne Victorian mansion have created magnificent rooms with European and oriental antiques, feather beds, down comforters, and exquisite wall coverings. Inspiration for the decor comes from the innkeepers' travels in the chateau region of France. Extravagant gourmet breakfasts served on fine china with sterling silver may feature eggs ranchero topped with a heavenly salsa or Belgian waffles with warmed strawberries.

HOST: Barbara Chambers

6 ROOMS, 6 pb

OPEN: ALL YEAR   **$95-155**

STANYAN PARK HOTEL
750 Stanyan St.
San Francisco, CA 94117
Tel:1-415-751-1000

SAN FRANCISCO `16`

A member of the National Register of Historic Places, this Victorian hotel, built in 1905, is located in the Haight-Ashbury district overlooking Golden Gate Park. Spacious comfortable rooms and the hospitable staff will make your stay a pleasant one.

30 ROOMS, 30 pb   6 SUITES, 6 pb

$78-170 ☕   OPEN: ALL YEAR   HOST: Brad Bihlmeyer

UNION STREET INN
2229 Union St.
San Francisco, CA 94123
Tel:1-415-346-0424

SAN FRANCISCO `17`

R

This colorful Edwardian home invites you to relax in the tranquility of a garden filled with lilacs, camelias, and violets—a sanctuary in the heart of San Francisco. Enjoy scrumptious homemade muffins for breakfast and later, complimentary wine.

6 ROOMS, 6 pb   1 COTTAGE, pb

$125-225 ☕   **SPA** OPEN: ALL YEAR   HOST: Helen Stewart

VICTORIAN INN ON THE PARK
301 Lyon St.
San Francisco, CA 94117
Tel:1-800-435-1967
1-415-931-1830

SAN FRANCISCO `18`

R

A registered historic landmark, this exquisitely restored inn, built in 1897, reflects classic Victorian elegance. Guest rooms have beautiful comforters and down pillows. The inn is close to Golden Gate Park and downtown. A delicious breakfast is served in the oak-paneled dining room.

12 ROOMS, 12 pb   1 SUITE, pb

$70-144 ☕ 🔥   OPEN: ALL YEAR   HOSTS: Lisa & William Benau

19 SAN FRANCISCO

WASHINGTON SQUARE INN
1660 Stockton St.
San Francisco, CA 94133
Tel:1-800-388-0220
or 1-415-981-4220

This inn offers all the charm and hospitality of a French country home, yet it is located in the heart of San Francisco's historic North Beach neighborhood, opposite Washington Square Park. Walk to Fisherman's Wharf, Chinatown, and Ghirardelli Square. Breakfast of flaky croissants, muffins, fresh fruit, and coffee, served in bed or in front of the hearth. Afternoon tea, wine, and hor d'oeuvres are served daily.

HOST: Brooks Bayly

15 ROOMS, 10 pb

OPEN: ALL YEAR

$85-180

20 WALNUT CREEK

MANSION AT LAKEWOOD
1056 Hacienda Dr.
Walnut Creek, CA 94598
Tel:1-800-477-7898
or 510-945-3600

This 1861 Victorian country manor is the ideal setting for a romantic retreat or business meeting. Two parlors, a majestic library, and an elegant dining room provide spacious comfort. Sparkling chandeliers and finely crafted furnishings complete the atmosphere. After morning coffee and pastries presented on fine china and silver, stroll through acres of green gardens with fragrant flowers. A short drive takes you to charming shops and restaurants.

HOST: Sharyn McCoy

5 ROOMS, 5 pb   2 SUITES, 2 pb

OPEN: ALL YEAR   SPA   **$85-250**

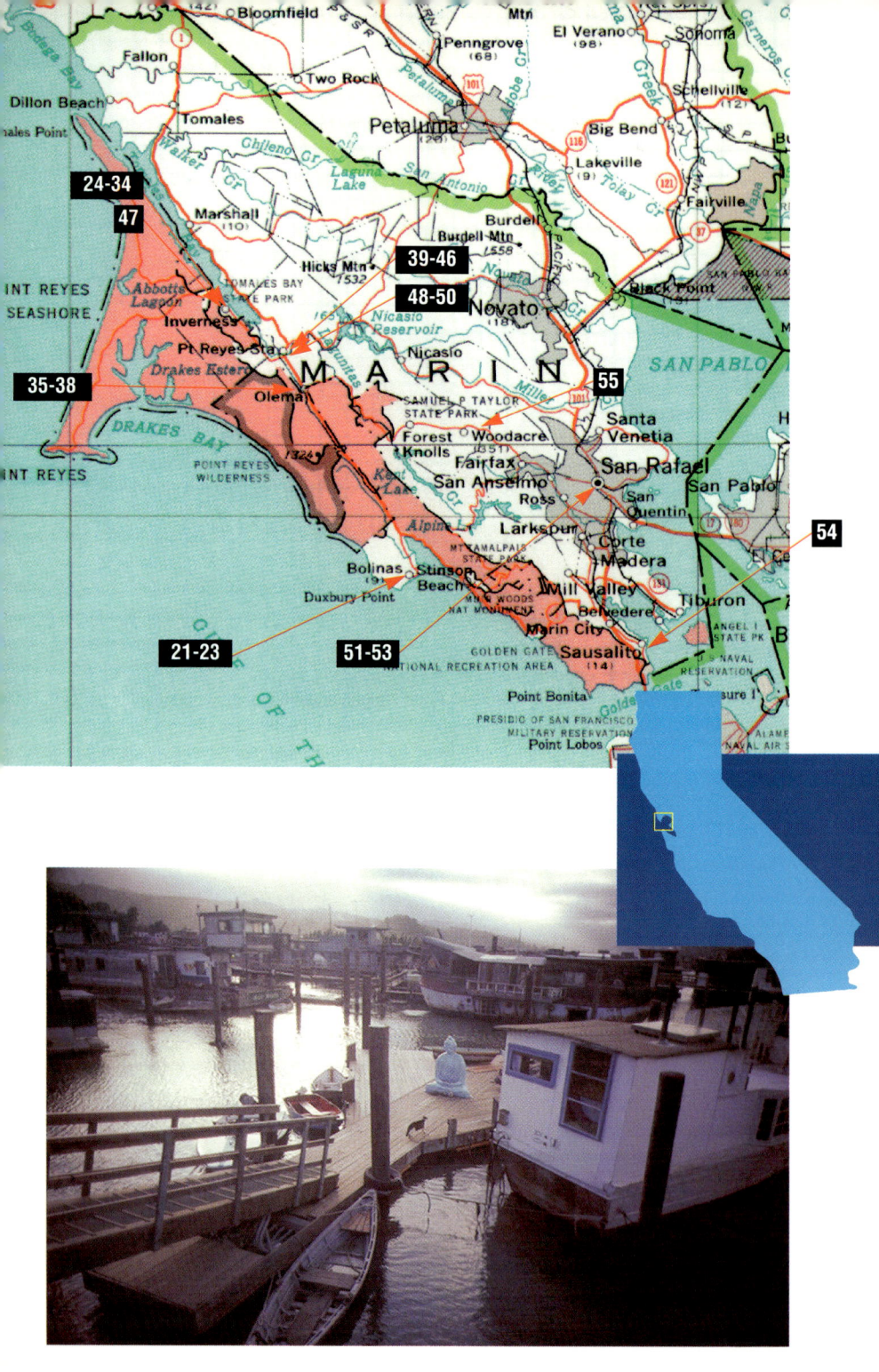

MARIN

& WEST MARIN COUNTIES

Travelling north from San Francisco across the Golden Gate Bridge brings you to legendary **Marin County.** Famed for its unique natural beauty, BMWs (Basic Marin Wheels), and ex-hippies-turned-entrepreneurs, this region offers something for everyone. The hills overlooking the bridge, the **Marin Headlands,** are known for their spectacular views of San Francisco and the bay. To best appreciate the natural assets of this area, you should explore the headlands by foot. Hiking on the extensive trails that wind through the foliage and rugged coastline is a favorite pastime for locals and tourists alike.

Immediately after crossing the bridge on Highway 101, take the Alexander exit from the freeway and explore the quaint waterfront town of **Sausalito,** whose name means "little willow" in Spanish. By the turn of the century, Sausalito had already become a haven for artists and writers.

Today it offers tourists a variety of art galleries, waterfront restaurants, elegant shops, parks, and even a flea market on weekends. The picturesque yacht harbor, home to whaling ships a century ago, now accommodates modern boat traffic, touring ferries, and commuter ferries to the city. Tourists and locals find the steep hillside above the town, combined with the waterfront setting, reminiscent of the French Riviera. Add to this the fantastic views of downtown San Francisco and you will understand why Sausalito is one of the most-visited places in Northern California.

A 5-mile (8 km) drive north brings you to **Mill Valley,** a town built in 1891 around a lumber mill. Today it is a cozy residential village with a variety of shops, restaurants, and outdoor cafes shaded by towering redwood trees. While strolling through town you may run into your favorite rock and blues musicians, actors, movie directors, and artists who have made this idyllic setting their home.

For breathtaking views of the city and ocean, hike on the spectacular trails of 2,571-foot (786 m) **Mount Tamalpais.** To get there, take Highway 1 toward Muir Woods until you see a Mount Tamalpais sign. Continuing on 6 miles (10 km) northwest brings you to the entrance to **Muir Woods,** a 427-acre (172 ha) grove of redwood trees, some of which are thousands of years old.

After wandering through the woods, head north on Highway 1 to the beach towns of Stinson and Bolinas. **Stinson Beach** has a 3-mile (5 km) white sand beach and a 53-acre (21 ha) state park. Swimming, surfing, and picnicking are popular activities during most of the year. A few miles north is the town of **Bolinas.** Surrounded by hills, this picturesque waterfront town is nestled between the ocean and a lagoon. You can find great clifftop hiking trails overlooking the ocean. Just offshore is the **Duxbury Reef,** the graveyard of many old sailing ships.

Twelve miles (19 km) north along Highway 1 lies the town of **Olema,** an Indian word meaning coyote. This little town used to be a part of a 9,000-acre (3,645 ha) Spanish rancho; today it is the crossroads for thousands of tourists who visit the **Point Reyes National Seashore** annually. Originally home to thousands of Coast Miwok Indians, this national park has 75,000 acres (30,375 ha) of rolling hills, beaches, lagoons, and tidepools. There are over 150 miles (240 km) of hiking, biking, and equestrian trails, as well as 25 miles (40 km) of ocean beaches. Over five hundred varieties of birds have been sighted in this birdwatchers' heaven. The natural beauty of this area is augmented by occasional cool, moisture-laden breezes that will enhance your enjoyment of a nice hot toddy!

Adjacent to the seashore are the towns of Point Reyes Station and Inverness, superb bases from which to explore the coastline. Separating these towns is **Tomales Bay,** believed to have been discovered by Sir Francis Drake in 1579. **Point Reyes Station,** now a favorite hangout for cyclists, hikers, and tourists, has catered to the dairy industry since the 1850s. As you will notice, millions of acres are still devoted to raising cattle (and the methane level). Away from the herds, the charming town features specialty shops, restaurants, and art galleries.

On the opposite side of the bay is **Inverness,** named by settler Judge James McMillan after a village in Scotland. Many street names reflect this Scottish influence. A fascinating event occurs here each winter when thousands of whales pass by the lighthouse as they migrate south from the Arctic on their way to Baja California, and again in April as they head north. Just join the party and the crowds at the lighthouse lookout. This pretty little town boasts several restaurants, shops, galleries, and numerous walks along the bay beaches.

After exploring this unique and beautiful area of California, head inland to **San Rafael,** Marin's county seat. Founded in 1817, the town grew up around the Mission San Rafael Arcangel. You will find an excellent variety of shops, restaurants, and historic places of interest. Architecture buffs will enjoy a visit to the **Marin Civic Center,** Frank Lloyd Wright's final design, just north of San Rafael off Highway 101.

ATTRACTIONS

Golden Gate National Recreation Area (Marin Headlands), call (415) 331-1540 for visitor information. **Point Reyes National Seashore,** call (415) 663-1092 for park information. **San Rafael Archangel Mission,** 1102 5th Ave., open daily 11-4.

RESTAURANTS $=under $10, $$=$10 to $20, $$$=over $20

BOLINAS
Blue Heron Inn
Warf Rd.
(415) 868-1102
American cuisine $$

INVERNESS
Barnaby's
12938 Sir Francis Drake
(415) 669-1114
California cuisine $$
Manka's
Argyl and Callendar Way
(415) 669-1034
Wild game, fish, grilled meats $$$

LARKSPUR
Marin Brewing Company
1809 Larkspur Landing Circle
(415) 461-4677
American cuisine, home brew $
Sushi Ko
1819 Larkspur Landing Circle
(415) 461-8400
Japanese cuisine $$

MARSHALL
Tony's Seafood
18863 Highway 1 N.
(415) 663-1107
American seafood $$

MUIR BEACH
Pelican Inn
10 Pacific Way
(415) 383-6000
Traditional English fare cuisine $$$

NICASIO
Rancho Nicasio
One Old Rancheria Rd.
(415) 662-2219
Continental cuisine $$

OLEMA
Olema Inn
10000 Sir Francis Drake
(415) 663-9559
Continental cuisine $$

SAN RAFAEL
Cafe Ristarante Italia
1236 4th St.
(415) 459-3977
Italian cuisine $$
My Thai
1230 4th St.
(415) 459-4455
Thai cuisine $$
Szechuan Village
720 B St.
(415) 454-2828
Szechuan Chinese cuisine$$

SAUSALITO
Angelino's
621 Bridgeway
(415) 331-5225
Italian cuisine $$
Casa Madrona
801 Bridgeway St.
(415) 331-5888
California cuisine $$$

Christophe Restaurant
1919 Bridgeway St.
(415) 332-9244
French cuisine $$$
Juan's
300 Valley
(415) 332-9322
Mexican cuisine $
Scomas
588 Bridgeway
(415) 332-9551
Seafood cuisine $$

STINSON BEACH
Stinson Beach Grill
3465 Shoreline Highway
(415) 868-2002
American cuisine $$

ONE FIFTY-FIVE PINE

BOLINAS 21

P.O. Box 62
Bolinas, CA 94924
Tel:1-415-868-0263

This private cottage at the southern tip of Point Reyes National Seashore has a spectacular view of the ocean. Enjoy the pine interior and huge stone fireplace, or walk three minutes to Agate beach. Romantic for two, cozy for four, the cottage can sleep six.

1 COTTAGE pb

$125-135 OPEN: ALL YEAR HOST: Karen Arthur

ROSE GARDEN COTTAGE

BOLINAS 22

P.O. Box 845
59 Altura Ave.
Bolinas, CA 94924
Tel:1-415-868-2209

Spectacular views and a warm fireplace await you in this cozy one-bedroom cottage with kitchen. Enjoy the peaceful surroundings and watch the birds soar as you breakfast on your private garden patio. Stroll on the nearby ocean beach and scenic trails.

1 COTTAGE pb

$80-100 OPEN: ALL YEAR HOSTS: Virginia & Richard Gavin

THOMAS' WHITE HOUSE INN

BOLINAS 23

P.O. Box 132
118 Kale Rd.
Bolinas, CA 94924
Tel:1-415-868-0279

This New England-style inn on two acres of clifftop gardens overlooks one of the most beautiful coastal areas in California. It offers a fireplace, a sun room, a country kitchen festooned with dried flowers, and an ocean view from every window.

2 ROOMS, 0 pb

$85-95 OPEN: ALL YEAR HOST: Jackie Thomas

24 INVERNESS

BLACKTHORNE INN
P.O. Box 712
266 Vallejo Ave.
Inverness, CA 94937
Tel:1-415-663-8621

Hidden away in the woods of Inverness is an inn that Sunset magazine called a "carpenter's fantasy." It resembles a giant treehouse with decks, whirlpool-spa, fireman's pole, and a spiral staircase that takes you to the Eagle's Nest. This romantic bedroom is for those who enjoy greeting the dawn. Enclosed in glass, with a private sundeck, this room affords spectacular views of the sky and treetops.

HOST: Susan Wigert

5 ROOMS, 3 pb

OPEN: ALL YEAR SPA $105-185

25 INVERNESS

DANCING COYOTE BEACH
P.O. Box 98
12794 Sir Francis Drake Blvd.
Inverness, CA 94937
Tel:1-415-669-7200

Situated in the midst of the Point Reyes National Seashore, these cottages make an ideal base for bicycling, hiking, whale or bird watching, or beachcombing. Each has a galley kitchen, skylights, fireplace, and views of the bay. Enjoy a romantic meal by the fire or wander into sleepy Inverness to enjoy one of several fine restaurants. Stroll along the private sandy beach and breakfast outdoors on your own private deck.

HOSTS: Bobbi Stumpf & Sherry King

1 STUDIO, 1 pb   3 COTTAGES, 3 pb

OPEN: ALL YEAR $100-125

DUCK LODGE COTTAGE
P.O. Box 562
12687 Sir Francis Drake Blvd.
Inverness, CA 94937
Tel:1-415-669-1520

INVERNESS **26**

The lodge, an intimate secluded retreat with captivating views and luxurious old-fashioned country charm, is situated on a wooded knoll overlooking Tomales Bay. Surround yourself with the luxury of a grand living room and elegant dining area, complete with turn-of-the-century furnishings.

2 ROOMS, 2 pb   1 COTTAGE, pb

$135-145   OPEN: ALL YEAR   HOST: Doreen Powell

FAIRWINDS FARM
P.O. Box 581
82 Drakes Summit
Inverness, CA 94937
Tel:1-415-663-9454

INVERNESS **27**

This large, secluded Inverness Ridge cottage affords direct access to a 68,000-acre national park. The farm, complete with barnyard animals, has a garden, a pond, a swing, and a playhouse for children. This roomy cottage can sleep six comfortably.

1 COTTAGE, 2 BEDROOMS, pb

$125   SPA   OPEN: ALL YEAR   HOST: Joyce Goldfield

HICKMAN HOUSE
P.O. Box 235
10 Miwok Way
Inverness, CA 94937
Tel:1-415-669-7428

INVERNESS **28**

Japanese antiques, bonsai, and beautiful woodwork surround you in quiet seclusion on twelve acres overlooking a wilderness valley. Watch the osprey, red tailed hawks, deer, and foxes from the spacious decks. Relax in the library and sitting rooms.

2 ROOMS, 2 pb   1 SUITE, pb

$90-140   OPEN: ALL YEAR   HOSTS: Gilly & Tom Hickman

MARIN & WEST MARIN

29 INVERNESS

HOSTS: Ellen & Howard Deixler

JAMBERRY COTTAGE
192 Hawthorne Way
Inverness, CA 94960
Tel:1-415-663-9543

In berry season, you can eat your way right up to the door of this private, intimate cottage. Meander along the flower-lined brook and end up in Inverness, where unique restaurants, art galleries, and shops abound.

1 COTTAGE, pb

OPEN: ALL YEAR   **$95**

30 INVERNESS

HOST: Lee & John Boyce-Smith

MOORINGS BED & BREAKFAST
P.O. Box 35
8 Pine Hill Drive
Inverness, CA 94937
Tel:1-415-669-1464

Overlooking Tomales Bay, and only a short drive from town, this contemporary home is convenient for hiking the trails of the Point Reyes National Seashore or exploring the nearby Coast Miwok Indian village. Guests enjoy a delicious breakfast served by the congenial hosts.

1 SUITE, pb

OPEN: ALL YEAR   **$75**

31 INVERNESS

HOST: Margaret Grade

MANKA'S INVERNESS LODGE
Argyle & Callender Way
Inverness, CA 94937
Tel:1-415-669-1034

Built as a hunting and fishing lodge, this elegant rustic inn and restaurant are tucked away in the hills overlooking Tomales Bay. This award-winning inn and restaurant were voted in the top ten by San Francisco Focus magazine readers for romance and cuisine.

8 ROOMS, 4 pb   2 COTTAGES, 2 pb

OPEN: ALL YEAR   **$65-145**

ROSEMARY COTTAGE

INVERNESS **32**

P.O. Box 273
75 Balboa Ave.
Inverness, CA 94937
Tel:1-415-663-9338

Hide away in this romantic French country cottage and wrap yourself in seclusion and beauty. The cottage features hand-crafted details, a wood-burning stove, full kitchen, private bath, large deck, and a garden. Sleeps four comfortably.

1 COTTAGE, pb

$105-150 SPA OPEN: ALL YEAR HOST: Suzanne Storch

TEN INVERNESS WAY

INVERNESS **33**

P.O. Box 63
10 Inverness Way
Inverness, CA 94937
Tel:1-415-669-1648

Classy comforts on the coast: oriental rugs, stone fireplace, strong coffee, and specialties like banana-buttermilk-buckwheat pancakes. Beachcomb, bike, and ride horseback at the Point Reyes National Seashore, then walk to dinner. "One of the niftiest inns in Northern California" -L.A. Times.

4 ROOMS, 4 pb   1 SUITES, pb

$90-140 SPA OPEN: ALL YEAR HOSTS: Mary Davies & Bonnie Fisk-Hayden

TREE HOUSE

INVERNESS **34**

73 Drakes Summit
Inverness, CA 94937
Tel:1-415-663-8720

This beautiful, custom-built home filled with family treasures is perched on a ridge-top affording spectacular views of the countryside. Experience Italian hospitality and a whirlpool-spa under the stars—and listen to the parrot sing "I left my heart in San Francisco."

3 ROOMS, 3 pb

$80-95 SPA OPEN: ALL YEAR HOST: Lisa Patsel

35 OLEMA

BEAR VALLEY INN
P.O. Box 33
88 Bear Valley Rd.
Olema, CA 94950
Tel:1-415-663-1777

Rendez-vous with the past in this classic 1899 Victorian ranch house, lovingly restored to its original beauty by the innkeepers. The parlor, with its woodstove, oak flooring and overstuffed chairs, offers a cozy spot to relax by the fire. The guest rooms feature antique beds, down comforters, and fresh flowers. Conveniently located in the historic town of Olema, the inn is one-half mile from the Point Reyes National Park Visitors Center.

HOSTS: JoAnne & Ron Nowell

3 ROOMS, 1 PRIV. BATH

OPEN: ALL YEAR

$60-140

36 OLEMA

OLEMA INN
P.O. Box 37
10,000 Sir Francis Drake Blvd.
Olema, CA 94950
Tel:1-415-663-9559

Originally part of the 9,000-acre ranch granted to Raphael Garcia by the Mexican government, this historic inn has been welcoming visitors since 1876. This Swiss family-run inn boasts an experienced staff and a superb restaurant. Dine on the garden patio. Overnight guests enjoy both gracious hospitality and the beauty of the nearby Point Reyes Seashore.

HOSTS: Marianne & Roger Braun

6 ROOMS, 6 pb

OPEN: ALL YEAR

$95-105

POINT REYES SEASHORE LODGE

OLEMA **37**

P.O. Box 39
10021 Highway 1
Point Reyes, CA 94950

Tel:1-415-663-9000

This elegantly re-created turn-of-the-century lodge offers stylish rooms and suites, many with fireplaces and whirlpool-spas. The suites feature sleeping lofts with European-type feather beds and are equipped with wet bars and refrigerators. This beautiful inn is ideally located next to the fabulous Point Reyes National Seashore. The area offers hundreds of miles of hiking and biking trails, lovely beaches, and gorgeous scenery.

 HOSTS: Judi & John Burkes

18 ROOMS, 48 pb   3 SUITES, 3 pb

$85-190   SPA   OPEN: ALL YEAR

ROUNDSTONE FARM

OLEMA **38**

P.O. Box 217
9940 Sir Francis Drake Blvd.
Point Reyes, CA 94950

Tel:1-415-663-1020

Surrounded by pastures where deer and horses peacefully graze, this board and batten cedar farmhouse was designed to take full advantage of the beautiful setting, wide open views and ever changing panorama. Wood-beamed ceilings and skylights add warmth and space to the custom-built home. Rooms are complete with cozy down comforters and European armoires. A hearty ranch breakfast with fresh juices, eggs and homemade scones is served each morning.

HOST: Inger Fisher

5 ROOMS, 5 pb

$95-125      OPEN: ALL YEAR

39 POINT REYES

HOSTS: Jeri Jacobsen & Herb Goldberg

BERRY PATCH COTTAGE
P.O. Box 712
68 Mesa Rd.
Point Reyes, CA 94956

Tel:1-415-663-1942

R

Hidden among fruit trees, berry bushes, and flowers, this country cottage has a library alcove, a redwood deck with views, and a unique potbellied stove. Guests can cook their own meals in the large, sunny kitchen. Walk or bicycle to town.

1 COTTAGE, 1 pb

OPEN: ALL YEAR $100

40 POINT REYES

HOST: Ewell McIsaac

THE COUNTRY HOUSE
P.O. Box 98
65 Manana Way
Point Reyes Station, CA 94956

Tel:1-415-663-1627

R

Hospitality is the hallmark of this rustic country home. Stay warm and cozy by the fireplace, stroll through the gardens, and enjoy the beautiful surroundings. Also featured are the delicious homemade breakfast and a children's book collection. As a vacation rental, the house can sleep ten.

3 ROOMS, 3 pb

OPEN: ALL YEAR $85-100

41 POINT REYES

HOST: Penelope Livingston

CRICKET COTTAGE
P.O. Box 627
18 Cypress Road
Point Reyes, CA 94956

Tel:1-415-663-9139

Relax in a private garden surrounded by a beautiful meadow or enjoy the whirlpool-spa beneath the stars. This rustic country cottage features original art, cozy furnishings, and a Franklin fireplace. Fresh eggs, homemade pastries, and orange juice are breakfast delights.

1 COTTAGE, 1 pb

OPEN: ALL YEAR SPA $115

FERRANDO'S HIDEAWAY
POINT REYES 42
P.O. Box 688
12010 Highway 1
Point Reyes, CA 94956
Tel:1-415-663-1966

R

Whether you stay in the cozy main house or in the secluded cottage, your visit here will be peaceful. Sit by the fireplace in the lounge, stroll through the spacious flower and vegetable garden, and then relax in the whirlpool-spa.

2 ROOMS, 2 pb   1 COTTAGE, 1 pb

$95-120   **SPA** OPEN: ALL YEAR HOSTS: Doris & Greg Ferrando

HOLLY TREE INN
POINT REYES 43
P.O. Box 642
3 Silverhills Rd.
Point Reyes, CA 94956
Tel:1-415-663-1554

R

Situated at the end of a wooded driveway and surrounded by gardens, this family-owned inn is peaceful and comfortable. Relax near the fireplace and enjoy the hospitality of your hosts. A cottage on the bay is available for solitude seekers.

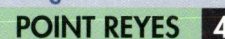

4 ROOMS, 4 pb   2 COTTAGES, 2 pb

$80-175   **SPA** OPEN: ALL YEAR HOSTS: Diane & Tom Balogh

JASMINE COTTAGE
POINT REYES 44
P.O. Box 56
11561 Highway 1
Point Reyes, CA 94956
Tel:1-415-663-1166

R

Enjoy this elegant country cottage all to yourself. This unique retreat offers sunny patios, beautiful views, and an open grassy meadow. If you're curious about the wonders of Point Reyes and the California coast, you can browse in the naturalist's library.

2 COTTAGES, 2 pb

$115   OPEN: ALL YEAR HOST: Karen Gray

45 POINT REYES

HOST: Sandy Fields

NEON ROSE
P.O. Box 632
76 Overlook
Point Reyes, CA 94956

Tel:1-415-663-9143

This lovely cottage overlooking Tomales Bay is ideal for those who wish to renew their spirits in a natural and peaceful environment. Santa Fe-inspired postmodern decor graces the interior. Prepare breakfast from supplies that are placed in the cottage.

1 COTTAGE, 1 pb

OPEN: ALL YEAR SPA **$125-150**

46 POINT REYES

HOST: Thomas Evans

POINT REYES COUNTRY INN & STABLES
P.O. Box 27
12050 Highway 1
Point Reyes, CA 94956

Tel:1-415-663-9696

A relaxing country Inn nestled in the rolling hill s adjacent to the Point Reyes National Seashore. Enjoy views of the Inverness ridge from your private balcony after a day of hiking and trail riding. Mountain bikes and horse stabling available.

5 ROOMS, 5 pb

OPEN: ALL YEAR SPA **$80-140**

47 POINT REYES

HOSTS: Terri Elaine & Richard Lailer

TERRI'S HOMESTAY
P.O. Box 113
Point Reyes, CA 94956

Tel:1-800-969-1289 or 1-415-663-1289

Gardens, birds, and a magnificent vista surround this sunny house, located in a wooded trailside setting. The natural beauty of the site is complemented by the colorful Central American decor. Professional massage services, which couples can receive simultaneously!

1 ROOM, 1 pb   1 SUITES, 1 pb

OPEN: ALL YEAR SPA **$75-126**

THIRTY-NINE CYPRESS

P.O. Box 176
39 Cypress Rd.
Point Reyes, CA 94956

Tel:1-415-663-1709

Warm welcomes, good cheer, and fantastic views of the Point Reyes Peninsula are trademarks of this hand-built cozy cottage. It is warmed by the sun and brightened by the beautiful paintings, prints, oriental rugs, and wood-paneled walls. Wake up to fresh-brewed coffee and feast on Julia's yummy egg casserole or wheat pancakes stuffed with fruit. During the day, hike on a wooded trail or picnic on the beach. Later, relax in the whirlpool-spa.

HOST: Julia Bartlett

3 ROOMS, 3 pb

$85-125 SPA OPEN: ALL YEAR

TRADEWINDS

P.O. Box 1117
12088 Highway 1
Point Reyes, CA 94956

Tel:1-415-663-9326

Situated on a sunny hillside, this comfortable ranch-style home provides a panoramic view of the surrounding country-side. The house was designed and built by the innkeeper in 1987. The luxurious accommodations combine hand-crafted wood with marble and tile. A spacious living room with cathedral ceilings and a woodstove opens onto a large sunny deck where you can relax and enjoy views of the horse pastures and surrounding hills.

HOST: John Walker

2 ROOMS, 2 pb

$90-110 SPA OPEN: ALL YEAR

50 POINT REYES

HOSTS: Virginia Drorbaugh & Tony Ragona

WINDSONG COTTAGE
P.O. Box 84
25 McDonald Lane
Point Reyes, CA 94956

Tel:1-415-663-9695

This unique cottage, with its pastoral and bay views, is a contemporary version of the yurt, a traditional dwelling of the nomadic tribes of Central Asia. The spacious interior, which includes a full kitchen, is comfortably furnished with family antiques and exotic details.

1 COTTAGE, 1 pb

OPEN: ALL YEAR   SPA   **$125**

51 SAN RAFAEL

HOSTS: Linda & Dan Cassidy

CASA SOLDAVINI
531 C Street
San Rafael, CA 94901

Tel:1-415-454-3140

Step back in time and enjoy the beauty that surrounds this 1930s Italian winemaker's home. The owners of this antique-filled inn invite their guests to play the piano, watch an old movie, or relax on the porch swing for a few quiet moments.

3 ROOMS, 2 pb

OPEN: ALL YEAR   **$65-90**

52 SAN RAFAEL

HOST: Carol Staley

FOUR TWENTY-FIVE MISSION
425 Mission Ave.
San Rafael, CA 94901

Tel:1-415-453-1365   R

You will be pampered in this homey setting, complete with landscaped yard and whirlpool-spa. The house is furnished in period antiques, and each bedroom has a character of its own. For a taste of the Orient, stay in the Cho Cho room.

4 ROOMS, 2 pb

OPEN: ALL YEAR   SPA   **$65-95**

PANAMA HOTEL
4 Bayview St.
San Rafael, CA 94901

Tel:1-800-899-3993
or 1-415-457-3993

SAN RAFAEL 53

Get a feel for Latin America's charm and intrigue in this urban villa. The rooms are a collage of color and comfort, and the restaurant offers delightful dishes. Romantics have the option of dining in their own room.

15 ROOMS, 9 pb

$45-110 OPEN: ALL YEAR HOST: Daniel Miller

LITTLE HARBOR VIEW
317 South St.
Sausalito, CA 94965

Tel:1-415-387-5595
or 1-415-331-3000

SAUSALITO 54

The romantic ambiance of these cozy guest suites is enhanced by the natural beauty of their secluded setting. Trees, flowers, and a lovely bay view add to the elegance of these light, airy, and tastefully furnished suites. Walk to town.

2 SUITES, 2 pb

$95-105 OPEN: ALL YEAR HOST: Christa C. Kerl-König

CHIKABUMI COTTAGE
P.O. Box 684
3 Laurel Ave.
Woodacre, CA 94973

Tel:1-415-488-4388

WOODACRE 55

Chikabumi (an Ainu word meaning "home of the birds") is a secluded cottage set among beautiful Douglas firs. Hike or ride horseback on the many nearby trails. A delicious breakfast is served in the main house or in your room. The kitchen will be fully stocked with a delicious breakfast.

1 COTTAGE, 1 pb

$75-95 SPA OPEN: ALL YEAR HOST: Jim Staley

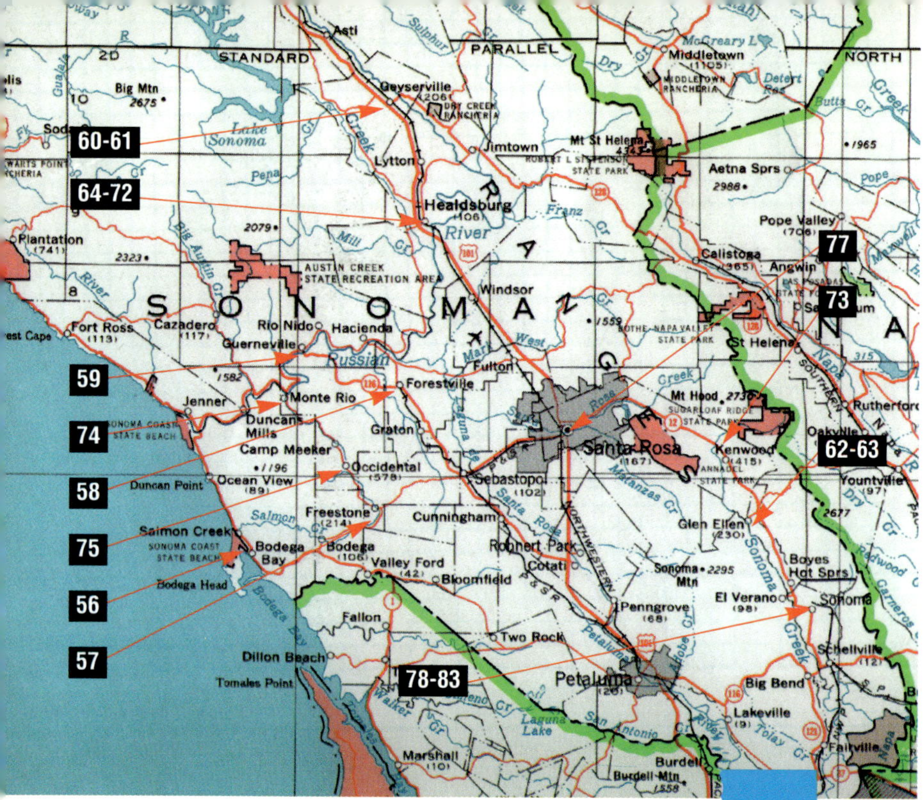

60-61

64-72

59

74

58

75

56

57

77

73

62-63

78-83

Asti
STANDARD PARALLEL
McCreary L.
Middletown
MIDDLETOWN
RANCHERIA
Desert
Res.
NORTH
Big Mtn
2675
Geyserville
(206)
DRY CREEK
RANCHERIA
Jimtown
Mt St Helena
4343
ROBERT L. STEVENSON
STATE PARK
1965
Dry
Cr.
Butts Cr.
Soda
Lake
Sonoma
Lytton
Healdsburg
(106)
Franz
Cr.
Aetna Sprs
2986
Pope
Pope Valley
(706)
Calistoga
3665
Angwin
SWARTS POINT
RANCHERIA
Pena
Cr.
River
RUSSIAN
2079
Mill Cr.
AUSTIN CREEK
STATE RECREATION AREA
2323
8
Windsor
559
BOTHE NAPA VALLEY
STATE PARK
St Helena
315
Plantation
(741)
Fort Ross
(113)
Cazadero
(117)
Rio Nido
Hacienda
Guerneville
Russian
West Cr.
Fulton
Mt Hood
2730
SUGARLOAF RIDGE
STATE PARK
Rutherford
est Cape
1582
Jenner
Monte Rio
Forestville
116
Santa Rosa
(167)
Kenwood
(415)
ANNADEL
STATE PARK
Oakville
(97)
Yountville
(97)
SONOMA COAST
STATE BEACH
Duncans
Mills
Camp Meeker
Graton
Glen Ellen
(230)
2677
Duncan Point
196
Ocean View
(89)
Occidental
(578)
Sebastopol
(102)
Cunningham
Salmon Creek
SONOMA COAST
STATE BEACH
Freestone
(214)
Bodega
Bodega
Bay
(106)
Valley Ford
(42)
Rohnert Park
Cotati
Sonoma Mtn.
2295
El Verano
(98)
Boyes
Hot Sprs
Sonoma
Schellville
(12)
Bodega Head
Fallon
Bloomfield
Penngrove
(68)
Big Bend
Dillon Beach
Two Rock
Petaluma
Lakeville
(9)
121
Fairville
Tomales Point
Marshall
(101)
Burdell
Burdell Mtn.
1558

44

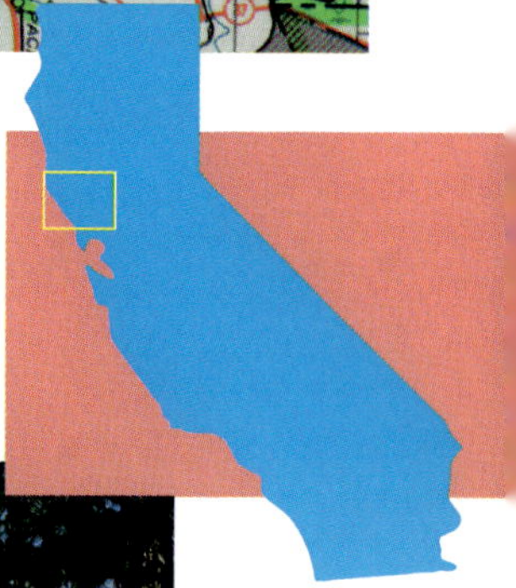

SONOMA
COUNTY

The topology, history, modern-day activities, and culture of Sonoma County are remarkably diverse. From its rugged coastline (once home to a Russian trading outpost), through the redwood forests lining the Russian River, to the Spanish mission town of Sonoma, the Valley of the Moon offers much beyond its international reputation for premium wine production. Rooted in such industries as fishing, lumber, and agriculture, Sonoma County today is a favorite area for nature lovers, gourmands, sports enthusiasts (biking, hiking, golfing, cycling, horseback riding—you name it), amateur historians, and anyone with a desire to experience the sheer breadth and beauty of its varied landscape.

The Sonoma coast was first settled by Tsarist Russians, who built a stockade at the site of Fort Ross. They married Pomo Indians and, later on, Spanish pioneers who came into the area. In the 1830s, when Mexico sent General Mariano Vallejo to secure the area, Sonoma County was divided into huge tracts, which were deeded as ranches to Vallejo's family and associates. This rich cultural tradition ultimately included wine makers from Hungarian nobility, American fortune-seekers, Italian grape-growers, and even smugglers who brought spirits in from Canada during the Prohibition era and hid among the rocky coves along the Sonoma coastline.

Start your tour of Sonoma County in **Bodega Bay,** a thriving village that gives you the opportunity to try deep-sea fishing—or to enjoy the catch of the day at a wonderful seafood restaurant on the waterfront. A few miles inland you will find the pretty town of **Freestone,** home of fourth- and fifth-generation California families, set amid wooded bluffs.

A forty-five minute drive to the south-east brings you to the bustling city of **Petaluma.** Once known as the Egg Capital of the World, Petaluma's west side boasts stately Victorian mansions, and its downtown area has the warmth and feeling of a bygone era. While the poultry farms now coexist with the dairy industry (the Egg and Butter Days Festival is held in May), Petaluma's roots are distinctly Hispanic. You can still visit the outpost home of General Vallejo at the **Petaluma Adobe State Historic Park.**

Travelling 15 miles (24 km) east brings you to historic **Sonoma.** Home of the Suisun Indians and the last of the Spanish missions, this town was the site of the famous Bear Flag Rebellion and features some of the best-preserved

examples of mission architecture. Its large central square is reminiscent of the days when General Vallejo himself strolled through the plaza. His Victorian home is open to the public. After a "surveying party" under the direction of Colonel John C. Fremont "liberated" Sonoma and proclaimed California a republic under U.S. domain, General Vallejo continued to participate in community and civic life there. Very soon thereafter Hungarian Agaston Haraszthy founded the Buena Vista Winery, thereby helping to establish Sonoma as the first major center of viticulture and wine making in California. Some of the varietals that Haraszthy helped establish, like zinfandel, can still be enjoyed at many of Sonoma's fine restaurants and shops.

Nine miles (14 km) north of Sonoma on Highway 12 is **Glen Ellen,** home of the famous novelist **Jack London.** It was London's novel Valley of the Moon that popularized the area's romantic alias. (It is thought that Sonoma is a corruption of an Indian word that means "valley of the moon.") Glen Ellen's climate is typical of this area: hot, sunny days, moderated by coastal influences, make it ideal for grape production. In addition to prosperous wineries, its proximity to hiking trails and a museum at Jack London State Park give the town its special appeal.

The county seat is **Santa Rosa,** just 16 miles (26 km) north. A hometown atmosphere combines with extensive shopping districts and a variety of cultural activities. The **Sonoma County Museum** and the **home and gardens of famous horticulturist Luther Burbank** are entertaining and educational diversions.

converted into elegant country inns, beloved by visitors and townsfolk alike. The **Healdsburg Museum** is rich with exhibits and memorabilia that bring the area's pioneer past alive.

On the outskirts of the Alexander Valley, on Highway 128, is the town of **Geyserville.** Here you can simply enjoy the mild days and evenings of the year-round temperate climate, savor country French cuisine, or even sign on as an "apprentice wine maker" and participate in the crush during the fall harvest.

Your trip concludes with a drive along the **Russian River** on Highway 116. Stands of ancient redwoods alternate with vineyards in this resort and river playground area. The river towns of **Guerneville, Monte Rio, Duncan Mills,** and **Forestville** offer family and adult resorts (where disco has replaced the big band music of an earlier era), in addition to hidden camping and canoeing enclaves. Driving on toward the ocean, you arrive at your final Sonoma County destination, the town of **Jenner.** Perched on a hillside overlooking the mouth of a river, Jenner is a small retreat community with great views of the surrounding area. It is located within minutes of spectacular coastal beaches and parks. Rich with marine life and pounded by thundering surf, these preserves give the traveller a full appreciation for the wonderful natural resources of the Valley of the Moon.

Buena Vista Winery, 18000 Old Winery Rd., slightly northeast of Sonoma, (707) 938-1266. **Healdsburg Museum,** 221 Matheson St., Healdsburg, open 12-5 except Sun. and Mon., free admission. **Jack London State Historic Park,** 2400 London Ranch Rd., Glen Ellen, (707) 938-5216, open daily 8-sunset, museum 10-5, $5 per car admission. **Petaluma Adobe State Historic Park,** 4 miles east of Petaluma at Adobe Rd. and Casa Grande Ave., open daily 10-5, small admission. **Sonoma Valley Visitors Bureau,** 453 1st St. East, Sonoma, (707) 996-1090.

RESTAURANTS S=under $10, $$=$10 to $20, $$$=over $20

BODEGA BAY
Inn at the Tides
800 Coast Highway
(707) 875-2751
California cuisine $$$

BOYES HOT SPRINGS
Papa Gayo
18625 Highway 12
(707) 935-0657
Mexican $

GEYSERVILLE
Chateau Souverain
400 Souverain Rd.
(707) 433-3141
American-French cuisine $$$

GLEN ELLEN
Amadeo
14301 Arnold Dr.
(707) 996-3077
Steak, seafood $$
Miel
13648 Arnold Dr.
(707) 938-4844
French cuisine $$

HEALDSBURG
Madrona Manor
1001 Westside Rd.
(800) 258-4003
(707) 433-4231
California cuisine $$$

SONOMA
Eastside Oysters Bar and Grill
133 E. Napa St.
(707) 939-1266
Grilled specialities $$
L'Esperance
464 First St.
(707) 996-2757
French cuisine $$
Pasta Nostra
139 E. NapaSt.
(707) 938-4166
Italian cuisine $$
Piattes
405 First St. W.
(707) 996-2351
Italian cuisine $$

Regina's at Sonoma Hotel
110 W. Spain St.
(707) 938-0254
New Orleans-style cuisine$$
Swiss Hotel
18 W. Spain St.
(707) 938-2884
Northern Italian cuisine $$
Winemaker
875 W. Napa St.
(707) 938-8489
European cuisine $$
Zino's
420 First St. E.
(707) 996-4466
Italian cuisine $$

Alderbrook Winery
2306 Magnolia Drive
Healdsburg, CA 95448
(707) 433-9154
Open: daily 10-5

Alexander Valley Fruit & Trading Co.
5110 Highway 128
Geyserville, CA 95441
(707) 433-1944
(800) 433-1944
Open: daily 10-5

Alexander Valley Vineyards
8644 Highway 128
Healdsburg, CA 95448
(707) 433-7209
Open: daily 10-5

Bellrose Vineyard
435 W. Dry Creek Road
Healdsburg, CA 95448
(707) 433-1637
Open: Tues thru Thurs 1-4:30
Fri thru Sun 11-4:30

Belvedere Winery
4035 Westside Road
Healdsburg, CA 95448
(707) 433-8236
Open: daily 10-4:30

Black Mountain & J.W. Morris Winery
101 Grant Ave.
Healdsburg, Ca 95448
(707) 431-7015
Open: Thurs thru Sun 10-4
Closed: Mon thru Wed

Buena Vista Winery
18000 Old Winery Road
Sonoma, CA 95476
(707) 938-1266
Open: daily 10-5

Davis Bynum Winery
8075 Westside Road
Healdsburg, CA 95448
(707) 433-5852
Open: daily 10-5

Chateau De Baun
5007 Fulton Road
Fulton, CA 95439
(707) 571-7500
Open: daily 10-5

Chateau Diana
6195 Dry Creek Road
Healdsburg, CA 95448
(707) 433-6992
Open: daily 11-4:30

Chateau St. Jean
8555 Sonoma Highway
Kenwood, CA 95452
(707) 833-4134
Open: daily 11-4:30

Chateau Souverain
400 Souverain Road
Geyserville, CA 95441
(707) 433-8281
Open: Tues thru Sun 10:30-5:30

Cline Cellars
24737 Arnold Drive
Sonoma, CA 95476
(707) 935-4310
Open: daily 10-6

Clos Du Bois
5 Fitch St.
Healdsburg, CA 95448
(707) 433-5576
Open: daily 10-4:30

De Loach Vineyards
1791 Olivet Road
Santa Rosa, CA 95401
(707) 526-9111
Open: daily 10-4:30

DeLorimier Winery
2001 Highway 128
Geyserville, CA 95441
(707) 443-7718
Open: Fri thru Mon

Domaine St. George Winery
1141 Grant Ave.
Healdsburg, CA 95448
(707) 433-5508
Open: daily 10-4

Dry Creek Vineyard
3770 Lambert Bridge Road
Healdsburg, CA 95448
(707) 433-1000
Open: daily 10:30-4:30

Ferrari-Carano Vineyards & Winery
8761 Dry Creek Road
Healdsburg, CA 95448
(707) 433-6700
Open: daily 10-5

Gloria Ferrer Champagne Caves
23555 Highway 121
Sonoma, CA 95476
(707) 996-7256
Open: daily 10:30-5:30

Field Stone Winery
10075 Highway 128
Healdsburg, CA 95448
(707) 433-7266
Open: daily 10-5

Foppiano Vineyards
12707 Old Redwood Highway
Healdsburg, CA 95448
(707) 433-7272
Open: daily 10-4:30

J. Fritz Cellars
24691 Dutcher Creek Road
Cloverdale, CA 95425
(707) 894-3389
Open: daily 11-4:30

Geyser Peak Winery
22281 Chianti Road
Geyserville, CA 95441
(707) 433-6585
Open: daily 10-5

Glen Ellen Winery
1883 London Ranch Road
Glen Ellen, CA 95442
(707) 935-3000
Open: daily 10-4:30

Gundlach Bundschu
Winery
2000 Denmark St.
Sonoma, CA 95476
(707) 938-5277
Open: daily 11-4:30

Hacienda Winery
1000 Vineyard Lane
Sonoma, CA 95476
(707) 938-3220
Open: daily 10-5

Kendall-Jackson Tasting
337 Healdsburg Ave.
Healdsburg, CA 95448
(707) 433-7102
Open: daily 10-5

Kenwood Vineyards
9592 Sonoma Highway
Kenwood, CA 95452
(707) 833-5891
Open: daily 10-4:30

Korbel Champagne Cellars
13250 River Road
Guerneville, CA 95446
(707) 887-2294
Open: daily 9-5

Lake Sonoma Winery
9990 Dry Creek Road
Geyserville, CA 95441
(800) 750-WINE
(707) 431-1550
Open: daily 10-5

Landmark Vineyards
101 Adobe Canyon Road
Kenwood, CA 95452
(707) 833-0053
Open: daily 10-4:30

Lytton Springs Winery
650 Lytton Springs Road
Healdsburg, CA 95448
(707) 433-7721
Open: daily 10-4

Mark West Vineyards
7000 Trenton-Healdsburg Road
Forestville, CA 95436
(707) 544-4813
Open: daily 10-5

Matanzas Creek Winery
6079 Bennett Valley Road
Santa Rosa, CA 95404
(707) 528-6464
Open: Mon thru Sat 10-4
Sun 12-4

Mazzocco Vineyards
1400 Lytton Springs Road
Healdsburg, CA 95448
(707) 433-9035
Open: daily 10-4

Mill Creek Vineyards
1401 Westside Road
Healdsburg, CA 95448
(707) 433-2121
Open: daily 10-4:30

Murphy-Goode Estate Winery
4001 Highway 128
Geyserville, CA 95441
(707) 431-7644
Open: daily 10:30-4:30

J. Pedroncelli Winery
1220 Canyon Road
Geyserville, CA 95441
(707) 857-3531
Open: daily 10-5

Piper Sonoma Cellars
11447 Old Redwood Highway
Healdsburg, CA 95448
(707) 433-8843
Open: daily 10-5

Ravenswood
18701 Gehricke Road
Sonoma, CA 95476
(707) 938-1960
Open: daily 10-4:30

Roche Winery
28700 Arnold Drive
Sonoma, CA 95476
(707) 935-7115
Open: daily 10-5

Rochioli Vineyard & Winery
6192 Westside Road
Healdsburg, CA 95448
(707) 433-2305
Open: daily 10-5

St. Francis Winery
8450 Sonoma Highway
Kenwood, CA 95452
(707) 833-4666
Open: daily 10-4:30

Sausal Winery
7370 Highway 128
Healdsburg, CA 95448
(707) 433-2285
Open: daily 10-4

Schug Carneros Estate Winery
602 Bonneau Road
Sonoma, CA 95476
(707) 939-9363
Open: daily 10-5

Sebastiani Vineyards
389 Fourth St. E.
Sonoma, CA 95476
(800) 888-5532
(707) 938-5532
Open: daily 10-5

Simi Winery
16275 Healdsburg Ave.
Healdsburg, CA 95448
(707) 433-6981
Open: daily 10-4:30

Sonoma Creek Winery
23355 Millerick Road
Sonoma, CA 95476
(707) 938-3031
Open: daily 11-4:30

Sotoyome Winery & Christopher Creek
641 Limerick Lane
Healdsburg, CA 95448
(707) 433-2001
Open: daily 11-5

Robert Stemmler Vineyards
3805 Lambert Bridge Road
Healdsburg, CA 95488
(707) 433-6334
Open: daily 10:30-4:30

Rodney Strong Vineyards
11455 Old Redwood Highway
Healdsburg, CA 95448
(707) 433-6511
Open: daily 10-5

Topolos at Russian River
5700 Gravenstein Highway N.
Forestville, CA 95436
(707) 887-1575
Open: daily 10-5:30

Trentadue Winery
19170 Geyserville Ave.
Geyserville, CA 95441
(707) 433-3104
Open: daily 10-5

Viansa Winery & Italian Marketplace
25200 Arnold Drive (Hwy.121)
Sonoma, CA 95476
(707) 935-4700
Open: daily 10-5

William Wheeler Winery
130 Plaza St.
Healdsburg, CA 95448
(707) 433-8786
Open: daily 11-5

White Oak Vineyards & Winery
208 Haydon St.
Healdsburg, CA 95448
(707) 433-8429
Open: Fri thru Sun 10-4

BAY HILL MANSION

P.O. Box 567
3919 Bay Hill Rd.
Bodega Bay, CA 94923
Tel:1-800-526-5927

R

This beautiful, contemporary Queen Anne-style mansion looks down over a sweeping panorama of the coast. Rooms are spacious, with high ceilings and elegant furnishings. Enjoy breakfast on the deck overlooking the ocean before a relaxing stroll to town and the beach.

6 ROOMS, 4 pb

$80-160  **SPA** **OPEN: ALL YEAR** **HOST: Frances Miller**

GREEN APPLE INN

520 Bohemian Hwy.
Freestone, CA 95472
Tel:1-707-874-2526

R

Located on five beautiful acres in the heart of the apple country, the inn is central to wineries and the coast. Enjoy bicycling, horseback riding, and fishing. This peaceful, New England-style farmhouse is furnished with heirloom antiques.

4 ROOMS, 4 pb   1 COTTAGE, pb

$82-90 **OPEN: ALL YEAR** **HOST: Rosemary & Rogers Hoffman**

THE FARMHOUSE INN

7871 River Rd.
Forestville, CA 95436
Tel:1-800-464-6642
or 1-707-887-3300

R

Set on six acres of rolling wine country, this meticulously restored turn-of-the-century farmhouse features luxurious guest rooms with whirlpool-spas and modern amenities. Some rooms have fireplaces, saunas, and wet bars. Elegant dining and special event planning available.

5 ROOMS, 5 pb   3 SUITES, 3 pb   **POOL**

$110-175 **SPA** **OPEN: ALL YEAR** **HOST: Rebecca Smith**

59 GUERNEVILLE

HOST: Lynn & Mark Crescione

CREEKSIDE INN
P.O. Box 2185
16180 Neeley Rd.
Guerneville, CA 95446
Tel:1-800-776-6586

Tucked away among the redwood trees, this charming inn, surrounded by rustic cottages and a creek, makes the perfect getaway. Stroll across Guernville's bridge to one of the Russian River beaches or visit Sonoma's fine wineries.

6 ROOMS, 0 pb   9 COTTAGE, 9 pb   **POOL**

OPEN: ALL YEAR   **$50-150**

60 GEYSERVILLE

HOST: Mary Jane & Jerry Campbell

CAMPBELL RANCH INN
1475 Canyon Rd.
Geyserville, CA 95441
Tel:1-707-857-3476

Enjoy strolling through the beautiful gardens, playing tennis and ping-pong, swimming, and cycling on the 35-acre grounds, or relax in the whirlpool-spa. The spacious rooms with private balconies overlook the surrounding vineyards. Eat breakfast and homemade desserts on the terrace.

4 ROOMS, 4 pb   1 COTTAGE, pb   **POOL**

OPEN: ALL YEAR   **SPA**   **$90-145**

61 GEYSERVILLE

HOST: Rosalie & Bob Hope

HOPE-MERRILL HOUSE
HOPE-BOSWORTH HOUSE
21253 Geyserville Ave.   P.O. Box 42
Geyserville, CA 95441
Tel:1-800-825-4BED (4233)

Featured in interior design magazines, these splendidly restored Victorian homes are furnished with exquisite antiques. Victorian furniture, fir floors, down comforters, whirlpool-spas, lush gardens with a gazebo, vineyards, and a heated pool will make your stay memorable. Prize-winning breakfast.

12 ROOMS, 11 pb   **POOL**

OPEN: ALL YEAR   **SPA**   **$95-135**

GLENELLY INN
GLEN ELLEN 62

5131 Warm Springs Rd.
Glen Ellen, CA 95442

Tel:1-707-996-6720

Situated in the quiet hamlet of Glen Ellen, this inn is a great place to watch the sun set over the Sonoma mountains. All of the beautifully decorated rooms open to the veranda or garden, and the spa is sublime. Throw off your Norwegian down comforter and begin your day with home-baked muffins, frittatas, souffles, quiches, oven pancakes, and fresh fruit from the garden.

HOST: Kristi Hallamore

8 ROOMS, 8 pb

$72-125 SPA OPEN: ALL YEAR

GAIGE HOUSE
GLEN ELLEN 63

13540 Arnold Dr.
Glen Ellen, CA 95442

Tel:1-707-935-0237

The decor of this landmark home, built around 1890, combines Victorian ambiance with a collection of early California art, antiques, and oriental rugs. Well situated for touring all the premium wine valleys, this inn makes a convenient base for maximizing your wine-country visit. Relax on the decks, swim in the pool, and enjoy the lovely gardens. The spacious rooms and indoor common areas are centrally heated and cooled.

HOST: Michol Tallent & Stephen Salvo

POOL

7 ROOMS, 7 pb   2 SUITES, 2 pb   1 COTTAGE, pb

$80-160 SPA OPEN: ALL YEAR

64 HEALDSBURG/WINDSOR

COUNTRY MEADOW INN
11360 Old Redwood Hwy.
Healdsburg/Windsor, CA 95492
Tel:1-800-238-1728

Share the informal country setting of this 1890 Victorian farmhouse, set amid gently rolling hills and open fields. Fruit trees, grape arbors, vegetable gardens, and terraced flower beds fill 6.5 acres of grounds. Comfortable guest rooms feature antiques, down comforters, and fresh flowers. Some have fireplaces and/or whirlpool-spas. Relax on the deck, by the pond, or in the pool. Enjoy the fresh abundant gourmet breakfast, built around local treats.

HOST: Sandy & Barry Weber

4 ROOMS, 4 pb   1 SUITE, pb   POOL

OPEN: ALL YEAR   SPA $75-165

65 HEALDSBURG

CALDERWOOD
P.O. Box 967
25 West Grant St.
Healdsburg, CA 95448
Tel:1-707-431-1110

Set behind ancient sentinel trees of cypress and spruce, this romantic and stately Queen Anne Victorian is a showcase of heirlooms, antique furnishings, glass, porcelain, and fine art. Down comforters and crisp linens add comfort and elegance. The elaborate, hand-crafted silkscreen Victorian-style wall and ceiling papers are an impressive touch. Gourmet cooking and entertaining are special passions of the hosts. Shops and restaurants are within walking distance.

HOST: Chris & Bob Maxwell

6 ROOMS, 6 pb

OPEN: ALL YEAR   SPA $95-150

CAMELIA INN
HEALDSBURG 66

211 North St.
Healdsburg, CA 95448
Tel:1-800-727-8182
or 1-707-433-8182

This elegant Italianate Victorian townhouse, built in 1869, features twin marble parlor fireplaces and an ornate mahogany dining room fireplace, which highlight the unique architectural features of the home. Take a dip in the pool, or walk to shops and wineries.

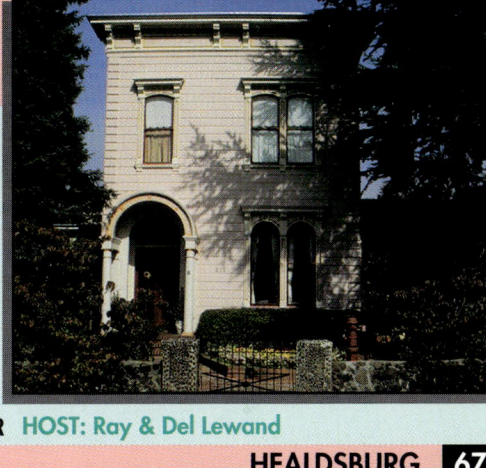

8 ROOMS, 8 pb **2 SUITES, 2 pb** **POOL**

$60-115  **SPA OPEN: ALL YEAR** HOST: Ray & Del Lewand

FRAMPTON HOUSE
HEALDSBURG 67

489 Powell Ave.
Healdsburg, CA 95448
Tel:1-707-433-5084

This Victorian inn, near the Russian River and surrounded by more than sixty wineries, has three luxurious guest rooms and a pool, whirlpool-spa, and sauna. Play ping-pong in the vine-covered arbor. Mountain bikes are at your disposal.

3 ROOMS, 3 pb **POOL**

$70-95 **SPA OPEN: ALL YEAR** HOST: Paula Bogle

THE GEORGE ALEXANDER HOUSE
HEALDSBURG 68

423 Matheson St.
Healdsburg, CA 95448
Tel:1-707-433-1358

This charming house, built in 1905, features exuberant late Victorian details, antiques, stained glass windows, and interesting art. It's within walking distance of the Russian River, shops, wine tasting, and fine dining. Or relax on the porch with your favorite book.

4 ROOMS, 4 pb

$80-160 **SPA OPEN: ALL YEAR** HOST: Phyllis & Christian Baldenhofer

SONOMA

69 HEALDSBURG

GRAPE LEAF INN
539 Johnson St.
Healdsburg, CA 95448
Tel:1-707-433-8140

Take an elegant step back in time in this beautifully restored 1900 Queen Anne Victorian home. Tall shade trees, lawns, and gardens provide the backdrop for this lovely inn located near downtown, wineries, Lake Sonoma, and the Russian River. Enjoy the scrumptious country breakfast and complimentary wine and cheese. The lovely guest rooms have skylight roof windows, air-conditioning, and whirlpool-spa or shower for two.

HOST: Karen & Terry Sweet

7 ROOMS, 7 pb

OPEN: ALL YEAR

SPA $85-130

70 HEALDSBURG

HEALDSBURG INN ON THE PLAZA
P.O. Box 1196
110 Matheson St.
Healdsburg, CA 95448
Tel:1-707-433-6991

Step back in time when you enter this 1900 Wells Fargo Express building in the heart of downtown. The tastefully appointed guest rooms, formerly professional offices, are decorated in American antiques. The solarium and roof garden provide a charming setting for a full breakfast and afternoon refreshments. Books, puzzles, games, and a TV are available in the lounge. Browse in the two gift shops, bakery, and art gallery on the main floor.

HOST: Genny Jenkins

9 ROOMS, 9 pb   1 SUITES, pb

OPEN: ALL YEAR

$55-155

58

MADRONA MANOR, A COUNTRY INN

P.O. Box 818
1001 Westside Rd.
Healdsburg, CA 95448
Tel:1-800-258-4003

There are a hundred wineries within a thirty minute drive of this magnificent country inn. Built in 1881, the majestic three-story, fifteen-room mansion contains its original antique furnishings. The mansion, the carriage house, and two other buildings offer eighteen bedrooms and three suites on eight acres of landscaped grounds with a swimming pool. All rooms are air conditioned, and the nationally acclaimed restaurant offers elegant candlelight dinners nightly. Relax. Enjoy.

HOST: John & Carol Muir

18 ROOMS, 18 pb   3 SUITES, 3 pb   **POOL**

$120-210

OPEN: ALL YEAR

RAFORD HOUSE

10630 Wohler Rd.
Healdsburg, CA 95448
Tel:1-707-887-9573

Originally built as a ranch home on fifteen hundred acres of hops, this splendid inn is a Sonoma County Historical Landmark. Today, the inn is surrounded by vineyards, orchards, and flowers. Enjoy a light country breakfast and complimentary wine and sherry. Antiques decorate the guest rooms, some of which have wood-burning fireplaces, decks overlooking the gardens, well-stocked libraries, and sitting rooms. Near many fine wineries, restaurants, historical points of interest, and the Russian River.

HOST: Gina & Vince Villenueve

8 ROOMS, 6 pb

$85-130

OPEN: ALL YEAR

73 KENWOOD

HOSTS: Roseann & Terry Grimm

KENWOOD INN
10400 Sonoma Hwy.
Kenwood, CA 95452
Tel:1-707-833-1293

R

The grounds of this romantic Italian villa boast flowers, trees, a swimming pool, and a shady grape arbor. When you walk into one of the four exquisite suites, complete with fireplace, you are greeted with a complimentary bottle of wine.

2 ROOMS, 2 pb   2 SUITES, 2 pb   **POOL**

OPEN: ALL YEAR   **SPA $125-225**

74 MONTE RIO

HOST: Michael Rusanowski

VILLAGE INN & LODGE
P.O. Box 850
20822 River Blvd.
Monte Rio, CA 95462
Tel:1-707-865-2304

R

This beautiful New England-style country inn is best known as "The Holiday Inn" from the famous movie of the same name, starring Bing Crosby. On the edge of the Russian River, the inn features river views, antiques, and dining on the terrace.

15 ROOMS, 5 pb   6 SUITES, 6 pb

OPEN: ALL YEAR   **$25-130**

75 OCCIDENTAL

HOST: Robert McDaniel

INN AT OCCIDENTAL
P.O. Box 857
3657 Church St.
Occidental, CA 95465
Tel:1-800-551-2292

R

You will find this remarkable inn in a sunny village in an enchanting redwood forest. This Victorian-style mansion, built in 1988, offers beautifully decorated rooms with private baths and its own intimate restaurant, which features the food and wines of Sonoma County.

7 ROOMS, 7 pb   1 SUITES, pb

OPEN: ALL YEAR   **$95-225**

CAVANAGH INN
10 Keller St.
Petaluma, CA 94952
Tel:1-707-765-4657

Built at the turn of the century, this redwood-paneled inn offers its guests a library full of books and games, a comfortable parlor with a fireplace, and a sunny glassed-in porch. The delightful full breakfast is served in the elegant dining room or on the deck in a garden setting. The inn is perfect for business functions, weddings, and other occasions. Historic downtown is just a short walk away.

HOST: Billie Erkel

7 ROOMS, 5 pb

$45-105   SPA   OPEN: ALL YEAR

THE GABLES INN
4257 Petaluma Hill Rd.
Santa Rosa, CA 95404
Tel:1-707-585-7777

Twelve-foot ceilings, three Italian marble fireplaces, and a mahogany spiral staircase are just a few of the elegant features of this Victorian inn. The Gables gets its name from the fifteen gables crowning the keyhole-shaped windows. Enjoy the brass beds and goose-down comforters in the guest rooms or the private creekside cottage. Visit the owl family in the 150-year-old barn, or cross the footbridge to wander in the meadow.

HOSTS: Judy & Mike Ogne

3 ROOMS, 3 pb   3 SUITES, 3 pb   1 COTTAGE, pb

$85-145   SPA   OPEN: ALL YEAR

SONOMA

78 SONOMA

HOST: Joe Leese

SONOMA CHALET
18935 5th St. West
Sonoma, CA 95476
Tel:1-707-938-3129

This Swiss-style chalet with country cottages is located in the beautiful Sonoma Valley. Romance abounds in antique-filled rooms complete with quilts and collectibles. A lovely breakfast is served outdoors. Listed in "Best Places to Kiss in the Bay Area."

2 ROOMS, 0 pb   1 SUITE, pb   3 COTTAGE, 3 pb

OPEN: ALL YEAR   SPA   **$75-125**

79 SONOMA

HOSTS: Dorene & John Musill

SONOMA HOTEL
110 West Spain St.
Sonoma, CA 95476
Tel:1-707-996-2996

This historic Victorian hotel, overlooking the downtown plaza, boasts antique rooms with European style-comfort. Some rooms have patios and sitting rooms. Enjoy drinks in the saloon or a delicious meal in the restaurant, which features contemporary country cuisine. Walk to shops and wineries.

17 ROOMS, 5 pb   1 SUITE, pb

OPEN: ALL YEAR   **$70-115**

80 SONOMA

HOST: Charles Papanteles

STONEGROVE
240 2nd St. East
Sonoma, CA 95476
Tel:1-707-939-8249

Fifteen bucolic acres surround this charming inn on Sonoma's historic east side. Stay in the large, comfortable studio, restored barn with kitchenette and deck entrance, or small antique stone house. Whirlpool-spa available. Walk two blocks to the plaza, dining, shops, and a winery.

1 ROOMS, pb   1 COTTAGE, pb

OPEN: ALL YEAR   SPA   **$75-85**

THISTLE DEW INN

171 West Spain St.
Sonoma, CA 95476
Tel:1-800 382-7895
1-707-938-2909

Located near Sonoma's historic town square, these two turn-of-the-century Victorians have exotic gardens, outdoor decks, living rooms with fireplaces, queen-sized beds, and ceiling fans. Soak in the whirlpool spa after a ride on the inn's complimentary bicycles.

6 ROOMS, 6 pb

$80-140   SPA   OPEN: ALL YEAR   HOSTS: Norma & Larry Barnett

TROJAN HORSE

19455 Sonoma Hwy.
Sonoma, CA 95476
Tel:1-707-996-2430

R

Originally the home of one of Sonoma's pioneer families, this beautifully restored inn decorated with antiques offers all of today's modern conveniences.   Soak in the whirlpool-spa in the garden or ride a bicycle to a winery.   Hosts weddings and business conferences.

6 ROOMS, 6 pb

$75-130   SPA   OPEN: ALL YEAR   HOSTS: Susan & Brian Scott

VICTORIAN GARDEN INN

316 East Napa St.
Sonoma, CA 95476
Tel:1-800-543-5339
1-707-996-5339

R

This lovely and unique 1880 Greek revival farmhouse is set on an acre of creekside gardens. Relax on the patio or by the pool and enjoy the hearty full breakfast. Walk to Sonoma Plaza, restaurants, wineries, and historic sites.

2 ROOMS, 2 pb   1 SUITES, pb   1 COTTAGE, pb

$79-139   SPA   OPEN: ALL YEAR   HOST: Donna Lewis

NAPA

C O U N T Y

The **Napa Valley** and **Lake County** regions of California offer a remarkable respite from busy urban schedules. Even with 25,000 acres (10,125 ha) of vineyards under cultivation and over two hundred wineries to visit, life here proceeds at a leisurely pace that is reminiscent of Europe's wine-growing regions, yet with an unmistakable feel of the Old West.

The traditions here date back over two hundred years to when Franciscan monks planted and tended European grape stock to make sacramental wine. More recently an entire industry has grown up around the pleasures of wine and unforgettable food in the towns along the **Silverado Trail,** which parallels Highway 29, the route that connects the southern portion of Napa County with the Clear Lake area. Winery maps are available in every town along the way, and most wineries are open year-round. In the spring, the wineries offer their new releases accompanied by regional delicacies that includes hand-made sausages, cheeses, and local fruits. In the fall, harvest festivals abound to celebrate the crush. Hot-air ballooning, cycling, and picnicking are favorite activities at any time, as is visiting the mineral-water spas at the valley's many hot-spring resorts.

Visits to wineries can be intimidating to the uninitiated, but the regimen is the same in most tasting rooms. Wine tasting is generally free, although a few wineries do charge a nominal fee. All tasting rooms display the wines they are pouring that day. They start you with the lighter white wines and then proceed to the richer reds. Often you will see a pitcher of water next to "spittoons," so that you can rinse your glass between samplings—a must. Some hosts also offer palate-cleansing crackers or bread. Wine tasting is not aimed at drinking. The amount of wine you are given is small, and it's not necessary to drink it all. Don't expect a "deal" on any wines you select for purchase—all you are guaranteed is the availability of the wine (especially important at the smaller boutiques and premium cellars), although you can often get a 20 percent discount on a case of twelve bottles.

Ballooning has reemerged only in the last decade as a sport and pastime. Gaily colored, heat-filled nylon envelopes safely carry passengers high above the vineyards and surrounding countryside. The only sound you can hear is the whoosh of the wind and your own happy laughter. Most ballooning begins at sunrise with a champagne breakfast in an open field where you can watch the balloonist (they are licensed!) prepare your craft. Ballooning is a popular gift for lovers of

all ages, and offers the guarantee of an exhilarating experience.

On a day when you are not ballooning or visiting wineries, definitely try a spa. Many offer a mud bath, followed by a shower and mineral bath; then on to a steam room and a massage. The mud is volcanic ash and water combined to make a thick paste, and the mineral water is from natural springs with temperatures high enough to relax even the tensest muscles. After this experience, you can float into a local restaurant for the best of relaxed dining.

Napa is the bustling county seat, where settlers first arrived in the 1830s. Farther north, **Yountville** was named for a North Carolinian, George Yount, who presided over a 12,000-acre (4,860 ha) Spanish land grant. Today it has the air of a European marketplace, with its acres of shops and restaurants that feature some of the area's best dining

presided over a 12,000-acre (4,860 ha) Spanish land grant. Today it has the air of a European marketplace, with its acres of shops and restaurants that feature some of the area's best dining and varietal wines. Major wineries line the route that takes you through **Oakville** and **Rutherford,** then on to **St. Helena**, home of author Robert Louis Stevenson and the **Silverado Museum**, which chronicles his life. North of St. Helena you'll find **Bale Grist Mill State Historic Park and Museum** and the 1,800-acre (725 ha) **Bothe-Napa Valley State Park**, with its miles of hiking trails through forests of redwood and madrone. **Calistoga** sits at the northern tip of the valley. The town offers geysers, warm springs and volcanic mud baths, a fossilized redwood forest dating back six million years, superb wineries, and a chance to view it all from a glider plane at 10,000 feet (3,058 m).

Lake County completes the tour, featuring fruit orchards and nut groves along slopes that gently taper down to Clear Lake and a hundred miles of beautiful shoreline. Fishing, boating, and resort life are unsurpassed. This area was once the home of the Pomo Indians who lived in the shadows of Mount Konochti, named for a legendary warrior chief. Today it is also home to an emerging wine industry of its own, and offers a lovely counterpoint to the Napa Valley.

Heading north on Highway 29, you'll meander through the towns encircling **Clear Lake** until you arrive at **Lakeport**, the county seat. Overlooking the northern expanse of the lake, nestled among oak-covered hills, resort life here ranges from the simple to the sumptuous. Enjoy award-winning wines and spectacular sunsets over the lake after a day of canoeing, water skiing, and bass fishing, as you reflect on a trip that has taken you through one of the richest agricultural areas in the world.

Bale Grist Mill State Historic Park and Museum, 3 miles north of St. Helena on Hwy. 29, (707) 942-4575, $2 adults, $1 children 7-18, open daily 10-5. **Napa Valley Conference & Visitors Bureau,** 1556 1st St., Napa, (707) 226-7459. **Napa Valley Wine Library Association/Silverado Museum,** 2 blocks west of Main on Adams St., Napa, open 12-4 daily except Monday.

RESTAURANTS $=under $10, $$=$10 to $20, $$$=over $20

CALISTOGA
All Seasons Cafe & Wine Shop
1400 Lincoln Ave.
(707) 942-9111
California cuisine $$-$$$
Calistoga Inn
1250 Lincoln Ave.
(707) 942-4101
California cuisine, home brew $
Checkers
1414 Loncoln Ave.
(707) 942-9300
Pizza, salads, pasta $
Valerianos
1457 Linclon Ave.
(707) 942-0606
Italian cuisine $$

KELSEYVILLE
Lakewood Restaurant
6330 Soda Bay
(707) 279-9450
French cuisine $$

LAKEPORT
Anthony's
2509 Lakeshore Blvd.
(707) 263-4905
Italian cuisine $$

LUCERNE
Bretwood Inn
6278 E. Hwy 20
(707) 274 2301
American fare, seafood $$

NAPA
La Boucane
1778 Second St.
(707) 253-1177
Classic French cuisine $$$
Mustards Grill
7399 St. Helena Highway
(707) 944-2424
California cuisine $$-$$$

ST. HELENA
Armadillo
1304 Main St.
(707) 936-8082
Mexican $$
Green Valley Cafe
1310 Main St.
(707) 963-7088
Italian cuisine $$
Rissa Oriental Cafe
1420 Main St.
(707) 963-7566
Eclectic Asian $
Showley's at Miramonte
1327 Railroad Ave.
(707) 963-1200
California cuisine $$
Terra Restaurant
1345 Railroad Ave.
(707) 963-8931
Italian-Japanese cuisine $$

Tra Vigne
1050 Charter Oak Ave.
(707) 963-4444
California-French-Italian cuisine $$
Trilogy
1234 Main St.
(707) 963-5507
California-French cuisine $$

YOUNTVILLE
Compadres Mexican Bar & Grill
6539 Washington St.
(707) 944-2406
Mexican with grilled specialties $$
Domaine Chandon
California Dr.
(707) 944-2892
California-French cuisine $$$
The French Laundry
Corner of Washington and Creek Sts.
(707) 944-2380
Country French cuisine $$$

S. Anderson Vineyard
1473 Yountville Cross Road
Yountville, CA 94599
(707) 944-8642
Open: daily 10-5

Beaulieu Vineyard
1960 St. Helena Highway
Rutherford, CA 94573
(707) 963-2411
Open: daily 10-5

Bergfield Winery
401 St. Helena Highway S.
St. Helena, CA 94574
(707) 963-7293
Open: daily 10-5

Beringer Vineyards
2000 Main St.
St. Helena, CA 94574
(707) 963-7115
Open: daily 9:30-6

Cakebread Cellars
8300 St. Helena Highway
Rutherford, CA 94573
(707) 963-5221
Open: daily 10-4

Carneros Alambic Distillery
1250 Cuttings Wharf Road
Napa, CA 94559
(707) 253-9055
Open: daily 10-5

Carneros Creek Winery
1285 Dealy Lane
Napa, CA 94559
(707) 253-9463
Open: daily 10-5

Casa Nuestra
3451 Silverado Trail N.
St. Helena, CA 94574
(707) 963-5783
Open: Fri. thru Sun. 11-5

Caymus Vineyards
8700 Conn Creek Road
Rutherford, CA 94573
(707) 963-4204
Open: daily 10-4

Chateau Montelena Winery
1429 Tubbs Lane
Calistoga, CA 94515
(707) 942-5105
Open: daily 10-4

Chimney Rock Winery
5350 Silverado Trail
Napa, CA 94558
(707) 257-2641
Open: daily 10-4

Clos Du Val
5330 Silverado Trail
Napa, CA 94558
(707) 252-6711
Open: daily 10-4

Clos Pegase
1060 Dunaweal Lane
Calistoga, CA 94515
(707) 942-4981
Open: daily 10:30-5

Codorniu Napa
1345 Henry Road
Napa, CA 94558
(707) 224-1668
Open: Mon. thru Thurs. 10-5
Fri. thru Sun. 10-3

Conn Creek Winery
8711 Silverado Trail
St. Helena, CA 94574
(707) 963-5133
Open: daily 10-5:30

Cosentino Winery
7415 St. Helena Highway
Yountville, CA 94599
(707) 944-1220
Open: daily 10-5:30

Cuvaison Winery
4550 Silverado Trail
Calistoga, CA 94515
(707) 942-6266
Open: daily 10-5

DeMoor Winery
7481 St. Helena Highway
Oakville, CA 94562
(707) 944-2565
Open: daily 10-5

Domaine Carneros
1240 Duhig Road
Napa, CA 94559
(707) 257-0101
Open: daily 10:30-5:30

Domaine Chandon
1 California Drive
Yountville, CA 94599
(707) 944-2280
Open: daily 11-6

Duckhorn Vinyards
3027 Silverado Trail
St. Helena, CA 94574
(707) 963-7108
Open: daily 9-5

Franciscan Oakville Estate
1178 Galleron Road
Rutherford, CA 94573
(707) 963-7111
Open: daily 10-5

Freemark Abbey Winery
3022 St. Helena Highway N.
St. Helena, CA 94574
(707) 963-9694 Ext. 14
Open: daily 10-4:30

Grgich Hills Cellar
1829 St. Helena Highway
Rutherford, CA 94573
(707) 963-2784
Open: daily 9:30-4:30

Guenoc Winery
21000 Butts Canyon Road
Middletown, CA 95461
(707) 987-2385
Open: Thurs. thru Sun. 10-4:30

Heitz Wine Cellars
436 St. Helena Highway S.
St. Helena, CA 94574
(707) 963-3542
Open: daily 11-4:30

The Hess Collection Winery
4411 Redwood Road
Napa, CA 94558
(707) 255-1144
Open: daily 10-4

Inglenook-Napa Valley
1991 St. Helena Highway
Rutherford, CA 94573
(707) 967-3300
Open: daily 10-5

Kendall-Jackson
600 Matthews Road
Lakeport, CA 95453
(707) 263-5299
Open: daily 11-5

Konocti Winery
Highway 29 at Thomas Frive
Kelseyville, CA 95451
(707) 279-8861
Open: daily 10-5

Hanns Kornell Champagne
1091 Larkmead Lane
Calistoga, CA 94574
(707) 963-1237
Open: daily 10-4:30

Charles Krug Winery
2800 St. Helena Highway
St. Helena, CA 94574
(707) 963-5057
Open: Thurs. thru Tues. 10-5

Lakespring Winery
2055 Hoffman Lane
Napa, CA 94558
(707) 944-2475
Open: daily 10:30-3:30

Markham Vineyards
2812 St. Helena Highway N.
St. Helena, CA 94574
(707) 963-5292
Open: daily 11-5

Milat Vineyards
1091 St. Helena Highway S.
St. Helena, CA 94574
(707) 963-0758
Open: daily 10-6

Robert Mondavi Winery
7801 St. Helena Highway
Oakville, CA 94562
(707) 963-9611
Open: daily 9-5

Mont St. John Cellars
5400 Old Sonoma Road
Napa, CA 94559
(707) 255- 8864
Open: daily 10-5

Mumm Napa Valley
8445 Silverado Trail
Rutherford, CA 94573
(707) 942-3434
Open: daily 11-6

Napa Creek Winery
1001 Silverado Trail
St. Helena, CA 94574
(707) 963-9456
Open: daily 10:30-4:30

Nichelini Winery
2950 Sage Canyon Road
St. Helena, CA 94574
(707) 963-0717
Open: daily 10-6

Robert Pepi Winery
7585 St. Helena Highway
Oakville, CA 94562
(707) 944-2807
Open: daily 10:30-4:30

Joseph Phelps Vineyards
200 Taplin Road
St. Helena, CA 94574
(707) 963-2745
Open: daily 9-4

Pine Ridge Winery
5901 Silverado Trail
Napa, CA 94558
(707) 253-7500
Open: daily 11-5

Raymond Vineyard and Cellar
849 Zinfandel Lane
St. Helena, CA 94574
(707) 963-8511
Open: daily 10-4

Round Hill Winery
1680 Silverado Trail
St. Helena, CA 94574
(707) 963-5251
Open: daily 10-4:30

Rutherford Hill Winery
200 Rutherford Hill Road
Rutherford, CA 94573
(707) 963-7194
Open: daily 10-4:30

Rutherford Vintners
1673 St. Helena Highway
Rutherford, CA 94573
(707) 963-4117
Open: daily 10-4:30

St. Clement Vineyards
2867 St. Helena Highway N.
St. Helena, CA 94574
(707) 963-7221
Open: daily 10-4

St. Supery Vineyards & Winery
8440 St. Helena Highway
Rutherford, CA 94573
(707) 963-4507
Open: daily 9:30-4:30

V. Sattui Winery
1111 White Lane
St. Helena, CA 94574,
(707) 963-7774
Open: daily 9-6

Sequoia Grove Vineyards
8338 St. Helena Highway
Rutherford, CA 94573
(707) 944-2945
Open: daily 11-5

Silver Oak Wine Cellars
915 Oakville Cross Road
Oakville, CA 94562
(707) 944-8808
Open: Mon thru Sat 10-4:30

Silverado Hill Cellars
3103 Silverado Trail
Napa, CA 94558
(707) 253-9306
Open: Wed thru Sun 11-5:30

Silverado Vineyards
6121 Silverado Trail
Napa, CA 94558
(707) 257-1770
Open: daily 11-4:30

Spring Mountain Vineyards
2805 Spring Mountain Road
St. Helena, CA 94574
(707) 963-5233
Open: daily 10-5

Stag's Leap Wine Cellars
5766 Silverado Trail
Napa, CA 94558
(707) 944-2020
Open: daily 10-4

Sterling Vineyards
1111 Dunaweal Lane
Calistoga, CA 94515
(707) 942-3344
Open: daily 10:30-4:30

Stonegate Winery
1183 Dunaweal Lane
Calistoga, CA 94515
(707) 942-6500
Open: daily 10:30-4:30

Sutter Home Winery
277 St. Helena Highway S.
St. Helena, CA 94574
(707) 963-3104
Open: daily 9-5

Trefethen Vineyards
1160 Oak Knoll Ave.
Napa, CA 94558
(707) 255-7700
Open: daily 10-4:30

Vichon Winery
1598 Oakville Grade
Oakville, CA 94562
(707) 944-2811
Open: daily 10-4:30

Villa Mt. Eden
620 Oakville Cross Road
Napa, CA 94558
(707) 944-2414
Open: daily 10-4

Wermuth Winery
3942 Silverado Trail,
Calistoga, CA 94515
(707) 942-5924
Open: daily 10-5

Whitehall Lane Winery
1563 St. Helena Higway S.
St. Helena, CA 94574
(707) 963-9454
Open: daily 11-5

ZD Wines
8383 Silverado Trail
Napa, CA 94558
(707) 963-5188
Open: daily 10-4:30

BRANNAN COTTAGE INN

109 Wapoo
Calistoga, CA 94515
Tel:1-707-942-4200

This award-winning inn, listed on the National Register of Historic Places, was built in 1860 by Sam Brannan, the founder of Calistoga. Light oak floors, primitive pine antiques, hand-painted stenciled walls, and fresh white wicker decorate this refreshing Victorian country cottage. Rooms have down comforters and private entrances. It's a two-minute walk to Main Street's spas, restaurants, and shops. A gourmet breakfast is served in the lovely gardens.

HOSTS: Mary, Earle & Rick

4 ROOMS, 4 pb	2 SUITES, 2 pb

$95-145

OPEN: ALL YEAR

CHRISTOPHER'S INN

1010 Foothill Blvd.
Calistoga, CA 94515
Tel:1-707-942-5755

In the heart of the Napa Valley wine country, this new country inn features Laura Ashley decor and selected antiques. Several of the elegantly appointed guest rooms have wood-burning fireplaces, and most have patio gardens. The wonderful breakfast is delivered to your room in a lovely basket. Inquire about the conference room—it's perfect for small seminars. Play croquet in the garden and walk to spas and downtown.

HOST: Christopher Layton

9 ROOMS, 9 pb	1 SUITES, pb

$100-165

OPEN: ALL YEAR

86 | CALISTOGA

HOST: Elaine Bryant

THE ELMS, A BED AND BREAKFAST INN
1300 Cedar St.
Calistoga, CA 94515
Tel:1-800-235-4316

This beautiful French Victorian home was built by Judge Palmer in 1871. Each room is uniquely decorated to reflect French and Victorian cultures. Giant elm trees grace the garden. Walk to shops, fine restaurants, and the many natural spas.

4 ROOMS, 4 pb   1 SUITE, pb

OPEN: ALL YEAR $85-200

87 | CALISTOGA

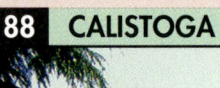
HOSTS: Doris & Gus Beckert

FOOTHILL HOUSE
3037 Foothill Blvd.
Calistoga, CA 94515
Tel:1-800-942-6933
or 1-707-942-6933

Nestled in the foothills north of Calistoga, this turn-of-the-century country house is surrounded by trees that shelter a variety of wildlife. Each suite and cottage has country antiques, four-poster bed, private entrance, small refrigerator, fireplace, and air conditioning. Some have whirlpool-spas.

3 SUITES, 3 pb   1 COTTAGE, pb

OPEN: ALL YEAR   SPA $110-250

88 | CALISTOGA

HOST: Ursula Tiber

LA CHAUMIERE
1301 Cedar St.
Calistoga, CA 94515
Tel:1-707-942-5139

This cozy country cottage is a haven of quiet privacy, where antiques, private decks, and a fireplace welcome you. Soak in the spa under a giant redwood or sample wines from the host's cellar. Walk to shops, restaurants, and spas.

2 ROOMS, 0 pb   1 COTTAGE, pb

OPEN: ALL YEAR   SPA $125-200

MEADOWLARK COUNTRY HOUSE

601 Petrified Forest Rd.
Calistoga, CA 94515
Tel:1-707-942-5651

R

Casual sophistication and understated elegance describe this country inn, which enjoys beautiful views of the twenty-acre grounds. English country antiques and comfortable contemporary furniture create a unique atmosphere ideal for retreats, meetings, and special functions. Relax by the pool.

4 ROOMS, 4 pb

POOL

$110-125

OPEN: ALL YEAR **HOST: Kurt Stevens**

THE PINK MANSION

1415 Foothill Blvd.
Calistoga, CA 94515
Tel:1-800-238-7465
or 1-707-942-0558

Guests enjoy the romance, comfort, and elegance of this turn-of-the-century home. One of Calistoga's most enduring landmarks, it features five distinctive rooms, among them the luxurious Rose Room Suite and the eclectic Oriental Room. Walk to town.

5 ROOMS, 5 pb

POOL

$85-155

OPEN: ALL YEAR **HOST: Jeff Seyfreid**

SCARLETT'S COUNTRY INN

3918 Silverado Trail
Calistoga, CA 94515
Tel:1-707-942-6669

R

This French country inn is a quiet retreat tucked away in a small canyon. Take a dip in the pool, pick fruit from the trees, read under the shade of a tall pine, or just relax in silence and privacy.

1 ROOMS, 1 pb   2 SUITES, 2 pb

POOL

$65-135

OPEN: ALL YEAR **HOST: Scarlett Dwyer**

92 CALISTOGA

HOSTS: Anita & Dennis Hubert

SLEEPY HOLLOW INN
911 Foothill Blvd.
Calistoga, CA 94515
Tel:1-707-942-4760

R

Nestled in a wooded setting, this lovely 1938 country-style inn is walking distance from spas and restaurants. Rooms are spacious, light, and airy. One guest room has a private kitchen, another has its own sunporch. Each room has a coffee pot.

2 ROOMS, 2 pb   1 SUITES, pb

OPEN: ALL YEAR   **$80-125**

93 CALISTOGA

HOSTS: Lani & Randy Gray

TRAILSIDE INN
4201 Silverado Trail
Calistoga, CA 94515
Tel:1-707-942-4106

R

This charming, centrally located 1930s farmhouse has three adjoining garden suites surrounded by trees and flowers. Comfortably decorated with quilts and antiques, each suite has a private entrance, porch, and kitchen. Breakfast fixings are provided for you to prepare at your leisure.

3 SUITES, 3 pb

OPEN: ALL YEAR   **SPA**   **$95-120**

94 CALISTOGA

HOSTS: Marina & Keith Dinsmoor

WISHING WELL INN
2653 Foothill Blvd.
Calistoga, CA 94515
Tel:1-707-942-5534

This 3.5-acre country vineyard estate has an elegant period interior and a spectacular view of the mountains. A full gourmet breakfast and evening wine and hors d'oeuvres are served poolside or on your private sun deck. Soak in the whirlpool-spa.

3 ROOMS, 3 pb

POOL

OPEN: ALL YEAR   **SPA**   **$90-150**

WASHINGTON STREET LODGING

CALISTOGA | 95

1605 Washington St.
Calistoga, CA 94515
Tel:1-707-942-6968

These cozy cottages in a private creekside setting offer relaxation and calm. Lodgings are complete with antique and country furnishings, private kitchens, and a beautiful garden view. Close to the center of town, the cottages provide a comfortable base from which to explore Calistoga's many attractions. Visit unique shops, dine in luxury at award-winning restaurants, and explore local wineries. Be sure to see Calistoga's famous spouting geyser, "Old Faithful."

5 COTTAGE, 5 pb

$80-90

R HOST: Joan Ranieri

OPEN: ALL YEAR

KRISTALBERG B& B

LUCERNE | 96

P.O. 1629
715 Bruner Dr.
Lucerne, CA 95458
Tel:1-707-274-8009

Kristalberg features spectacular views of Clear Lake from its mountain perch opposite Mount Konocti. Enjoy a bird's-eye view of a beautiful panorama of lake, mountains, and forest from this elegant eagle's nest. European / Victorian decor, warm hospitality, tasty, nutrtitious gourmet breakfast; Host speaks German, Spanish and French. Hike the trails, swim in the lake or just relax and watch the sun go down.

R HOST: Merv Myers

3 ROOMS, 3 pb

$55-150

SPA OPEN: ALL YEAR

97 LAKEPORT

HOSTS: Ginny & Don Carmody

THE WOODEN BRIDGE B&B
1441 Oakwood Court
Lakeport, CA 95453
Tel:1-707-263-9125

Ⓡ

This elegant inn is situated on five secluded acres of meadows studded with oak trees and a variety of wildflowers. Enjoy afternoon refreshments while relaxing in a large sitting-dining room that features a wood-burning stove for winter warmth.

2 ROOMS, 2 pb

OPEN: ALL YEAR $105-125

98 NAPA

HOSTS: Carol & Jim Beazley

BEAZLEY HOUSE
1910 First St.
Napa, CA 94559
Tel:1-800-559-1649 CAL
or 1-707-257-1649

Ⓡ

Beazley House, Napa's first B&B (built circa 1902), is a landmark mansion and carriage house. It is surrounded by beautiful gardens. Some of the elegant rooms have a private whirlpool-spa and a fireplace. Breakfast is a delicious California buffet.

11 ROOMS, 11 pb

OPEN: ALL YEAR SPA $105-185

99 NAPA

HOSTS: Susan & Tom Ridley

BROOKSIDE VINEYARD
3194 Redwood Rd.
Napa, CA 94558
Tel:1-707-944-1661

Ⓡ

This California Mission-style inn is also a working vineyard that produces premium-quality Chardonnay grapes. Enjoy breakfast in the gazebo surrounded by fragrant gardens and vineyards. Complimentary wine and cheese are served beside the swimming pool in the afternoon.

2 ROOMS, 2 pb   1 SUITE, pb

POOL

OPEN: ALL YEAR $85-105

CHURCHILL MANOR

485 Brown St.
Napa, CA 94559
Tel:1-707-253-7733

Each distinctive room in this 1889 grand mansion is tastefully furnished with antiques. Play croquet in the side garden, discover old-town Napa on a tandem bicycle, or relax with soft music on the expansive veranda. Afternoon fresh-baked cookies and evening wines and cheeses are served for your enjoyment. Breakfast, served in the marble-floored sun room, consists of French toast, fresh fruit, gourmet omelettes, fresh-squeezed juice, home-baked muffins, nut breads, and croissants.

R **HOSTS: Joanna & Brian Jensen**

10 ROOMS, 10 pb
$75-160 SPA OPEN: ALL YEAR

COUNTRY GARDEN INN

1815 Siverado Trail
Napa, CA 94558
Tel:1-707-255-1197

Situated on 1.5 acres of mature woodland riverside property, this English country-style inn is surrounded by trees, flowers, a garden terrace, and a rose garden with lily pond and fountain. Many of the elegant rooms have pine furniture, poster beds, fireplaces, whirlpool-spas, and balconies overlooking the garden. Creative champagne breakfast, evening hors d'oeuvres, and desserts are served. Complimentary wine is brought to your room.

R **HOSTS: Lisa & George Smith**

8 ROOMS, 8 pb
$105-190 SPA OPEN: ALL YEAR

102 NAPA

CANDLELIGHT INN
1045 Easum Drive
Napa, CA 94558
Tel:1-800-788-0236
or 1-707-257-3717

Built in 1929, this elegant English Tudor home is surrounded by an acre of trees and lawns in a serene country setting. Guest suites are cozy and tastefully decorated. The inn is close to the delights of the area and is just minutes from the wine train. Your hosts will share Napa Valley's secrets during the afternoon social hour, and will serve you a candlelight breakfast in the dining room overlooking the garden.

HOSTS: Carol & Joe Farace

9 ROOMS, 9 pb

OPEN: ALL YEAR 🍴☕🔥 **SPA** **$112-150**

103 NAPA

HOSPITALITY HOUSE B&B
4455 LindaVista Ave.
Napa, CA 94558
Tel:1-707-226-5092

Away from traffic and close the adventures of the valley. This two-story colonial home boasts contemporary furnishings and is surrounded by five acres with beautiful gardens. Guests may lounge on the patio, explore nearby wineries or take in the view—from a hot-air balloon. Enjoy a delicious breakfast in the morning and complimentary refreshments in the afternoon. Learn about the wine country from your hostess, a lifelong resident of Napa.

HOSTS: Dorothy & Harry Wojcik

3 ROOMS, 1 pb

OPEN: ALL YEAR ☕ **$75-85**

LA BELLE EPOQUE

NAPA 104

1386 Calistoga Ave.
Napa, CA 94559

Tel:1-707-257-2161

Journey into the beauty and romance of this 1893 Victorian mansion. An exquisite collection of fine period antiques and original stained glass windows add elegance to the spacious and tastefully decorated accommodations. Wines from the owner's cellar and hors d'oeuvres are served nightly. Breakfast is served by the fireplace or on the sun porch, where you are surrounded by ferns, orchids, and african violets. A bedroom with a cozy fireplace is available.

HOSTS: Claudia & Merlin Wedepohl

6 ROOMS, 6 pb

$110-145

OPEN: ALL YEAR

LA RESIDENCE COUNTRY INN

NAPA 105

4066 St. Helena Hwy
Napa, CA 94558

Tel:1-707-253-0337

Located on two acres between Napa and Yountville, this inn is situated in the heart of the Wine Country. Built in 1870, the Gothic mansion offers rooms with private baths, sitting areas, and fireplaces. The entire home is furnished in American antiques, with queen-size beds and designer decorations. Enjoy the wine hour hosted by the innkeepers each evening, and don't forget your swimsuit for the whirlpool-spa and heated swimming pool.

HOSTS: David Jackson & Craig Claussen

20 ROOMS, 18 pb

$75-170

POOL

SPA **OPEN: ALL YEAR**

NAPA & LAKE

106 NAPA

HOSTS: Carol & Doug Moraleo

NAPA INN
1137 Warren St.
Napa, CA 94559
Tel:1-800-435-1144

R

Lovingly restored and furnished from the owner's personal antique collection, this stately inn rests on a quiet, tree-lined street in the historic city of Napa. In true Victorian fashion, "afternoon tea" is served at 3 P.M. each day.

3 ROOMS, 3 pb   2 SUITES, 2 pb

OPEN: ALL YEAR SPA **$95-140**

107 NAPA

HOST: Diane Dumaine

OLD WORLD INN
1301 Jefferson St.
Napa, CA 94559
Tel:1-707-257-0112

R

For a holiday of romance and gourmet delights, plan a stay at this charming inn. You can relax in the outdoor spa or choose a room with a sunken spa tub. You will be pampered with home-baked treats from breakfast until bedtime.

8 ROOMS, 8 pb

OPEN: ALL YEAR SPA **$100-140**

108 NAPA

HOSTS: Ethel & Ron Stahlecker

STAHLECKER HOUSE B&B
1042 Easum Dr.
Napa, CA 94558
Tel:1-707-257-1588

R

This quiet, secluded country inn is located just minutes from wineries. Rooms feature canopied beds, antique furnishings, and fresh flowers. Enjoy a delicious gourmet breakfast and relax on the sun deck overlooking the gardens and trees, or in the cozy reading room with fireplace.

3 ROOMS, 3 pb

OPEN: ALL YEAR **$90-125**

RANCHO CAYMUS INN
RUTHERFORD 109

P.O. 78
1140 Rutherford Rd.
Rutherford, CA 94573
Tel:1-800-845-1777

This inn was named after the first land grant in the Napa Valley, awarded in 1836. Its early California hacienda-style architecture is reminiscent of that period, with the guest rooms surrounding a beautiful central courtyard. All rooms are suites, and twenty-two have adobe-style beehive fireplaces. Located in the heart of the Napa Valley midway between Yountville and St. Helena, Rancho Caymus makes a perfect base for touring the wine country.

HOST: Tony Prince

26 ROOMS, 26 pb

$95-295 SPA OPEN: ALL YEAR

AUBERGE BRISEBOIS
ST. HELENA 110

271 Via Monte
St. Helena, CA 94574
Tel:1-707-963-4658

Spectacular views of surrounding wineries captivate the visitor to this secluded residence in the heart of the Napa Valley. Relax in the hammock or by the pool, stay in a room with a forest view, and enjoy candlelight breakfasts in the elegant dining room. The house is full of contemporary stained glass and sculptures created by the artist/innkeeper. Your relaxed, friendly hostess will provide inside information on local wineries, activities, and restaurants.

HOST: Diane Brisebois Peterson

2 ROOMS, 2 pb

$75-110 POOL

SPA OPEN: ALL YEAR

111 ST. HELENA

HOST: Jane Gibson

AMBROSE BIERCE HOUSE
1515 Main St.
St. Helena, CA 94574
Tel:1-707-963-3003

®

Author of The Devil's Dictionary, Ambrose Bierce's former home was built in 1872. Combine the history with one of the wine country's most enchanting B&B's. Filled wih antique brass beds, claw foot tubs and Victorian furnishings. Walk to wineries, shops and fine restaurants.

3 ROOMS, 3 pb

OPEN: ALL YEAR 🍽☕🍴   **$99-139**

112 ST. HELENA

HOST: Jami Bartels

BARTELS RANCH & COUNTRY INN
1200 Conn Valley Rd.
St. Helena, CA 94574
Tel:1-800-932-4002
or 1-707-963-4001

®

On a hundred acres of rolling meadows, this nationally recognized country estate offers a library, games, bicycles, and a pool. The charming rooms have private entrances. One has a whirlpool-spa, sauna, fireplace, and deck. Indulge in the hearty breakfast and refreshments.

3 ROOMS, 3 pb   1 SUITE, pb

OPEN: ALL YEAR ☕ 🔥 **SPA** **$115-275**

113 ST. HELENA

HOST: Genny Jenkins

CINNAMON BEAR
1407 Kearney St.
St. Helena, CA 94574
Tel:1-800-491-2327
or 1-707-963-4653

®

Originally the home of the mayor of St. Helena, this quaint inn is furnished with fine antiques and oriental carpets. Stuffed bears will keep you company, thanks to the owner's son. Enjoy the bountiful country breakfast, afternoon refreshments, games, and books.

4 ROOMS, 4 pb

OPEN: ALL YEAR 🍽☕🍴🔥   **$55-145**

CHESTLESON HOUSE

ST. HELENA **114**

1417 Kearney St.
St. Helena, CA 94574
Tel:1-707-963-2238

This comfortable Victorian home is located in a quiet residential neighborhood a short walk from charming shops and excellent restaurants. Guest rooms are cozy and old-fashioned. Enjoy refreshments and hors d'oeuvres by a crackling fire or on the porch and awaken to a mouth-watering breakfast prepared by the host, a former caterer and cooking teacher. Host will provide information about off-the-beaten-track wineries.

HOST: Jackie Sweet

4 ROOMS, 4 pb

$78-135 SPA OPEN: ALL YEAR

THE INK HOUSE

ST. HELENA **115**

1575 St. Helena Hwy.
St. Helena, CA 94574
Tel:1-800-553-4343
or 1-707-963-3890

Listed in the National Register of Historic Places, this Italianate Victorian was featured in Elvis Presley's 1959 movie, Wild in the Country. It has a restored 1870 pump organ, concert grand piano, and glass-walled observatory with a sweeping 360° view of the surrounding hills and vineyards. Stained glass windows, white wicker furniture, period antiques, handmade quilts, and lace curtains grace the interior. Enjoy bicycling, billiards, movies, and in-house massages.

HOSTS: Ernie Veniegas & Jim Annis

4 ROOMS, 4 pb   1 COTTAGE, pb

$90-160 OPEN: ALL YEAR

116 ST. HELENA

OLIVER HOUSE COUNTRY INN
2970 SIlverado Trail
St. Helena, CA 94574
Tel:1-800-682-7888
or 1-707-963-4089

Set against the foothills over-looking acres of surrounding vineyards, the warm country decor of this lovely chalet reflects its English and Swiss history. Tastefully furnished with beautiful antiques and feather beds, each room has french doors that open onto a balcony with vineyard views. Relax in the comfortable old-fashioned parlor or curl up by the fire. Breakfast is served on the balcony or in the cheery country kitchen.

HOSTS: Clara & Richard Oliver

3 ROOMS, 3 pb   1 COTTAGE, pb

OPEN: ALL YEAR $85-195

117 ST. HELENA

RUSTRIDGE RANCH & WINERY
2910 Lower Chiles Valley Rd.
St. Helena, CA 94574
Tel:1-800-788-0263
or 1-707-965-9353

Located in the foothills east of the Napa Valley, Rustridge Ranch and winery is the perfect destination for a relaxing vacation, a romantic getaway, or a group retreat. Guest rooms are complete with feather beds and southwestern decor. Several rooms open to a deck overlooking majestic oak trees, others have panoramic views of the valley. This impressive inn offers horses to be pet, wonderful places for walking, and a working winery to explore.

HOSTS: Susan & Jim Fresquez

5 ROOMS, 3 pb

OPEN: ALL YEAR   SPA   POOL $72-140

ROSE GARDEN INN
**1277 St. Helena Hwy.
St. Helena, CA 94574**
Tel:1-707-963-4417

This lovely turn-of-the-century farmhouse is a cozy hideaway, yet central to the Napa wineries, hot-air ballooning, unique shops, and fine restaurants. Guest rooms are spacious and charming, with an atmosphere of relaxation. Breakfast is a delight, featuring fresh-brewed coffee, delicious pastries, and seasonal fresh fruit. Unwind by the living room fireplace with a good book, stroll in the peaceful gardens, and tour the surrounding vineyards.

HOSTS: Joanne & Tom Contreras

3 ROOMS, 3 pb
$110-130

OPEN: ALL YEAR

SPANISH VILLA
**474 Glass Mountain Rd.
St. Helena, CA 94574**
Tel:1-707-963-74833

Nestled in a wooded valley, this spacious inn is a short, scenic drive from Calistoga's mud baths, glider rides, and world-famous wineries such as Christian Brothers and Beringer. Look out onto the patio through the elegant arched windows of "La Galleria," the villa's sitting room. Each spacious guest room features a king-sized bed and Tiffany lamps. The surrounding country roads are perfect for jogging and cycling.

R **HOSTS: Roy Bissember & Barbara Gates**

2 ROOMS, 2 pb   2 SUITES, 2 pb
$95-125

OPEN: ALL YEAR

120 ST. HELENA

SHADY OAKS COUNTRY INN
399 Zinfandel Lane
St. Helena, CA 94574
Tel:1-707-963-1190

HOSTS: Lisa & John Runnells

Experience the romance and warm hospitality of our secluded country inn, located among the finest wineries and restaurants in Napa Valley. Where life is simpler and the pace relaxed, guests will be pampered each evening with wine and cheeses as your hosts assist you in selecting the perfect place to dine. Enjoy a full gourmet champagne breakfast served fireside or on a Roman pillared patio. The immaculate antique filled rooms boast fine linens.

4 ROOMS, 4 pb

OPEN: ALL YEAR

$75-145

121 ST. HELENA

VILLA ST. HELENA
2727 Sulphur Springs Ave.
St. Helena, CA 94574
Tel:1-707-963-2514

HOSTS: Carolyn & Ralph Cotton

This secluded twenty-acre estate is a Mediterranean-style villa hidden in the hills of the Mayacamas Mountains above St. Helena. Eclectic period-style furniture, a blue delft tile fireplace in the cozy wood-paneled library, the beamed-ceiling living room, and the discreet entrances from the verandas into each bedroom epitomize country elegance. Some guest rooms have fireplaces. Enjoy breakfast in the solarium, relax in thegardens or walk the trails.

3 ROOMS, 3 pb

OPEN: ALL YEAR

$145-225

WINE COUNTRY COTTAGE
P.O. BOX 295
400 Meadowood Lane
St. Helena, CA 94574
Tel:1-707-963-0852

Relax amid elm, pine, and oak trees in this 1895 Victorian mansion and charming secluded cottage. Spacious rooms in the main house have lovely garden views. The cottage features a kitchen, patio, and living room. Located in the heart of the Napa Valley.

2 ROOMS, 1 pb   1 COTTAGE, pb

$95-135   OPEN: ALL YEAR   HOST: Jan Strong

ZINFANDEL INN
800 Zinfandel Lane
St. Helena, CA 94574
Tel:1-707-963-3512

In the heart of the wine country, this elegant stone English Tudor inn looks like a castle in the vineyards. It has fireplaces, whirlpool tubs, feather beds, stained glass windows, balconies, and an enchanting garden with an aviary. The hosts will gladly spoil you.

3 ROOMS, 3 pb

$125-200   SPA   OPEN: ALL YEAR   HOSTS: Diane & Jerry Payton

MAGNOLIA HOTEL
6529 Yount St.
Yountville, CA 94599
Tel:1-800-788-0369 USA
or 1-707-944-2056

Once a bordello and center for bootlegging activities, the Magnolia Hotel is now a family-operated twelve-room hotel. Take a break from touring the wineries and swim in the pool, lounge on the lawn, or rejuvenate in the whirlpool-spa.

13 ROOMS, 13 pb

$89-189   POOL   SPA   OPEN: ALL YEAR   HOSTS: Bonnie & Bruce Locken

125 YOUNTVILLE

HOSTS: Louise & John Packard

OLEANDER HOUSE
P.O. 2937
7433 St. Helena Hwy.
Yountville, CA 94599
Tel:1-800-788-0357 or 1-707-944-8315

This Country French two-story home, located in the heart of the Napa Valley, combines old-world design with modern amenities. Guests enjoy spacious bedrooms with high ceilings, balconies, fireplaces, antiques, and Laura Ashley decor. Indulge in a scrumptious gourmet breakfast.

4 ROOMS, 4 pb

OPEN: ALL YEAR  **$115-160**

126 YOUNTVILLE

HOSTS: Cheryl & Sybil Maddox

SYBRON HOUSE
7400 St. Helena Hwy.
Yountville, CA 94599
Tel:1-707-944-2785

Perched on a hill overlooking the beautiful Napa Valley, this impressive house offers a large parlor with a fireplace and a wet bar. After breakfast outdoors on the redwood deck, play tennis on the private court and take in the view.

4 ROOMS, 4 pb

OPEN: ALL YEAR  **$100-150**

127 YOUNTVILLE

HOST: Diane Bartholomew

WEBBER PLACE
P.O. 2873
6610 Webber Street
Yountville, CA 94599
Tel:1-707-944-8384

Homey and unpretentious, this 1850 farmhouse has charming guest rooms with brass beds, antique quilts, and views of the treetops. One room has its own entrance and veranda with a hammock. Delicious country breakfast. Walk to shops, wineries, and restaurants.

3 ROOMS, 1 pb   1 SUITE, pb

OPEN: ALL YEAR  **$69-119**

156

132-137

144-153

140-143

128-129

131

130

138-139

154-155

Westport

Fort Bragg

Mendocino

Little River

Albion

Elk

Pt. Arena

Gualala

Boonville

MENDOCINO

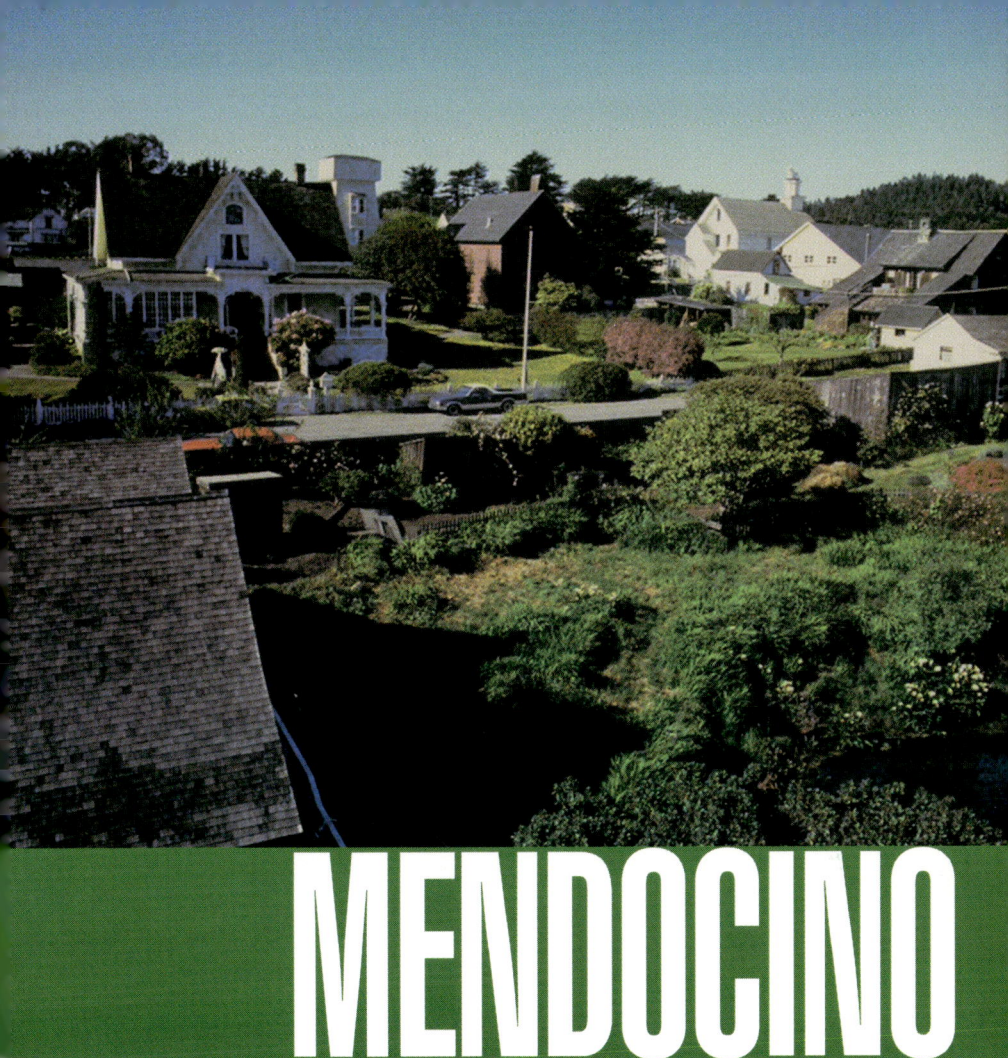

MENDOCINO
COUNTY

Deep green forests, blue waters, and weathered barns create the atmosphere in Mendocino County, where artists, tourists, fishermen, and nature-lovers congregate to enjoy the gorgeous scenery and nineteenth-century charm. Stretching from the Gualala River in the south to Point No Pass in the north, Mendocino County's spectacular coastal journey along Highway 1 begins at the town of **Gualala,** named by the Pomo Indians. A successful lumber town in the 1860s and 1870s, today Gualala offers fishing facilities and a variety of shops, restaurants, and comfortable accommodations. Cultural attractions include theater, musical performances, art galleries, and exhibits.

Farther north, **Point Arena** offers more elaborate fishing facilities, including a public pier and boat-launching area used by commercial fishermen and sport-fishing enthusiasts alike. The town, which dates back to 1859, offers a variety of shops and restaurants. During the booming lumber days, Point Arena was one of the most thriving towns between San Francisco and Eureka. One mile from town is a 115-foot (35 m) lighthouse, built in 1870. Drive inland 20-miles (32 km) from Point Arena to the apple- and wine-growing area of **Anderson Valley** and the secluded farming town of **Boonville,** named after the early settler W.W. Boon. Eight miles (13 km) west of town, **Hendy Woods State Park** contains a primeval redwood forest and provides campsites overlooking the Navarro River. Return to the coast and drive a few miles north to **Manchester,** a small town that is a center for farming, dairy cattle, and sheep ranching.

Elk is 14 miles (22 km) north of Manchester. It is built along the cliff tops and overlooks spectacular outcroppings of rocks, pounded by the crashing ocean surf. A lumber town until 1931, it had a dozen saloons and several hotels in its heyday. Today it is a picturesque town with many bed and breakfast inns and shops. Its state beach is reached by a wide footpath.

Eight miles (13 km) north on the Albion River is the quaint town of **Albion**, with a harbor that is home to a small fishing fleet. From Albion, Highway 1 winds northward through strips of farmland, sheep ranches, and rolling stretches of forested hillsides climbing steeply into the interior. Enjoy the spectacular vistas of rocky inlets and scattered beaches with pounding surf. A drive of a few miles brings you to **Little River,** with its collection of beautiful Victorian houses, most of which offer accommodations. **Van Damme State Park,** with its scenic walking trails, winds along the cliff tops.

A 3-mile (5 km) drive north brings you to the charming historical town of **Mendocino,** located at the mouth of Big River. Settled by lumber men in the 1850s, it became a major outlet for the vast redwood forests that surrounded the area. Local mills flourished for nearly a hundred years. Attracted by the area's natural beauty and inexpensive housing, artists discovered the town, and have contributed to the restoration of the Cape Cod-style and Victorian-era homes. Today Mendocino has a delightful collection of art galleries, quaint shops, excellent restaurants, and cozy inns. Tourists may enjoy exploring the secluded little coves and beaches or hiking on the miles of trails with coastal views. Watch the grey whale migrations in December and March, and enjoy the **Mendocino Coast Botanical Gardens,** where several thousand varieties of native and cultivated plants grow.

Ten miles (16 km) north of Mendocino is the town of **Fort Bragg.** The biggest lumber town in the area, it boasts a large commercial fishing fleet that sails out of the Noyo River harbor in search of salmon and crab. Fort Bragg is a bustling town with an interesting history and many activities. Be sure to ride the **Skunk Train** through the redwoods, a 40-mile (64 km) journey to the town of **Willits.** The track was laid in the 1800s for the logging industry and the train engines were originally fueled by gas, hence the name Skunk Train.

The tiny town of **Cleone,** located 3 miles (5 km) north of Fort Bragg, is the gateway to **MacKerricher State Park,** which has a beach, a freshwater lake, sand dunes, and seventy campsites. Farther north is **Westport,** with its wonderful ocean views and memories of days gone by.

Mendocino Coast Botanical Gardens, off Highway 1, between Mendocino and Fort Bragg, (707) 964-4352, open daily Apr.-Oct. 9-5, Nov.-Mar. 9-4, $5 adults, $4 senior citizens, $3 children 13-17. **Point Arena Lighthouse,** 65 miles north of Point Reyes, (707) 882-2777, open daily 11-2, except December, 10-3:30 summer weekends, $2 adults, $.50 children under 12. **Skunk Train (California Western Railroad),** (707) 964-6371, Fort Bragg-Willits: half-day trips in winter depart daily at 10 and 2, in summer 9:20 and 1:35, $18.50 adults, $9 children 5-11, reservations suggested for summer and holidays.

RESTAURANTS $=under $10, $$=$10 to $20, $$$=over $20

ALBION
Ledford House
3000 N. Highway 1
(707) 937-0282
New American cuisine $$

FORT BRAGG
Rendez-Vous Inn
647 N. Main St.
(707) 964-8142
California-Continental cuisine $$
The Wharf
780 N. Harbor Dr. on the wharf
(707)964-4283
Seafood, steaks, pasta $$

GUALALA
Old Milano
38300 Highway 1
(707) 884-3256
Eclectic California cuisine $$-$$$
St. Orres
2.5 miles north of downtown
Gualala on east side of Highway 1
(707) 884-3335
North Coast Country cuisine $$$
(fixed price)

LITTLE RIVER
Little River Inn
7751 N. Highway 1
(707) 937-5942
California cuisine $$
Little River Restaurant
7750 N. Highway 1
(707) 937-4945
California-French cuisine $$

MENDOCINO
Café Beaujolais
961 Ukiah
(707) 937-5614
French cuisine $-$$
Mac Callum House
45020 Albion St.
(707) 937-5763
Fresh Mediterranean cuisine $$

POINT ARENA
The Galley
790 Port St.
(707) 882-2189
Seafood/varied menu $-$$

Christine Woods Winery
3155 Highway 128
Philo, CA 95466
(707) 895-2115
Open: daily 11-6

Fetzer Vineyards
13601 Eastside Road
Hopland, CA 95449
(707) 744-1250
Open: daily 8:30-5

Fetzer Visitor Center & Tasting Room
13500 S. Highway 101
Hopland, CA 95449
(707) 744-1737
Open: daily 8:30-5

Handley Cellars
3151 Highway 128
Philo, CA 95466
(707) 895-3876
Open: daily 11-6

Hidden Cellars Winery
1500 Ruddick-Cunningham
Road, Ukiah, CA 95482
(707) 462-0301
Open: Mon. thru Fri. 10-4

Husch Vineyards
4400 Highway 128
Philo, CA 95466
(707) 895-3216
Open: daily 10-6

Jepson Vineyards
10400 S. Highway 101
Ukiah, CA 95482
(707) 468-8936
Open: daily 10-5

Kendall-Jackson Tasting Room
5500 Highway 128
Philo, CA 95466
(707) 895-3009
Open: Open Tues. thru Sun. 11-5

Konrad Estate
3620 Road B
Redwood Valley, CA 95470
(707) 485-0323
Open: daily 10-4

Navarro Vineyards
5601 Highway 128
Philo, CA 95466
(707) 895-3686
Open: daily 10-6

Obester Winery
9200 Highway 128
Philo, CA 95466
(707) 895-3814
Open: daily 10-5

Parducci Wine Cellars
501 Parducci Road
Ukiah, CA 95482
(707) 462-3828
Open: daily 9-5

Roederer Estate
4501 Highway 128
Philo, CA 95466
(707) 895-2288
Open: Fri. thru Mon. 11-4

Scharffenberger Cellars
8501 Highway 128
Philo, CA 95466
(707) 895-2065
Open: daily 11-5

ALBION RIVER INN

P.O. Box 100
3790 North Highway 1
Albion, CA 95410

Tel:1-707-937-1919

The romantic New England-style cottages of this inn are perched on a ten-acre bluff overlooking beautiful Albion Cove, where the Albion River and the forest meet the sea. Relax in the contemporary, spacious rooms, many of which have ocean views, telescopes, and tubs-for-two. Enjoy a hearty breakfast of eggs, homemade bread, and granola in the inn's excellent restaurant, which is also open for dinner every night.

HOSTS: Flurry Healy & Peter Wells

20 ROOMS, 20 pb

$85-225   SPA   OPEN: ALL YEAR

FENSALDEN INN

P.O. Box 99
33810 Navarro Ridge Rd.
Albion, CA 95410

Tel:1-707-937-4042

The panoramic view of the ocean, cypress trees, and deer feeding in the meadow captivates all who enter this beautiful inn set on twenty acres of the Mendocino Coast. Spacious and elegant guest rooms are furnished with antiques. Some have fireplaces, ocean and ridge views, sitting rooms, and private decks. Private kitchens are available in two of the suites. The inn offers a quiet respite in a peaceful environment. Walk to the ocean or relax in the garden.

HOSTS: Frances & Scott Brazil

5 ROOMS, 5 pb   2 SUITES, 2 pb   1 COTTAGE, pb

$75-145   OPEN: ALL YEAR

MENDOCINO

130 BOONVILLE

ANDERSON CREEK INN
P.O. Box 217
12050 Anderson Valley Way
Boonville, CA 95415
Tel:1-800-LLAMA-02 or 1-707-895-3091

This country inn, nestled deep in a valley at the junction of two creeks, is surrounded by lush mountains and scenic beauty in this coastal, redwood, wine-growing valley. This romantic adult getaway is located away from the highway in a pastoral setting. Enjoy the dogs, cats, llamas and sheep. Hike the trails or simply relax by the pool. A short drive through the redwoods will bring you to the ocean.

HOSTS: Lee & Ed Lewis

4 ROOMS, 4 pb
OPEN: ALL YEAR   SPA   POOL $140-195

131 ELK

ELK COVE INN
P.O. Box 367
6300 South Highway 1
Elk, CA 95432
Tel:1-707-877-3321

This charming 1883 Victorian, nestled in peaceful seclusion atop a bluff overlooking the ocean, offers unique lodging and gourmet breakfasts in the European tradition. The main house features ocean-view dining rooms, upstairs rooms with large dormer windows and window seats, a cozy parlor, and ocean-view deck. Behind the main house, four cabins, two with fireplaces, command spectacular ocean vistas. Enjoy sitting in the gazebo or strolling along the path to an expansive driftwood-strewn beach.

HOST: Hildrun-Uta Triebess

4 ROOMS, 4 pb   4 COTTAGE, 4 pb
OPEN: ALL YEAR $108-148

AVALON HOUSE
561 Stewart St.
Fort Bragg, CA 95437
Tel:1-707-964-5555

FORT BRAGG `132`

R

Built at the turn of the century, this intimate inn has been restored to preserve the unique details of its California Craftsman style. Antiques fill the guest rooms, some of which have fireplaces, decks, whirlpool-spas and ocean views.

6 ROOMS, 6 pb

$70-135 **SPA OPEN: ALL YEAR HOST: Anne Sorrells**

CLEONE LODGE INN
24600 North Highway 1
Fort Bragg, CA 95437
Tel:1-707-964-2788
Northern Cal. only 1-800-400-2189

FORT BRAGG `133`

This ranch-style inn offers the discerning traveller a quiet setting on five acres of wooded grounds. The main lodge consists of comfortable units with cozy interiors; a separate beach house and cottage are also available. Bed & breakfast plan is optional and spa provided at additional cost.

7 ROOMS, 7 pb   3 SUITE, 3pb   2 COTTAGES,2pb

$74-107 **SPA OPEN: ALL YEAR HOST: Lar Krug**

GREY WHALE
615 North Main St.
Fort Bragg, CA 95437
Tel:1-800-382-7244

FORT BRAGG `134`

R

"Comfortably Posh" is how one guest described the inn's casually elegant decor. This 1915 Mendocino Coast Landmark has been beautifully restored and furnished. Enjoy a romantic room with a blue ocean view or a warm fireplace. Prize-winning coffee cake.

14 ROOMS, 14 pb

$55-140 **SPA OPEN: ALL YEAR HOST: Colette Bailey**

MENDOCINO

135 FORT BRAGG

JUGHANDLE BEACH INN
32980 Gibney Lane
Fort Bragg, CA 95437
Tel:1-707-961-9600

Built in 1883, this beautifully restored Victorian farmhouse overlooks the ocean on the impressive Mendocino coast. Sleep in comfortable, gabled attic rooms carefully decorated with country antiques. In the morning, wake up to a delicious home-cooked breakfast complete with fresh pastries, juices and eggs. Walk in ocean meadows and watch the passing whales in December and March. The owners invite guests to share their relaxed country life.

HOSTS: Sue & Jerry Schlect

4 ROOMS, 4 pb

OPEN: ALL YEAR

$65-95

136 FORT BRAGG

OLD STEWART HOUSE INN
511 Stewart St.
Fort Bragg, CA 95437
Tel:1-800-287-8392
or 1-707-961-0775

A knight in shining armor will greet you in this delightful Victorian inn, built in 1876 by a wealthy partner in one of Fort Bragg's founding lumber mills. The inn has been restored to its original charm with beautiful wall paper, antique furnishings and fine window treatments. Relax in the comfortable guest rooms and make new friends in the spacious parlor. Walk to shops, art galleries, and restaurants.

HOST: Darrell Galli

4 ROOMS, 4 pb   2 COTTAGE, 2 pb

OPEN: ALL YEAR   SPA

$65-95

PUDDING CREEK INN
700 North Main St.
Fort Bragg, CA 95437
Tel:1-800-227-9529

FORT BRAGG 137

This inn was built in 1884 by a Russian count who, according to legend, buried his mysteriously acquired riches on the property. Newly renovated, antique-filled rooms are romantically named and decorated with unique style. Breakfasts are memorable. Walk to shops.

10 ROOMS, 10 pb

$65-125   OPEN: ALL YEAR   HOSTS: Carole & Garry Anloff

NORTH COAST COUNTRY INN
34591 South Highway 1
Gualala, CA 95445
Tel:1-800-995-4537
or 1-707-884-4537

GUALALA 138

These rustic redwood buildings are set on a forested hillside overlooking the coast. Each spacious guest room has bed-sitting, dining, and kitchenette areas, a wood-burning fireplace, and a deck with ocean views. Relax in the lovely gardens and hot tubs.

4 ROOMS, 4 pb

$135   SPA   OPEN: ALL YEAR   HOSTS: Nancy & Loren Flanagan

WHALE WATCH INN BY THE SEA
35100 Highway 1
Gualala, CA 95445
Tel:1-800-WHALE-42
or 1-707-884-3667

GUALALA 139

Luxurious contemporary rooms and suites with fireplaces and breathtaking ocean views, some with two-person whirlpool-spas and kitchens, are set on 2.5 acres of cliffside oceanfront property with beautiful gardens. Voted "Top Ten B&B" by San Francisco Focus Magazine.

12 ROOMS, 12 pb   6 SUITES, 6 pb

$160-275   SPA   OPEN: ALL YEAR   HOSTS: Kazuko & Jim Popplewell

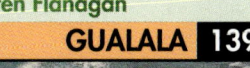

140 LITTLE RIVER

GLENDEVEN
8221 North Highway 1
Little River, CA 95456
Tel:1-707-937-0083

Stay in an 1867 farmhouse, barnhouse, suite, or cozy annex when you visit this intimate country inn overlooking Little River Bay. The casual yet elegant atmosphere is apparent in the inn's decor — a combination of fine antiques, contemporary crafts, and special attention to detail. Fireplaced rooms, lovely garden views and a sense of serenity make this a perfect place from which to explore the spectacular coast and nearby charming village of Mendocino.

HOSTS: Jay & Janet deVries

R

7 ROOMS, 7 pb   3 SUITES, 3 pb

OPEN: ALL YEAR $160

141 LITTLE RIVER

THE INN AT SCHOOLHOUSE CREEK
7051 North Highway 1
Little River, CA 95456
Tel:1-707-937-5525

Located on ten acres of spectacular gardens, meadows and forest, this delightful inn has offered lodging since the 1930s. All of the separate country-style cottages and rooms have ocean views, and most have fireplaces. Breakfast is available at a small additional cost in the communal dining room. Walk to the ocean and Van Damme State Park, or drive thirty minutes to wine tasting and the Skunk Train.

HOSTS: Linda Wilson & Peter Fearey

R

7 SUITES, 7 pb   5 COTTAGES, 5 pb

OPEN: ALL YEAR $60-115

STEVENSWOOD LODGE

8211 Highway 1 P.O. Box 170
Little River, CA 95460

Tel:1-800-421-2810
or 1-707-937-2810

This elegant Scandinavian-style country estate has luxurious contemporary suites with ocean and forest views, fireplaces, cable television, and stocked refrigerators. Admire the art gallery and take advantage of the modern executive conference facilities, which accommodate ten. Wander the forest trails to the beach, or walk to the nearby shops, restaurants, and art galleries. The Automobile Association of America has given this lodge a four-diamond rating.

HOSTS: Vera & Robert Zimmer

1 ROOMS, 1 pb   9 SUITES, 9 pb

$95-195   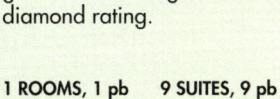   OPEN: ALL YEAR

THE VICTORIAN FARMHOUSE

P.O. Box 357
7001 North Highway 1
Little River, CA 95456

Tel:1-707-937-0697

Built in 1877, this inn has been renovated and furnished in period antiques to enhance its beauty and Victorian charm. Some of the beautifully appointed rooms have fireplaces. Sherry is served each evening in the parlor, and breakfast is delivered to your room. Enjoy the private apple orchard and flower gardens. You can take a short drive to art galleries, boutiques, and restaurants, or walk to the ocean.

HOSTS: Carol & George Molnar

10 ROOMS, 10 pb   1 COTTAGE, pb

$70-120   OPEN: ALL YEAR

144 MENDOCINO

HOSTS: Sallie & Jake McConnell-Zahavi

AGATE COVE INN
11201 North Lansing St. P.O. 1150
Mendocino, CA 95460
Tel:1-800-527-3111
or 1-707-937-0551

These romantic cottages all enjoy spectacular ocean views, fireplaces, private decks, four-poster beds, handmade quilts, and country decor. The cottages are surrounded by beautifully landscaped gardens. Sumptuous breakfasts are served in the dining room overlooking the ocean.

10 COTTAGES, 10 pb

OPEN: ALL YEAR 🍴☕|🏊 SPA $75-175

145 MENDOCINO

HOST: Linda & Bill Howarth

BREWERY GULCH INN
9350 Highway 1
Mendocino, CA 95460
Tel:1-707-937-4752   R

Established in the 1860s, Brewery Gulch is said to be the oldest farm on the Mendocino coast. Furnished with antiques and cozy comforters, each room has its own unique attraction. Breakfast is served when you want it in farm-hearty portions.

4 ROOMS, 2 pb   1 SUITE, pb

OPEN: ALL YEAR 🍴☕|🏊 $65-115

146 MENDOCINO

HOSTS: Arlene & Jim Moorehead

JOSHUA GRINDLE INN
P.O. Box 647
44800 Little Lake Rd.
Mendocino, CA 95460
Tel:1-707-937-4143

Set on two acres, this New England-style inn offers views of the historic village and the ocean. Spacious accommodations feature Early American and Shaker antiques. Some rooms have ocean views, others have fireplaces. Walk to galleries, shops, restaurants, and the beach.

10 ROOMS, 10 pb

OPEN: ALL YEAR 🍴☕|🏊 $80-150

JOHN DOUGHERTY HOUSE

P.O. Box 817
571 Ukiah St.
Mendocino, CA 95460

Tel:1-707-937-5266

One of the oldest houses in Mendocino, this inn, constructed in 1867, features period country antiques and ocean and bay views. Most rooms have color cable television, a small refrigerator, a wood-burning stove, and hand-stenciled walls. The delicious full breakfast is served by the fireplace in the sitting room. Relax in the English gardens or on the verandas, with their ocean views. Walk to many fine restaurants and boutiques.

HOSTS: Marion & David Wells

2 ROOMS, 2 pb   3 SUITES, 3 pb   1 COTTAGE, pb

$95-145   OPEN: ALL YEAR

MacCALLUM HOUSE INN

P.O. Box 206
45020 Albion St.
Mendocino, CA 95460

Tel:1-707-937-0289

Built in 1882, this carefully preserved inn brings back the Victorian era in its full splendor. Original Tiffany lamps and intricate Persian rugs add authentic touches to the taste-fully decorated guest rooms. Some rooms have bay views and fireplaces. Sip a cocktail on the porch by the bar and enjoy the ocean view. The restaurant offers creative cuisine served beside huge old cobblestone fireplaces. Walk to shops, galleries, restaurants, and the beach.

HOSTS: Melanie & Joe Reding

20 ROOMS, 8 pb   1 SUITE, pb

$75-180   OPEN: ALL YEAR

149 MENDOCINO

HOSTS: Margie & Bud Kamb

MENDOCINO FARMHOUSE
P.O. Box 247
43410 Compche-Ukiah Rd.
Mendocino, CA 95460
Tel:1-707-937-0241

A secret place for the traveller with a taste for quiet seclusion. Beautiful gardens and stately redwoods surround this comfortable Victorian farmhouse. The inn is "off the beaten path," yet close to the ocean and the quaint village of Mendocino.

3 ROOMS, 3 pb   2 COTTAGE, 2 pb

OPEN: ALL YEAR $75-100

150 MENDOCINO

HOST: Rachel Binah

RACHEL'S INN
P.O. Box 134
2 miles south of Mendocino at Little River
Mendocino, CA 95460   **R**
Tel:1-707-937-0088

This inn, surrounded by informal gardens and century-old cypress trees, borders the adjoining Van Damme State Park. Watch seals and whales from the nearby cliffs overlooking the ocean, or follow the gently winding path down to the beach.

7 ROOMS, 7 pb   2 SUITES, 2 pb

OPEN: ALL YEAR $96-165

151 MENDOCINO

HOSTS: Barbara & Monte Reed

REED MANOR
P.O. Box 127
off Palette Dr.
Mendocino, CA 95460   **R**
Tel:1-707-937-5446

For those who desire the ultimate in luxury and privacy. The inn has the only Four Diamond AAA rating in the village of Mendocino. Each of the guest rooms has a fireplace and a whirlpool tub. The decks of ocean- and village-view rooms are equipped with telescopes.

4 ROOMS, 4 pb   1 SUITE, pb

OPEN: ALL YEAR   SPA $175-350

SEAGULL INN

P.O. Box 317
44594 Albion St.
Mendocino, CA 95460

Tel:1-707-937-5204

The Seagull Inn is located in the heart of the charming and beautiful Mendocino village. A converted townhouse, this is one of Mendocino's oldest bed and breakfast inns. The innkeeper does not require a two-night weekend minimum, and she offers the best bargain in the village: a cozy room in The Shed. All other rooms are cheerful and spacious. Enjoy the lovely gardens. Walk to shops, galleries and restaurants.

HOSTS: Marlene McIntyre & Bill Yearous

9 ROOMS, 8 pb

$35-105 OPEN: ALL YEAR

STANFORD INN BY THE SEA

P.O. Box 487
Hwy.1 & Comptche-Ukiah Rd.
Mendocino, CA 95460

Tel:1-800-331-8884 or 1-707-937-5615

This elegant and rustic lodge is situated on a meadow that slopes toward the sea. Accommodations include wood-burning fireplaces, down comforters, refrigerators, coffee makers, and all the amenities expected of the finest hotels. A true country inn, the Stanford is the home of California certified organic Big River nurseries and Big River llamas. The inn also offers canoes, kayaks, and bicycles for exploring, and an indoor swimming pool, sauna, and spa.

HOSTS: Joan & Jeff Stanford

23 ROOMS, 23 pb   3 SUITES, 3 pb   POOL

$160-250   SPA   OPEN: ALL YEAR

MENDOCINO

154 POINT ARENA

HOSTS: Vicky & John Tanti

WHARFMASTER'S INN
P.O. Box 674
785 Port Rd.
Point Arena, CA 95468
Tel:1-800-932-4031

Included in the National Register of Historic Places, this serene blufftop retreat overlooking the port was built in 1870 as the home of the Point Arena wharf master. This inn is beautifully renovated and retains much of the original ornamentation, such as turned posts and elaborate window moldings. Enjoy spectacular ocean views, courtyards, private decks, fireplaces, in-room whirlpool-spas, and poster beds. Walk to mountain trails, fine shops, and restaurants.

23 ROOMS, 23 pb   1 SUITE, pb   1-3 ROOM HOUSE

OPEN: ALL YEAR   SPA $95-350

155 POINT ARENA

HOSTS: Merita Whatley & Richard Wasseman

COAST GUARD HOUSE
695 Arena Cove P.O. Box 117
Point Arena, CA 95468
Tel:1-800-524-9320
or 1-707-882-2442

This former life-saving station can rescue you from the hustle and bustle of city life. The two-story inn sits on a hillside overlooking the Pacific Ocean at Arena Cove. You can fish from the public pier just below the inn, and the grounds are an excellent place to watch the California grey whales. In the evening, join the other guests around the fireplace in the living room. Explore nearby galleries and shops or dine in one of the fine local restaurants.

6 ROOMS, 4 pb

OPEN: ALL YEAR   SPA $75-145

HOWARD CREEK RANCH

P.O. Box 121
40501 North Highway 1
Westport, CA 95488

Tel:1-707-964-6725

Bordered by miles of wilderness, beach, and mountains, this historic 1867 oceanfront ranch offers beautiful views and cabins filled with antiques and fireplaces. Go horseback riding nearby and then pamper yourself in the hot tub and sauna. For a real treat, indulge in a professional massage. After a delicious ranch breakfast, stroll through the flower gardens to the 75-foot swinging bridge over Howard Creek to the beach.

HOSTS: Sally & Charles Grigg

POOL

4 ROOMS, 2 pb   2 SUITES, 2 pb   3 COTTAGE, 3 pb

$50-115   SPA   OPEN: ALL YEAR

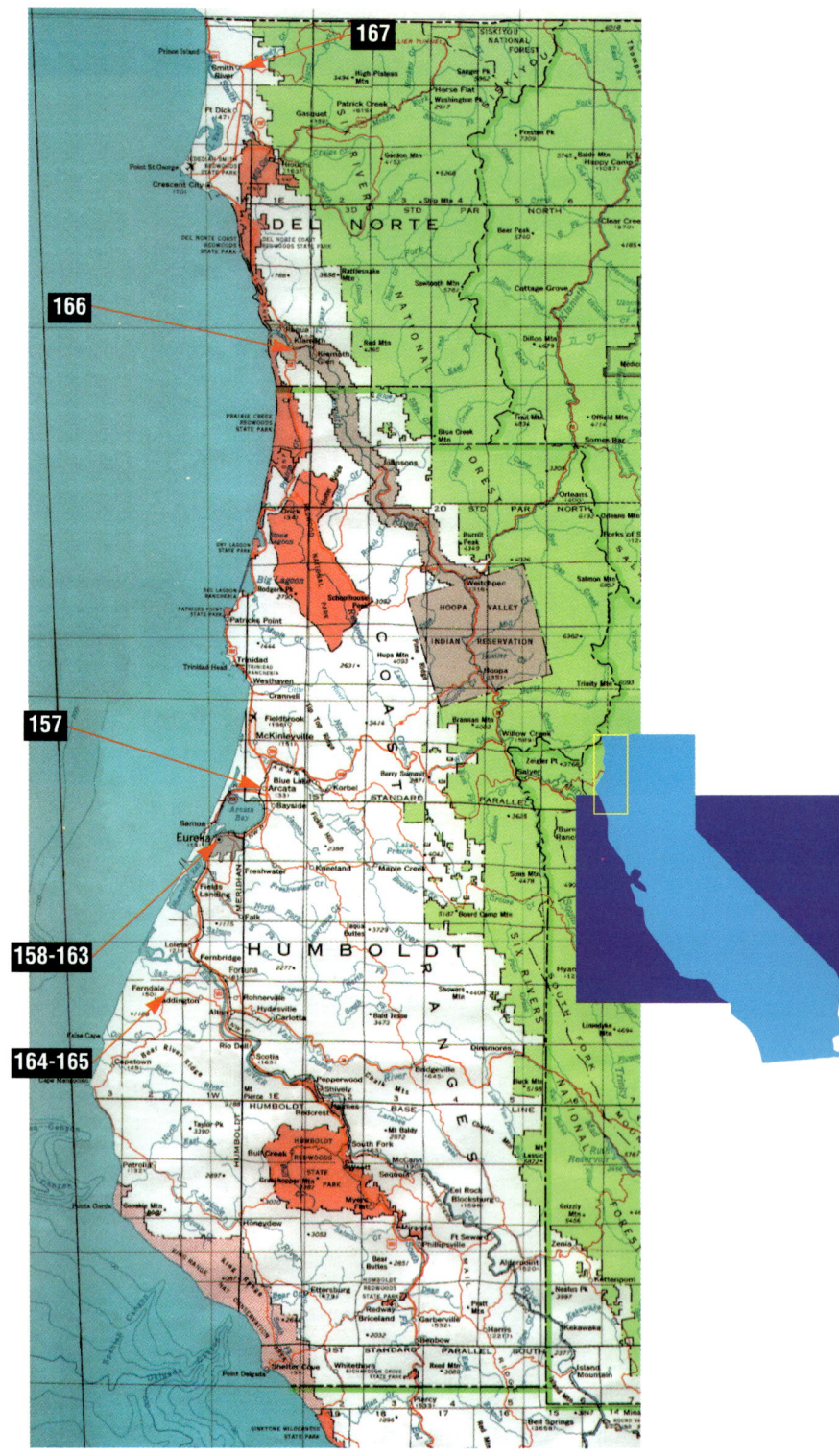

167

166

157

158-163

164-165

HUMBOLDT
& DEL NORTE COUNTIES

Travellers to Humboldt County come to see the forest and the trees—this is Redwood Country. Misty woods and an isolated coast that reveal haunting seascapes enhance the mystique of the huge ancient trees (some date back more than two thousand years). A host of state parks showcase these giants, some of which tower more than 325 feet (99 m) over the awestruck visitor. Hiking, fishing, and hunting are popular activities with local residents as well as tourists.

The coastline between Rockport and Eureka is named the **Lost Coast** because of its isolation and inaccessibility—the King Range prevented state engineers from building a highway along this portion of the coast. It takes a hearty camper to explore the Lost Coast, but anyone can picnic in **Humboldt Redwood State Park** or enjoy a scenic drive on the Avenue of the Giants.

Shortly after leaving Rockport, head inland to pick up Highway 101. Travel north past the Benbow Inn, where the **Eel River** is dammed during the summer to form **Benbow Lake,** a great place to swim on a hot day. After a dip, move on to the town of **Garberville,** a center for adventure. Explore the surrounding countryside—**Humboldt Redwood State Park, the King Range Wilderness, Sinkyone Wilderness State Park,** and more.

Fifty miles (80 km) north of Garberville you will find yourself in **Ferndale.** Located 5 miles (8 km) from the ocean, and surrounded by forested hills and farmlands, the entire town is a State Historical Landmark. In any direction you look, you will see beautiful, well-preserved Victorian homes. Jerry Hulse, travel editor of the Los Angeles Times, has described Ferndale as "California's best preserved Victorian village." Charming shops, art galleries, a repertory theater, and a museum complete the picture.

Eureka, a historic seaport thirty minutes north of Ferndale, is the largest town in Humboldt County. The **Old Town district** near the waterfront is worth a visit, and more than a hundred distinctive Victorian homes are a reminder of the town's prosperous past. Covered bridges and Native American culture and handicrafts give the area a flavor of the Old West. What was once a wild logging and fishing community today offers all the comforts of a modern city. Excellent hotels, inns, restaurants, and a variety of entertainment are here for your enjoyment.

Highway 101 reunites with the coast near Eureka and takes you northward to **Arcata,** home of **Humboldt State University.** This unique town has an informal, relaxed, youthful atmosphere, reminiscent of the 1960s, complete with cafes, restaurants, and a thriving nightlife. Founded in 1850, Arcata originally served as a supply town for the gold fields in the Trinity Alps and the lumber camps all around the area. It was also the setting for many stories of the Wild West by author Brett Harte.

After enjoying the spoils of civilization, head back to nature as Highway 101 continues north. First up is **Patrick's Point State Park,** a prime spot for whale watching and tidepool exploring. Next you come to **Redwood National Park,** populated by trees, bears, elk, fish, and (according to legend) the ape-man "Bigfoot." The most impressive specimens of redwood trees are found in this park, which covers more than 100,000 acres (40,500 ha) and includes 8 miles (13 km) of coastal roads and 120 miles (192 km) of trails. The world's tallest tree, at a towering 367 feet (112 m), is found in this park. Many people will tell you that this is the best area in California for fishing and hiking. It certainly provides an incredible farewell to a county blessed by Mother Nature.

A short drive over the Del Norte county line brings you to the town of **Klamath** and the **Klamath River,** one of the most powerful rivers in the United States. Every year, from August to late fall, the river attracts fishermen in pursuit of steelhead and king salmon. There are over two thousand public and private campsites in the surrounding area. A few miles north of Klamath, be on the lookout for Paul Bunyan, who towers over the highway in front of the **Trees of Mystery storyland park.** At the end of a nature trail an Indian museum offers the world's largest private collection of Native American artifacts, including weapons, clothing, baskets, and tools.

Next travel north to **Crescent City,** the last major town on the northern coast of California. Named for its crescent-shaped beach, the town serves as the northern gateway to Redwood National Park. If you get up early you can watch the fishing fleet unloading its daily catch of salmon, Dungeness crab, and shrimp at the **Citizens' Dock.** You can also explore the **Battery Point Lighthouse.** Built in 1856, this is the oldest working lighthouse on the Pacific Coast; it also houses a museum that is open seasonally at low tide. Crescent City is home to the **World Championship Crescent Crab Races,** held each year in February.

ATTRACTIONS

Battery Point Lighthouse, Crescent City, (707) 464-3089, open Wed.-Sun. 10-4, $2 adults, $.50 children under 12. **Humboldt Redwoods State Park,** (707) 946-2311. **Patrick's Point State Park,** 25 miles north of Eureka, (707) 677-3570, $5 per car, $4 seniors, $12 camping. **Redwood National Park,** Redwood National Park Headquarters, 1111 2nd St., Crescent City, (707) 464-6101.

RESTAURANTS $=under $10, $$=$10 to $20, $$$=over $20

ARCATA
Abbruzzi
Jacoby's Storehouse in Arcata Plaza
(707) 826-2345
Italian cuisine $$
Casa de qué Pasa
(707) 822-3441
854 Ninth St.
Mexican health food $
Ottavio's
7th and F Sts.
(707) 822-4021
Continental cuisine $$

EUREKA
Bay City Grill
508 Henderson
(707) 444-9069
Grill specialties $$
Hotel Carter
301 L St.
(707) 444-8062
Sophisticated regional cuisine $$
Sea Grill
316 East St.
(707) 443-7187
Fresh seafood $$

FERNDALE
Bi, Bo and the Bear
460 Main St.
(707) 786-9484
Casual fine dining $$
Stagedoor
Main St. (next door to theater)
(707) 786-4675
Gourmet salads, soups, sandwiches $
Victorian Village Inn
Main and Ocean
(707) 786-4949
California cuisine $$

LADY ANNE VICTORIAN INN ARCATA 157

901 14th St.
Arcata, CA 95521

Tel:1-707-822-2797

From the serene glass veranda to the three inviting parlors, the feeling of this Victorian mansion is one of relaxation. Guest rooms are light and airy, furnished with antiques, English stained glass, and delicate lace curtains. For some excitement and fine dining, the university and downtown plaza are a short walk away. Your host, Sam, was Arcata's mayor and will gladly share his knowledge of the many historical and natural sites of Humboldt county.

HOSTS: Sharon & Sam Pennisi

5 ROOMS, 0 pb   1 COTTAGE, pb

$65-105   OPEN: ALL YEAR

THE CARTER HOUSE EUREKA 158

3rd & L Sts.
Eureka, CA 95501

Tel:1-707-444-8062
or 1-707-445-1390

Painstakingly renovated by the owner, this Victorian house demonstrates understated elegance. Tasteful antiques, oriental rugs, polished oak floors, contemporary paintings, and ceramics by local artists enhance the light, airy interior. Marble fireplaces and large bay windows add an extra dimension. Also famous for its cuisine, the inn offers specialty dinners and breakfasts, featuring an almond and apple tart. Service to and from the airport is available in a 1958 Bentley limousine.

HOSTS: Christi & Mark Carter

29 ROOMS, 27 pb

$95-185   SPA OPEN: ALL YEAR

159 EUREKA

HOSTS: Sue & Gene Clinesmith

DALY INN
1125 H Street
Eureka, CA 95501

Tel:1-800-321-9656
or 1-707-445-3638

R

Relive turn-of-the-century elegance in this 1905 Colonial Revival home. Each room has a unique character and intriguing history. Breakfast in the dining room, garden patio, or sunlit breakfast parlor, then take a short drive to the majestic redwoods.

5 ROOMS, 4 pb

OPEN: ALL YEAR **$65-125**

160 EUREKA

HOST: Janice Escott

HOLLANDER HOUSE
2436 E Street
Eureka, CA 95501

Tel:1-707-443-2419

R

This landmark Queen Victorian, built in 1906 of heart redwood, has spacious, sun-filled rooms complete with antiques and artifacts from around the world. A tantalizing gourmet breakfast is served by the owner, a local talk-radio food show host.

3 ROOMS, 1 pb

OPEN: ALL YEAR **$55-125**

161 EUREKA

HOSTS: Diane & Leigh Benson

OLD TOWN BED & BREAKFAST INN
1521 Third Street
Eureka, CA 95501

Tel:1-800-331-5098
or 1-707-445-3951

R

This 1871 Victorian inn, with its plush period ambiance, is located in the Old Town national historic district. Indulge in a huge gourmet breakfast. Walk to restaurants and shops. The warm, hospitable, and fun-loving innkeepers will keep you entertained.

7 ROOMS, 5 pb

OPEN: ALL YEAR **SPA** **$75-185**

SHANNON HOUSE
EUREKA 162

2154 Spring St.
Eureka, CA 95501
Tel:1-707-443-8130

R

In a quiet residential neighborhood, this 1891 Victorian home is a haven for travellers seeking comfort, quiet, and relaxation. The gracious hosts offer afternoon tea and a delicious breakfast in their formal dining room. Repose in the parlor with a good book.

3 ROOMS, 1 pb

$55-75

OPEN: ALL YEAR **HOSTS: Barbara & David Shannon**

A WEAVER'S INN
EUREKA 163

1440 B Street
Eureka, CA 95501
Tel:1-707-443-8119

R

This 1883 Queen Anne Victorian is the home of a renowned weaver and pianist. Guests can get in on the fun by taking a turn at the piano, spinning wheel, or loom. Unique antiques and comfortable furniture complete the warm atmosphere.

3 ROOMS, 1 pb   1 SUITE, pb

$45-85

OPEN: ALL YEAR **HOSTS: Dorothy & Bob Swendeman**

THE GINGERBREAD MANSION
FERNDALE 164

P.O. Box 40
400 Berding St.
Ferndale, CA 95536
Tel:1-707-786-4000

Victorian elegance abounds in this turn-of-the-century inn, which offers nine large, romantic guest rooms with private baths. Completely decorated with antiques, the inn features four parlors, afternoon tea, use of bicycles, bedside chocolates, and a formal English garden.

9 ROOMS, 9 pb

$110-185

OPEN: ALL YEAR **HOST: Ken Torbert**

HUMBOLDT & DEL NORTE

165 FERNDALE

HOSTS: Norma & Ken Bessingpas

THE SHAW HOUSE
703 Main St.
Ferndale, CA 95536
Tel:1-707-786-9958

The owners of this gorgeous country inn, which is listed in the National Register of Historic Places, will make your stay a memorable one. Relax by the creek, nap in the lush garden, or drive the scenic five miles to the coast.

6 ROOMS, 6 pb

OPEN: ALL YEAR $65-125

166 KLAMATH

HOSTS: Donna & Paul Hamby

REQUA INN
451 Requa Rd.
Klamath, CA 95548
Tel:1-707-482-8205

This 1914 historical inn is situated in the heart of Redwood National Park, overlooking the Klamath River. Beaches and hiking trails are nearby, and a fine dining room provides delicious food for guests in a peaceful setting.

10 ROOMS, 10 pb

OPEN: APRIL-OCT $60-85

167 SMITH RIVER

HOST: Tony Rubio

CASA RUBIO
17285 Crissey Rd.
Smith River, CA 95567
California-Oregon State Line
Tel:1-707-487-4313

R

Once experienced, never forgotten. This ocean-front oasis is tucked away on a secluded beach near the mouth of the Winchuck River. The completely private accommodations and lush landscaping provide "at home" coziness. Enjoy the ocean view from your private deck.

2 ROOMS, 2 pb

OPEN: ALL YEAR $75-95

BIG TREE

	FT.	MTRS.
HEIGHT	304	92.6
DIAMETER	21.6	6.6
CIRCUMFERENCE	68	20.7
ESTIMATED AGE	1500 YRS.	

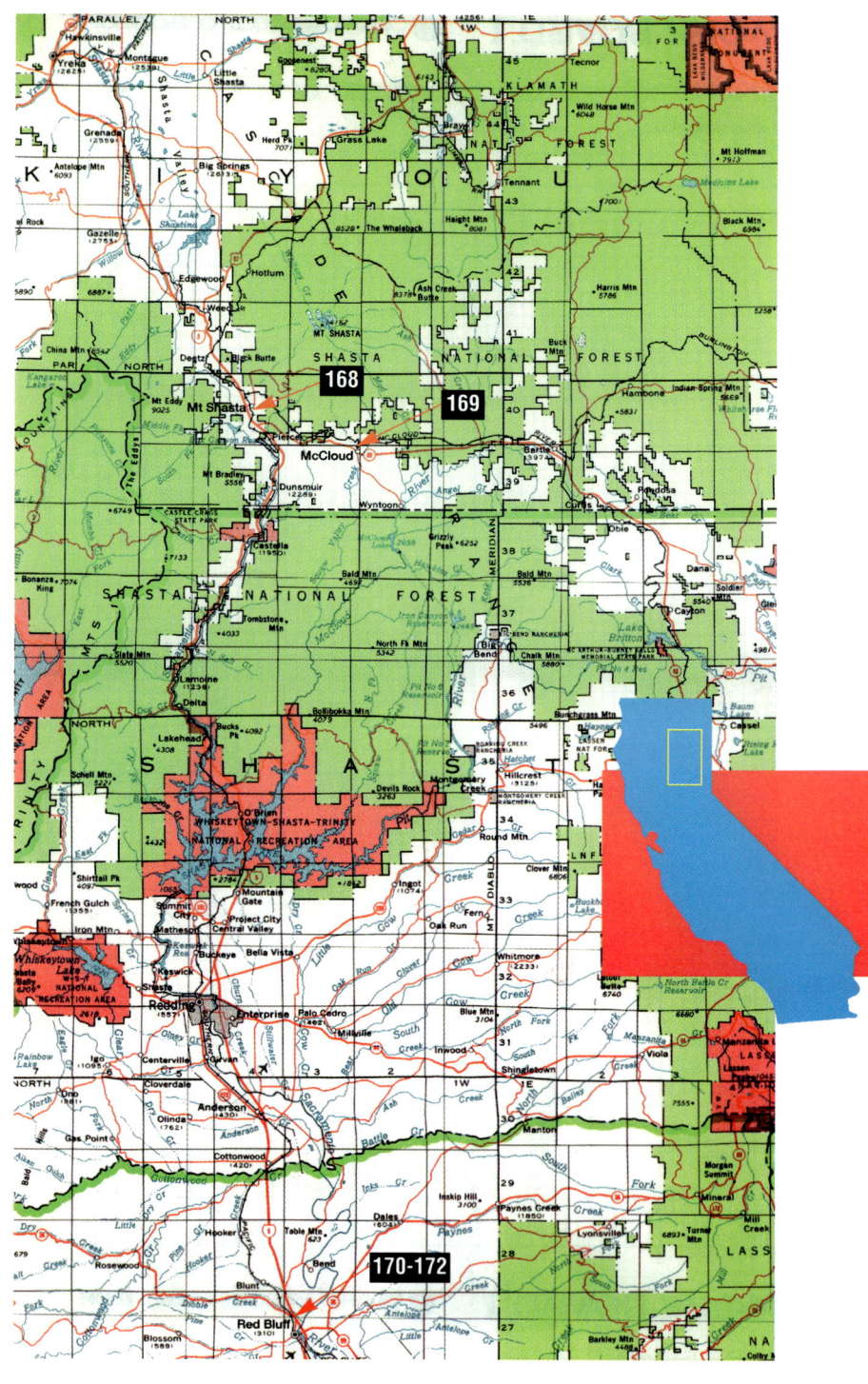

SHASTA

& THE CASCADES

This wild and magnificent area contains two volcanic mountains, the dormant 14,162-foot (4,316 m) **Mount Shasta** and the active 10,457-foot (3,187 m) **Mount Lassen.** Visitors can find white-water rivers, glaciers, forests, alpine lakes, deep canyons, and beautiful farmland. Since the population of the area is under 250,000, everyone who visits or resides here can really enjoy uncrowded natural splendor.

Horseback riding, hiking, fishing, skiing, golfing, mountain climbing, hunting, gold panning, and white-water rafting are some of the many activities available. This is also a great place to bring your camera, since you can explore six national forests, a national park, six state parks, the **Trinity Alps,** and the **Cascade Range**. If you are looking for modern conveniences, there are several large towns and cities to enjoy, starting in the north with **Yreka.** Yreka, the Indian name for Mt. Shasta, was a base camp for gold miners in 1851. It survived a fire in 1871, the rough and tumble of the Wild West, and the Chinese tong wars. Today you can enjoy the shops and restaurants of the old restored commercial buildings on **Miner Street,** or walk around the nationally registered historic district, with its many fine Victorian homes.

A thirty-minute drive to the south brings you to the town of **Mount Shasta,** nestled at the base of the mountain of the same name. Mount Shasta is a resort town that offers accommodations, shops, restaurants, and a spectacular view of the snow-capped mountain. It is also adjacent to **Lake Siskiyou,** a popular place for water sports and recreation. **McCloud,** located 10 miles (16 km) to the east, is a unique historic lumber town. Built over a century ago, it still captures the imagination with its old buildings and museum. Most of the inns in town were originally the homes of mill employees.

An hour's drive to the south brings you to the bustling city of **Redding,** located on the **Sacramento River.** Try canoeing on the river, or visit the **Redding Museum** and art center. The **Carter House Natural Science Museum** has displays featuring native animals. The nearby **Shasta-Trinity National Forest** includes 1,400 miles (2,258 km)

of trails, mountains, and lakes. **Shasta Dam,** 14 miles (22 km) northwest of Redding, is well worth a visit. **Shasta State Historic Park,** 6 miles (10 km) west of town, was once a successful gold-mining town. Today it offers restored buildings and museums, an old courthouse, a barn, a stagecoach, and a picnic area.

Red Bluff, a short hop to the south, is named after the colored sand and gravel banks along the Sacramento River. It is also the gateway to **Lassen Volcanic National Park.** The residential section of town, with its elegant tree-lined avenues, provides a perfect setting for countless Victorian homes, many of which bear informational plaques stating the age and pertinent historical information of the structure. Be sure to visit the **William B. Ide Adobe State Historic Park.** In 1846 this was the home of the founder and president of the California Republic. Mr. Ide was one of twenty-four settlers who led a revolt against the Mexican occupation. California was an independent country for twenty-six days, until the outbreak of the Mexican-American War and the subsequent liberation of the area by U.S. troops. Red Bluff, with 11,000 inhabitants, is the last major town on your tour of the Shasta-Cascade wilderness area.

ATTRACTIONS

Carter House Natural Science Museum, Caldwell Park, Redding, (916) 225-4125, open Tues.-Sun. 10-5, $1 adults, $.50 children. **Lassen Volcanic National Park,** Mineral, (916) 595-4444. **Redding Museum of Art and History,** Caldwell Park, 56 Quartz Hill Rd., Redding, (916) 225-4155, open Tues.-Sun. in summer 10-5, Sun.-Fri. 12-5 Sept.-May, Sat. 10-5. **Shasta Dam Visitor Information,** Redding, (916) 275-1554. **Shasta State Historic Park,** Shasta, (916) 225-2065, museum open Mar.-Oct., Thurs.-Mon. 10-5, $2 adults, $1 children 6-17. **Shasta Trinity National Forest,** 2400 Washington Ave., Redding, (916) 246-5313. **William B. Ide Adobe State Historic Park,** 21659 Adobe Rd., Red Bluff, (916) 527-5927, home open 11-4 summer, park and picnic facilities open all year 8 to sunset, $2 adults, $1 children 6-17.

McCLOUD

The McCloud Guest House Restaurant
606 W. Colombero Dr.
(916) 964-3160
Elegant, fine dining $$

MT. SHASTA

Lily's
1013 S. Mt. Shasta Blvd.
(916) 926-3372
Steaks, seafood, pasta $$

Michael's
313 N. Mt. Shasta Blvd.
(916) 926-5288
Continental cuisine $$

RED BLUFF

Coyote Canyon
2001 Main St.
(916) 527-2684
Hearty American fare $

The Green Barn
5 Chestnut Ave.
(916) 527-3161
All-American food $

Zorba's
645 Antelope Blvd.
(916) 527-2223
Greek $

MOUNT SHASTA RANCH
1008 W. A. Barr Rd.
Mount Shasta, CA 96067
Tel:1-916-926-3870

Built in 1923 by H.D. "Curley" Brown as a thoroughbred horse ranch, this inn offers spacious rooms with mountain views. Specialties are a delicious country-style breakfast and afternoon refreshments. Play pool, or watch the sunset from the veranda.

9 ROOMS, 4 pb   1 COTTAGE, pb

$45-75   **SPA**   **OPEN: ALL YEAR**   **HOSTS: Mary & Bill Larsen**

McCLOUD GUEST HOUSE
P.O. 1510
606 W. Colombero Dr.
McCloud, CA 96057
Tel:1-916-964-3160

On the first floor of this large country home is one of Siskiyou County's finest dining establishments. The second floor is for overnight guests, where a large parlor with a pool table is surrounded by beautifully decorated private rooms.

5 ROOMS, 5 pb

$75-90   **OPEN: ALL YEAR**   **HOSTS: Pat & Patti, Bill & Dennis**

BUTTONS & BOWS
427 Washington
Red Bluff, CA 96080
Tel:1-916-527-6405

This 1882 Victorian home, with its unique touch of buttons and bows, is the ideal place for a retreat. It's an easy walk to the Sacramento River and downtown. Rocking chairs and antiques add homey, old-fashioned charm.

3 ROOMS, 0 pb

$60-65   **SPA**   **OPEN: ALL YEAR**   **HOSTS: Betty & Marvin Johnson**

171 RED BLUFF

JEFFERSON HOUSE
1236 Jefferson St.
Red Bluff, CA 96080
Tel:1-916-527-4133

Situated on a quiet tree-lined street, this lovingly restored home offers a Victorian tea garden and a sun room. Breakfast in the formal dining room is a delightful experience. Antique shops and a Victorian museum are within walking distance. With a little luck and proper timing, while relaxing on the veranda, you may see the old Southern Pacific steam train as it makes its way up and down the valley.

HOSTS: Kay & Fred Webb

3 ROOMS, 1 pb

OPEN: ALL YEAR

$45-65

172 RED BLUFF

JETER VICTORIAN INN
1107 Jefferson St.
Red Bluff, CA 96080
Tel:1-916-527-7574

The rooms in this elegant Victorian home are furnished with exquisite antiques, reminding you of a bygone era. This comfortable guest house is located in a quite residential neighborhood, a short walk from the center of town. A romantic getaway in a private spa awaits you in the Imperial Room. After a delicious breakfast, explore the nearby shops and attractions.

HOST: Mary & Bill Dunlap

5 ROOMS, 3 pb   1 COTTAGE, pb

OPEN: ALL YEAR

SPA $55-140

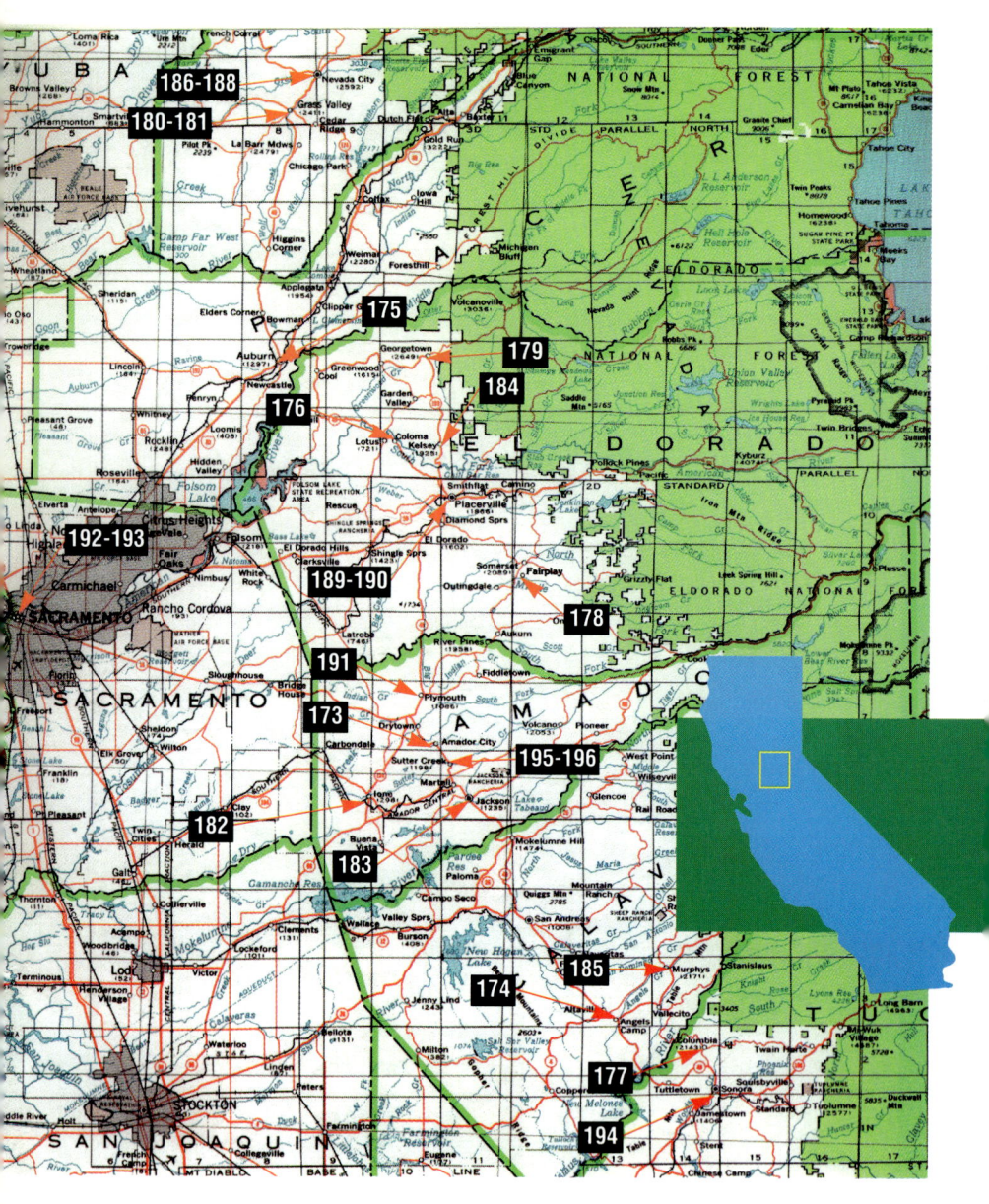

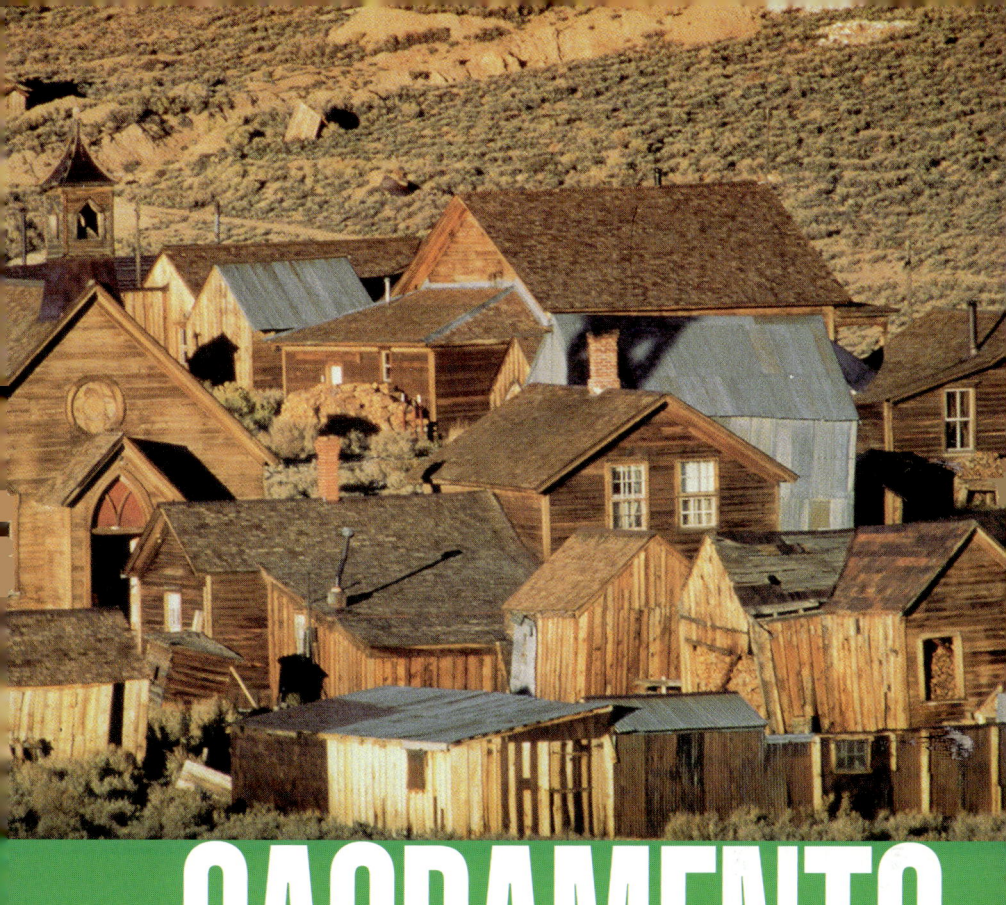

SACRAMENTO
& THE GOLD COUNTRY

The discovery of gold by John Marshall at **Sutter's Mill** precipitated the greatest mass migration in U.S. history. With the "argonauts" came the Pony Express, the transcontinental railroad, and the telegraph—all of which terminated in **Sacramento.** Located on the **American River** and home of John Sutter, a Swiss-German entrepreneur whose mill set the stage for the California gold rush of 1849, Sacramento was the primary supply center for the mines of the **Mother Lode.**

Today Sacramento's beautiful tree-lined streets are home to the **State Capitol** and **Fairgrounds,** lush parks featuring thousands of varieties of plants from around the world, the **California State Railroad Museum,** classical art galleries, and the completely restored **Sutter's Fort.**

Architectural styles range from the handsome old homes of the late 1800s to the Roman-Classic style of the capitol building. Built of granite and white sandstone, trimmed in onyx and marble, the capitol sits atop a gentle slope in a 40-acre (16 ha) park and is a showcase for tile mosaics, lovely murals, and statuary. In other parts of the city, carefully preserved historic sections such as **Old Sacramento** evoke the days when miners crowded into the city to buy supplies and lose their fortunes in gambling parlors and dance halls.

Upon leaving Sacramento, gold-seekers typically fanned out to the little towns and hamlets along the "golden necklace" of the Mother Lode, Route 49. Running through the heart of the gold country, Route 49 can be reached by driving northeast on Interstate 80 to the town of **Auburn.** Loop west to Route 49 and Nevada City, where you will begin the historic journey by travelling southwest to **Jamestown.**

In the years immediately following the discovery of gold, over 100,000 people—mostly men—descended on this region. The lure of riches was so strong that some eastern communities lost large portions of their populations. Prospectors formed camps on every stream and hill, wandering throughout the area by the thousands. Over the course of a decade, placer mining gave way to labor- and capital-intensive operations that reached deep into the earth. Many of the boom towns eventually fell into ruin or disappeared entirely, leaving little except for relics and memories of the noisy, crowded, thriving communities. The towns that still stand along Route 49 are wonderful testimonies to this era. Each has its own place in history, offering magical glimpses into the past and colorful celebrations reminiscent of days gone by.

The topology of the area is extremely varied, from river bottoms and rolling farmland to alpine forests and foothills. You can go hiking and river rafting, visit Mother Lode vineyards for wine tastings, explore restored camptowns and hardrock mines, or enjoy great food and entertainment. You can even pan for gold!

Nevada City provides a great introduction to your travels. The entire business district has been registered as a National Historic Landmark. Stop by the Chamber of Commerce to pick up a walking tour map and a calendar of events—the town hosts special activities and events every month throughout the year. Then head over to the **National Hotel** for a Pisco Punch—a favorite of travellers who arrived by stagecoach. The materials provided by the Chamber of Commerce, as in all of the Gold Country towns, will help you plan a special day. The Chamber of Commerce should be your first stop in all of these communities.

Just south of Nevada City, the green meadows that later became **Grass Valley** were discovered by livestock that had strayed from the campsite of a group of overland voyagers. When the travellers found their foraging cattle, they also found an area that held the secret of rich gold-bearing quartz veins deep within the earth. Home of famous gold-rush personality Lola Montez, who toppled the reign of a Bavarian king before fleeing to California, and child actress Lotta Crabtree, Grass Valley is near the **Empire Mine State Historic Park.** The Empire operated continuously for over a hundred years, and was the oldest and richest source of gold in the state. It is open for tours from April through November.

Auburn is a thriving city formed by the hardwood trees and fruit orchards that dot the surrounding foothills. Old Town in Auburn features innumerable reminders of its history, including the old **Placer County Courthouse.** So many mule teams and stagecoaches crisscrossed the routes leading to the mines that highwaymen and robbers camped along the trails in anticipation of easy riches.

Farther on, **Georgetown** lies at the edge of the true Mother Lode. Originally called Growlersburg, it was a supply center for thousands of miners and looks much as it did when grizzled men from such camps as Volcanoville and Sailors' Slide roamed the main street. Adjacent to **Coloma** is **Marshall Gold Discovery State Historic Park,** with its reconstructed buildings and fabulous exhibits. It is the site of **Sutter's Mill** and the discovery of gold by John Marshall, who later moved to nearby Kelsey and ran a blacksmith shop.

Placerville is the next major junction. Home of the excellent **El Dorado County Museum,** it was a stopover for those who travelled the overland trail and a pivot point for the **Pony Express.** Just over the hill is tiny **Fairplay,** a small nugget of history set on oak-studded slopes.

The next cluster of towns includes **Plymouth, Amador City, Sutter Creek, Ione,** and **Jackson,** all located in one of the oldest wine-producing areas of the state, **Amador County,** named after a wealthy rancher. Gold and wine were chief products of this county and thus played important historical roles. Today wineries abound and provide a flavorful backdrop to the fascinating stories behind each of these rough-and-ready communities.

Your tour of the Gold Country ends with **Angels Camp** and the towns of **Columbia, Sonora, Jamestown, and Mariposa.** This is the part of the Mother Lode frequented by some of the most colorful figures of the gold rush, including Black Bart, Joaquin Murietta, Mark Twain, Brett Harte, Horatio Alger, and even Ulysses S. Grant. Tradition is still maintained in these parts, including the Jumping Frog Jubilee at Angels Camp, immortalized in Mark Twain's famous story. Held each May, anyone can enter—they will even supply the frog! Each town has an interesting tale, and they are all beautifully situated in the western Sierra.

Columbia is a state park and completely reconstructed Gold Rush town. It provides an amazing array of attractions and is populated by people who regularly dress in period costumes to bring alive the spirit and feeling of a town dating back to the mid-1800s. One of the most-visited spots in the Gold Country, it makes a wonderful conclusion to your journey through the Mother Lode.

SACRAMENTO

California State Railroad Museum, 125 I St., (916) 448-4466, open daily 10-5, $5 adults, $2 children 6-12. **Governor's Mansion,** 16th and H Sts., (916) 323-3047, tours on the hour 10-4, $2 adults, $1 children 6-17. **Old Sacramento Visitor Information Center,** 1104 Front St., (916) 442-7644, open daily 9-5. **State Capitol,** Capitol Ave. and 10th St., (916) 324-0333, open daily 9-4 spring/summer, weekdays 9-5, 10-5 fall/winter. **Sutter's Fort State Historic Park,** 2701 L St., (916) 445-4422, open daily 10-4, $2 adults, $1 children 6-17.

GOLD COUNTRY

Columbia State Historic Park, Columbia, (209) 532-4301, exhibits and demonstrations daily 10-6, museum open 8-5. **El Dorado County Museum,** in fairgrounds north of U.S. 50, Placerville, open Wed.-Sat. 10-4, Sun. 1-4 in summer. **Empire Mine State Historic Park,** 10791 E. Empire St. (Empire St. exit south from Hwy. 49), near Grass Valley, (916) 273-8522, open daily in summer 9-6, daily in winter 10-5. **Marshall Gold Discovery State Historic Park,** Coloma, (916) 622-3470, open daily 8-sunset, $5 per car, museum open daily 10-5 in summer, 10:30-4:30 Labor Day-Memorial Day. **Nevada City Chamber of Commerce,** 132 Main St., Nevada City, (916) 265-2692.

RESTAURANTS

S=under $10,   SS=$10 to $20,   SSS=over $20

AMADOR CITY

Ballad's
14220 Highway 49
(209) 267-5403
California cuisine $$

Imperial Hotel
14202 Highway 49
(209) 267-9172
California cuisine $$

COLUMBIA

Columbia City Hotel
Main St.
(209) 532-1479
California-French cuisine $$$

El Sombrero
11256 State
(209) 533-9123
Family-style Mexican food $

Stage Coach Inn
Perris Ferry Road
(209) 532-5816
Family-style American fare $$

NEVADA CITY

Cirino's
309 Broad St.
(209) 265-2246
Italian $

Friar Tuck's
111 North Pine
(209) 265-2262
California cuisine, seafood $$

Michael's Garden Restaurant
216 Main St.
(209) 265-6660
California cuisine, seafood $$

Selaya's
320 Broad St.
(209) 265-5697
Continental cuisine $$

SACRAMENTO

Americo's
2000 Capitol Ave.
(916) 442-8119
Italian cuisine $$

Capitol Grill
28th and N Sts.
(916) 736-0744
Steaks, seafood $$

Paragary's
1401 28th St.
(916) 457-5737
Pizza oven, seafood, pastas $-$$

SONORA

Banny's Cafe
14751 Mono Way
(209) 533-4709
Bistro-style California cuisine $$

City Hotel
Main St.
(209) 532-1479
Fixed menu, seasonal $$

Hemingway's Cafe
362 S. Stewart
(209) 532-4900
Continental cuisine, weekend musical theater $$

La Torre Restaurant
39 N. Washington
(209) 533-9181
Italian and other specialties $$

Cache Cellars
Pedrick Road
Davis, CA 95616
(916) 756-6068
Open: Sat.+ Sun. 10-4

Cache Creek Winery
36380 County Road 21
Woodland, CA 95695
(916) 662-2578
Open: Sat.+ Sun. 1-5

R & J Cook
Netherlands Road
Clarksburg, CA 95612
(916) 775-1234
Open: Sat.+ Sun. 12-5

Delicato Vineyards
Highway 99 at French Camp
Road, Manteca, CA 95336
(209) 239-1215
Open: daily 9-5:30

Franzia Winery
17000 E. Highway 120
Ripon, CA 95366
(209) 599-6511
Open: daily 10-5

Giumarra Vineyards
11220 Edison Highway
Edison, CA 93220
(805) 395-7153
Open: Tues. thru Sat. 9-4

Madrona Vineyards
High Hill Road
Camino, CA 95709
(916) 644-5948
Open: daily 11-5

Milliaire Winery
276 Main St.
Murphys, CA 95247
(209) 728-1658
Open: daily 11-4:30

Montevina Wines
20680 Shenandoah School Road
Plymouth, CA 95669
(209) 245-6942
Open: daily 11-4

Nevada City Winery
321 Spring St.
Nevada City, CA 95959
(916) 265-9463
Open: daily 12-5

Oak Ridge Vineyards
6100 E. Highway 12
Lodi, CA 95240
(209)369-4758
Open: daily 9-5

Phillips Farms Winery
4580 W. Highway 12
Lodi, CA 95242
(209) 368-7384
Open: daily 9-5

The R.H. Phillips Vineyard
County roads 87 and 12A
Esparto, CA 95627
(916) 662-3215
Open: daily 8-5

Santino Wines
12225 Steiner Road
Plymouth, CA 95669
(209) 245-6979
Open: daily 11:30-4:30

Shenandoah Vineyards
12300 Steiner Road
Plymouth, CA 95669
(209) 245-4455
Open: daily 10-5

Sobon Estate
14430 Shenandoah Road
Plymouth, CA 95669
(209) 245-6554
Open: daily 10-5

Stevenot Winery
2690 San Domingo Road
Murphys, CA 95247
(209) 728-3436
Open: daily 10-5

Story Vineyard
10525 Bell Road
Plymouth, CA 95669
(209) 245-6208
Open: Sat.+ Sun. 11-5

Windwalker Vineyards
7360 Perry Creek Road
Somerset, CA 95684
(209) 245-4054
Open: Sat.+ Sun. 11-5

Wooden Valley Winery
4756 Suisun Valley Road
Suisun, CA 94585
(707) 864-0730
Open: Tues. thru Sun. 9-5

IMPERIAL HOTEL
P.O. Box 195
14202 Highway 49
Amador, CA 95601
Tel:1-209-267-9172

AMADOR **173**

This newly restored hotel epitomizes affordable luxury in a Victorian atmosphere with modern amenities. Unwind at the bar or on the secluded patio surrounded by flowers. The restaurant specializes in Continental cuisine, serving dinner every evening and Sunday brunch.

6 ROOMS, 6 pb

$60-90

OPEN: ALL YEAR   HOSTS: Dave Martin & Bruce Sherrill

COOPER HOUSE
P.O. Box 1388
1184 Church St.
Angels Camp, CA 95222
Tel:1-209-736-2145

ANGELS CAMP **174**

Built in 1911 and carefully restored, this rustic home features antiques, a magnificent greenstone fireplace, and original artwork by local artists. A spacious veranda overlooks the garden path that leads to a gazebo. Each room features unique decor. Walk to shops and restaurants.

3 ROOMS, 3 pb

$80-90

OPEN: ALL YEAR   HOSTS: Thomas & Katherine Reese

LINCOLN HOUSE
191 Lincoln Way
Auburn, CA 95603
Tel:1-916-885-8880

AUBURN **175**

"There are no strangers here, only friends you have not met." In addition to the friendly atmosphere, the house is tastefully decorated with antiques and historical artifacts. Wander through nearby Old Town Auburn, or read in front of the fireplace.

3 ROOMS, 2 pb   1 SUITES, pb   **POOL**

$70-100

OPEN: ALL YEAR   HOSTS: Leslie & Stan Fronczak

176 COLOMA

THE COLOMA COUNTRY INN

P.O. Box 502
345 High St.
Coloma, CA 95613

Tel:1-916-622-6919

This beautiful inn, built in 1852, is nestled in a park filled with historic Gold Rush sites. It is also one of the oldest remaining structures in town. Enjoy fresh lemonade in the gazebo, pick blackberries, or stroll through the park. In the morning, enjoy breakfast overlooking the pond. The adventurous can escape in a hot air balloon piloted by the host or go white-water river rafting.

HOSTS: Cindi & Alan Ehrgott

5 ROOMS, 3 pb

OPEN: ALL YEAR $79-89

177 COLUMBIA

COLUMBIA CITY HOTEL

P.O. Box 1870
Main St. Columbia State Historic Park
Columbia, CA 95310

Tel:1-209-532-1479

This 1860s historic inn provides both comfort and fun. Each guest room is appointed with antiques that convey a genuine feeling of the Gold Rush era. The inn is complete with an intimate dining room. "The Gold Country medal goes to this hotel...the dinner menu is multicultural and impressive...the wine list is fabulous," says The Wall Street Journal. Guests can explore the old town or pan for gold.

HOST: Tom Bender

10 ROOMS, 10 pb

OPEN: ALL YEAR $65-90

7UP GUEST RANCH

FAIRPLAY | 178

P.O. Box 304
8060 Fairplay Rd.
Fairplay, CA 95684

Tel:1-209-245-5450

Escape to a country retreat, away from the fast-paced life of the city. Step back in time and find serenity in this secluded, historic, 1930s restored Western guest ranch. Tucked away are log cabins, each with two distinctively different private rooms. Contemporary and period furnishings of the Old West accent each room. A delicious "country ranch" breakfast with homemade biscuits and ranch-fresh eggs is served in the main lodge or on the terrace.

R HOSTS: Alice & Michael Chazen

4 ROOMS, 4 pb

$89   OPEN: ALL YEAR

AMERICAN RIVER INN

GEORGETOWN | 179

Orleans & Main   P.O. Box 43
Georgetown, CA 95634

Tel:1-800-245-6566
or 1-916-333-4499

This historic inn was a popular stagecoach stop during the gold rush era. Relax in the elegant parlor and enjoy the complimentary wine and cheese served each evening. Cool off in the mountain pool, or relax in the spa. Stroll in the gardens, enjoy the putting green, or play croquet, badminton, ping-pong and bocce ball. Rafting trips, hot air ballooning, fishing and golf are available nearby. The Inn can accommodate groups and provide elegant wedding and meeting facilities.

R HOSTS: Maria & Will Collin

18 ROOMS, 10 pb   6 SUITES, 6 pb   **POOL**

$80-150   SPA OPEN: ALL YEAR

180 GRASS VALLEY

HOSTS: Sue & Tom Myers

MURPHY'S INN
318 Neal St.
Grass Valley, CA 95945
Tel:1-916-273-6873

R

This opulent inn, located in the heart of the historic district, was built in 1866 by one of the Mother Lode's famous gold barons. Antiques, lace curtains, and floral wallpaper decorate the interior. Unwind in the pool and spa. Walk to shops and restaurants.

5 ROOMS, 5 pb   3 SUITES, 3 pb

OPEN: ALL YEAR   **SPA**   **$75-135**

181 GRASS VALLEY

HOSTS: Margaret Swan & Howard Levine

SWAN-LEVINE HOUSE
328 South Church
Grass Valley, CA 95945
Tel:1-916-272-1873

The owners of this impressive Victorian home are artists and collectors who operate a studio and a gallery to display the fine art of printmaking. The atmosphere is relaxed, and the house is furnished with a collection of art and antiques.

3 ROOMS, 3 pb

OPEN: ALL YEAR   **$75-85**

182 IONE

HOSTS: Patricia & Melisande

THE HEIRLOOM
P.O. 322
214 Shakeley Lane
Ione, CA 95640
Tel:1-209-274-4468

R

Inspired by the Gold Rush of 1848, this southern antebellum-style home is filled with antiques and family heirlooms and surrounded by a romantic English garden. Distinctive furniture and hand-crafted accessories accent each room; skylights and balconies add a special ambiance.

6 ROOMS, 4 pb

OPEN: ALL YEAR   **$55-85**

WEDGEWOOD INN

JACKSON | **183**

11941 Narcissus Rd.
Jackson, CA 95642
Tel:1-209-296-4300

Treat yourself to romantic elegance combined with generous hospitality. This charming Victorian replica tucked away on wooded acreage offers a terraced garden park, spectacular gazebo, hammocks, horseshoes, and croquet. Inside, guests are surrounded by family heirloom antiques, stained glass, Victorian lampshades and needle work crafted by your hosts. A delicious gourmet breakfast is served in the dining room by candlelight.

R **HOSTS: Jeannine & Vic Beltz**

5 ROOMS, 5 pb   1 COTTAGE, pb

$75-130

OPEN: ALL YEAR

MOUNTAINSIDE

KELSEY | **184**

P.O. Box 165
5821 Spanish Flat Rd.
Kelsey, CA 95643
Tel:1-800-237-0832

Situated on a peaceful mountaintop amid eighty acres of forest, this home is tastefully appointed with 1920s furnishings. Enjoy the 180-degree view of the foothills from the veranda, or relax in front of the fireplace in the spacious parlor. An authentic country breakfast is served in the dining room or on the breakfast deck. The parlor can accommodate large groups or parties and the home is open for weddings.

R **HOST: Mary Ellen & Paul Mello**

4 ROOMS, 4 pb

$70-75

SPA OPEN: ALL YEAR

185 MURPHYS

HOSTS: Barbara & Bob Costa

DUNBAR HOUSE 1880
271 Jones St. P.O.1375
Murphys, CA 95247

Tel:1-800-225-3764 ext.321
or 1-209-728-2897

R

Your date with history begins the moment you arrive at this beautiful 1880 Italianate Victorian inn. Enjoy an afternoon appetizer buffet with local wines. Savor a full country breakfast by the fire, in the beautiful garden, or in the privacy of your room.

3 ROOMS, 3 pb   1 SUITE, pb

OPEN: ALL YEAR   SPA   **$105-145**

186 NEVADA CITY

HOSTS: Jan & Ted Kendall

THE KENDALL HOUSE
534 Spring St.
Nevada City, CA 95959

Tel:1-916-265-0405

R

This California farmhouse-style home dates back to the 1860s. Your friendly innkeepers invite you to experience a unique balance of pre-Victorian architecture with modern amenities. You'll also enjoy the contemporary pool, lovely gardens, peaceful neighborhood, and nearby shops.

4 ROOMS, 4 pb   1 COTTAGE, pb   **POOL**

OPEN: ALL YEAR   **$98-150**

187 NEVADA CITY

HOST: Deborah Dane

THE PARSONAGE
427 Broad St.
Nevada City, CA 95959

Tel:1-916-265-9478

R

Located in the historic district of "The Queen of the Northern Mines," this Methodist parsonage was converted to a bed and breakfast inn and furnished with pioneer family antiques Old-fashioned graces include Haviland china on an exquisite Sheridan dining table.

3 ROOMS, 3 pb   1 COTTAGE, pb

OPEN: ALL YEAR   SPA   **$65-95**

THE RED CASTLE INN

109 Prospect St.
Nevada City, CA 95959

Tel:1-916-265-5135

This 1860 Gothic Revival brick mansion is a historic landmark that overlooks the city. Sparkling chandeliers enchant the antique-filled rooms. Admire the owner's extensive library and collection of Gold Rush memorabilia and California art. Listen to strains of Mozart echoing through the lofty hallways. Close to gold-mining museums, theaters, shops, galleries, and restaurants. "Would top my list of places to stay in the Gold Country. Nothing else quite compares with it." - Gourmet Magazine

HOSTS: Mary Louise & Conley Weaver

4 ROOMS, 4 pb   3 SUITES, 3 pb

$65-140   OPEN: ALL YEAR

CHICHESTER-McKEE HOUSE

800 Spring St.
Placerville, CA 95667

Tel:1-800-831-4008

This elegant Victorian inn is filled with turn-of-the-century charm. Admire the antique Story Book Doll collection, stained glass windows, exquisite fireplaces, and unique lighting. Wake up to the aroma of coffee, fresh-baked muffins and coffee cake. The area surrounding the inn is rich in history, offers breathtaking natural beauty, and contains many interesting shops and attractions, such as white-water rafting and hot-air ballooning.

HOSTS: Doreen & Bill Thornhill

3 ROOMS, 3 private wash basins & toilets, shd. bath

$75-80   OPEN: ALL YEAR

190 PLACERVILLE

HOST: Dorothy Irvin

RIVER ROCK INN
1756 Georgetown Dr.
Placerville, CA 95667
Tel:1-916-622-7640 **R**

Spacious and comfortable, this inn has a large deck with an uninterrupted view of the American River. After a hearty breakfast, you can go fishing, take a white-water raft trip down the river, or pan for gold.

4 ROOMS, 2 pb   1 SUITES, pb

OPEN: ALL YEAR   **SPA**   **$75-90**

191 PLYMOUTH

HOST: Bobbi Deever

AMADOR HARVEST INN & VINEYARD
12455 Steiner Rd.
Plymouth, CA 95669
Tel:1-209-245-5512

Tucked serenely amid the vineyards of Shenandoah Valley, this inn is a comfortable and contemporary farm house on the grounds of the owner's vineyard. Each guest room has its own style. Enjoy the wildlife or play croquet by the pond.

4 ROOMS, 4 pb

OPEN: ALL YEAR   **$85-110**

192 SACRAMENTO

HOSTS: Susanne & Ken Ventura

AUNT ABIGAIL'S
2120 G Street
Sacramento, CA 95816
Tel:1-800-858-1568
or 1-916-441-5007

This stately mansion is one of Sacramento's loveliest. Vacationers and business travellers alike will be pampered, spoiled, and overfed in this elegant inn. Breakfast is a gourmet delight, with award-winning baked goods. Guests can walk to many fine restaurants.

6 ROOMS, 4 pb

OPEN: ALL YEAR   **SPA**   **$75-135**

AMBER HOUSE

1315 22nd St.
Sacramento, CA 95816

Tel:1-800-755-6526
or 1-916-444-8085

Just eight blocks from the capitol, on a quiet street of historic homes, Amber House offers the perfect blend of elegance, comfort, and friendly hospitality. Whether you desire a cozy hideaway or a spectacular minisuite with an elegant marble bath and whirlpool-spa for two, you will be served a delicious gourmet breakfast (in your room if you wish), an early-morning coffee tray, evening beverages, and all the personal attention you could wish.

HOSTS: Jane Ramey & Michael Richardson

7 ROOMS, 7 pb   1 SUITE, pb

$85-195   SPA   OPEN: ALL YEAR

SERENITY

15305 Bear Cub Dr.
Sonora, CA 95370

Tel:1-800-426-1441
or 1-209-533-1441

The pastoral setting, bountiful breakfasts, charming rooms, and crackling fires are some of the things that attract guests to this comfortable inn. The guest rooms, library, and living and dining rooms are individually appointed with antiques, reproductions, fine woodwork, and needle art to create a peaceful, romantic atmosphere. Relax on the veranda while you enjoy afternoon refreshments, listen to the wind whistling through the trees, or stroll through the wooded grounds.

HOSTS: Charlotte & Fred Hoover

4 ROOMS, 4 pb

$65-80   OPEN: ALL YEAR

195 SUTTER CREEK

THE FOXES IN SUTTER CREEK
P.O. Box 159
77 Main St.
Sutter Creek, CA 95685
Tel: 1-209-267-5882

This impeccably restored award-winning Victorian home from the Gold Rush era earns its reputation with its exquisite furnishings and period antiques. Garden views, private baths, fireplaces, A/C and covered parking offer extra appeal. Personal service is a trademark. Foxes features cooked-to-order breakfasts brought to your room on silver service. Close to quaint shops, museums, wineries, and nature, it makes the perfect getaway.

HOSTS: Min & Pete Fox

6 SUITES, 6 pb

OPEN: ALL YEAR

$95-140

196 SUTTER CREEK

SUTTER CREEK INN
P.O. Box 385
75 Main St.
Sutter Creek, CA 95685
Tel: 1-209-267-5606

This comfortable old inn offers tastefully decorated rooms, some with fireplaces and swinging beds. A large living room filled with comfy sofas and a collection of over three thousand books are sure to appeal to the avid reader. Walk in the beautiful gardens or schedule a relaxing massage. Afternoon refreshments include homemade cookies and lemonade served by a crackling fire in the kitchen. For the curious, handwriting analysis is available by appointment.

HOST: Jane Way

R

8 ROOMS, 8 pb   11 COTTAGE, 11 pb

OPEN: ALL YEAR

$50-135

A
218
Tahoe City
Twin Peaks
Tahoe Pines
Homewood
Tahoma
Meeks Bay
South Lake Tahoe
Camp Richardson
LAKE TAHOE

B
Groveland
202-203
Coulterville
199
MARIPOSA
Mariposa
209-216
Fish Camp
200-201
Ahwahnee
197
Oakhurst
217
NATIONAL PARK
MADERA
FRESNO
INYO NATIONAL FOREST
Mammoth Lakes
206-208
Bishop
198
SIERRA NATIONAL FOREST
SEQUOIA NATIONAL FOREST
205
Giant Forest

A
B
C

204
Kernville
C
Isabella Lake
Weldon
Onyx

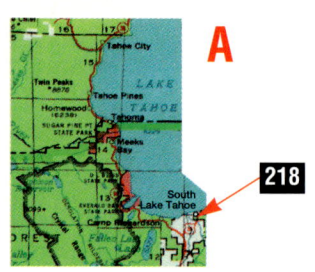

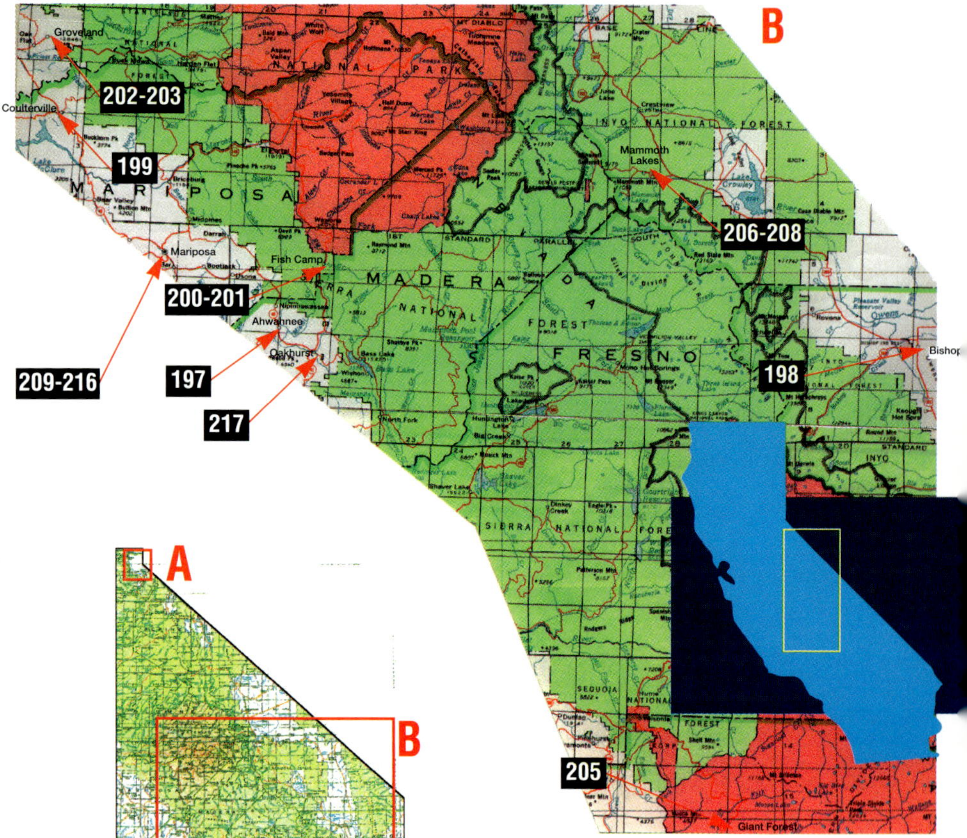

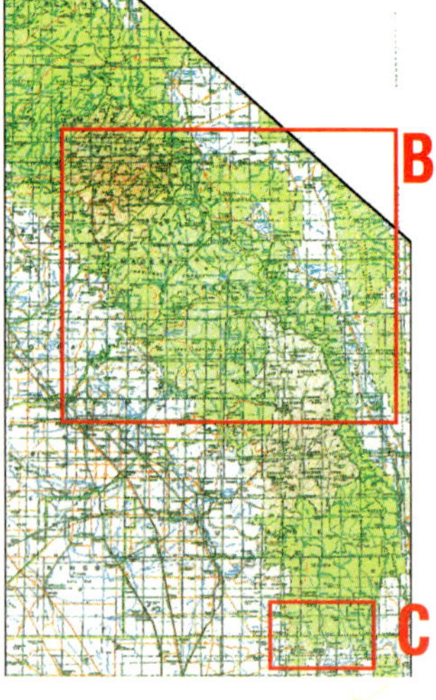

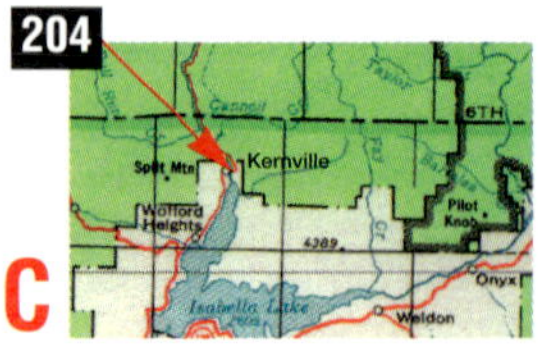

YOSEMITE
KINGS CANYON & THE HIGH SIERRAS

Crisp alpine air, crashing waterfalls, crystalline lakes of deep blues and greens, and towering forests prevail in the Sierra Nevada, where outdoor recreation is at its exhilarating best. This largest single mountain range in the country offers everything from gambling casinos to snow and water skiing, as well as breathtaking hikes in the unparalleled Yosemite Valley.

We begin our tour at **Lake Tahoe,** where snow-capped mountains frame the stunningly beautiful lake that welcomes boaters, anglers, and any other water sports enthusiasts who can withstand the perpetually chilly waters. The town of Lake Tahoe is divided into four sections, the South, West, North, and East shores; the South and North shores are more popular. **South Shore** is the most action-packed and heavily populated area, with restaurants, shopping centers, and accommodations lining State Highway 50 past the state line into Nevada, where you can gamble and enjoy the cabaret shows at Caeser's, Harrah's, and Harvey's, throughout the day and night. **Heavenly Valley** ski resort is easily accessible from the south. **Tahoe City** at **North Shore,** located at the junction of State Highways 28 and 89, is the center for skiers who pack the slopes at the **Squaw Valley** and **Alpine Meadows** ski resorts.

South of Tahoe and only 24 miles (38 km) from Yosemite is the old gold mining town of **Groveland.** Eleven miles (18 km) south is **Coulterville,** a photogenic little town that has some unique adobe structures and was once the home of Buffalo Bill's brothers. Heading southeast is **Mariposa,** with its fine Gold Rush era architecture and the **California State Mining and Mineral Museum,** which houses gems, minerals, artifacts, and photographs that document the mining industry. High up in the mountains, 30 miles (48 km) southeast, is the forested village of **Ahwahnee.** The town of **Oakhurst** is located at the southern tip of State Highway 49. Just north is **Fish Camp,** a pleasant gateway to the southern entrance of Yosemite National Park that features the **Yosemite Mountain-Sugar Pine Railroad;** you can a ride an old logger steam train through the **Sierra National Forest.**

The final destination on this trip is **Yosemite National Park** and **Yosemite Valley,** which will take your breath away in more ways than one. Magical, awe-inspiring beauty and spectacular hiking opportunities will have you hooked. Yosemite Valley: Don't leave for home without visiting it! Bring your camera and take lots of photos, but you will find it impossible to re-create the feeling of standing in the most perfect valley a glacier could carve.

Water falls thousands of feet down the rocky cliffs into the tranquil green carpet of the meadows below. Sand-colored cliffs are a stark contrast to the verdant forests. In winter, revel in the glorious snow-covered scenes. Sublime spring bring a colorful renaissance of activity, complete with raging torrents of crystal-clear water cascading down from above. Blissful warmth and long hikes under blue skies rejuvenate the soul in summer. Autumn treats us to vibrant colors in a crisp, clear backdrop. Yosemite may change with the seasons, but its beauty never ceases to captivate.

Yosemite Valley is the gem in the center of the national park of the same name, which features many wonderful areas of great natural beauty. Yosemite contains 360 miles (576 km) of roads and 750 miles (1200 km) of trails. Although it attracts three million visitors a year, it is still easy to find solitude on the mountain trails. The numerous villages, especially in the valley itself, offer boutiques, restaurants, valley information centers, sports equipment shops and rentals and, of course, a variety of accommodations.

Half Dome and **El Capitan** are the most famous peaks in the valley. Half Dome, at 8,842 feet (2,700 m), is a striking angular mass that forms a spectacular cliff 2,000 feet (600 m) high. El Capitan rises 3,593 feet (1,100 m) and is the largest granite monolith in the world. **Glacier Point** offers a breathtaking panorama of the High Sierra. **Mariposa Grove** is the largest grove of giant sequoias in the park, featuring the impressive **Grizzly Giant** at 30 feet (9 m) in diameter and 210 feet (64 m) in height. **Tioga Pass,** north of the valley, rises to 9,945 feet (3,030 m), making it the highest road in

California, and one of the most beautiful drives anywhere in the United States. This road brings you to **Tuolumne Meadows,** the largest alpine meadow in the Sierra.

Just past Lee Vining Junction off Highway 395 is salty **Mono Lake,** a resting spot and breeding ground for gulls and other water fowl. Lately there has been an ecological movement to save Mono Lake, as a major water project has siphoned the water from the lake to dangerously low levels. Environmentalists and ecologists are fighting for the restoration of the lake and a return to its original condition. Visit the State Reserve on the south shore to find out more about the unique geological history of the lake and the birds that make their home there.

Twenty-five miles (40 km) south of Mono Lake is the resort town of **Mammoth Lakes,** known for its impeccable and challenging ski slopes during the winter and early spring months, and for its hiking trails in summer. Be sure to see **Devils Postpile National Monument,** a unique geologic formation; take a ride on the aerial tram for a view from above.

In the southern Sierra, towering trees, crystal lakes, echoing canyons, and rippling streams greet the visitor at **Kings Canyon** and **Sequoia National Parks.** Backpackers, hikers, anglers, and horseback riders can enjoy miles of unspoiled trails and rivers. **General Grant Grove** in Kings Canyon contains almost all of the park's facilities. Sequoia National Park has the largest number of giant sequoias in California. The highlight of the park is the **General Sherman Tree,** which wins the prize for the largest living thing in the world, at 102 feet (31 m) in base circumference, 36.5 feet (11 m) in diameter, and 275 feet (84 m) in height.

Kernville, at the southern tip of Sequoia National Park, is a rustic mountain village adjacent to **Lake Isabella.** It makes a nice stopover point for exploring the national parks.

ATTRACTIONS

California State Mining and Mineral Museum, in fairgrounds on State 49 1.5 miles south of its junction with State 140, Mariposa, open daily 10-6, Sun. until 4, moderate admission. **Lake Tahoe Visitors Authority,** South Lake Tahoe, (916) 544-5050, (800) 288-2463. **Mammoth Lakes Visitor Information Center,** Mammoth Lakes, (800) 367-6572. **National Park Service,** Information Office, Yosemite National Park, (209) 372-0265, (209) 372-0264 for a recording. **North Lake Tahoe Visitors and Convention Bureau,** Tahoe City, (916) 583-3494, (800) 824-6348. **Sequoia and Kings Canyon National Parks,** Three Rivers, (209) 565-3456, (209) 565-3351 for a recording, open daily 8-4:30. **Yosemite Camping and Recreation,** (209) 372-4845. **Visitors Center,** Yosemite Village, (209) 372-0299, open daily 9-5, with extended hours in summer. **Yosemite Area Road Conditions,** (209) 372-4605. **Yosemite Mountain-Sugar Pine Railroad,** 56001 State 41, Fish Camp, (209) 683-7273, call for schedule and prices.

FISH CAMP
Narrow Gauge Inn
48571 Highway 41
(209) 683-7720
American fare, closed for winter $$
Wawona Hotel
Yosemite National Park
(209) 375-6556
American fare $$

GROVELAND
Groveland Restaurant
Groveland Hotel
18767 Main St.
(209) 962-4000
Continental cuisine $$
Pine Mountain Lake Country Club
Mueller Dr.
(209) 962-8638
Classic American cuisine $$-$$$

MAMMOTH
Angel's
Corner of Main St. and Sierra Blvd.
(619) 934-7427
Barbeque $$
Nevado's
Main St. at Minaret
(619) 934-4466
Steaks, pasta, seafood $$-$$$
Rafters
Old Mammoth Rd. next to Sierra
Nevada Inn
(619) 934-2537
Continental cuisine $$-$$$
The Stove
Old Mammoth Road next to
Mammoth Creek Park
(619) 934-2812
Country cooking $-$$

MARIPOSA
Charles Street Dinner House
Hwy 140 and Seventh St.
(209) 966-2366
Steaks, seafood $$-$$$
Sugar Pine
Hwy 140
(209) 966-3816
Steaks, seafood $$

OAKHURST
Erna's Elderberry House
Estate by the Elderberries
48688 Victoria Lane
(209) 683-6800
European-California cuisine $$$

THE HOMESTEAD

41110 Road 600
Ahwahnee, CA 93601
Tel:1-209-683-0495

AHWAHNEE 197

This retreat offers private cottages on 160 acres, overlooking a panoramic sierra view. The interiors are decorated with modern and antique furnishings, giving each cottage its own unique ambiance. The horse lay-over facilities and outdoor barbecue complement the country atmosphere.

4 COTTAGE, 4 pb

$125   **OPEN: ALL YEAR**   **HOSTS: Cindy Brooks & Larry Ends**

CHALFANT HOUSE

213 Academy St.
Bishop, CA 93514
Tel:1-619-872-1790

BISHOP 198

This beautifully restored 1898 house offers tastefully furnished guest rooms with handmade quilts, ceiling fans, lovely antiques, and central air. Suites have parlors and television. Full kitchen available. Indulge in the gourmet breakfasts and old-fashioned ice cream sundaes in the evening.

4 ROOMS, 4 pb   3 SUITES, 3 pb

$50-90   **OPEN: ALL YEAR**   **HOSTS: Sally & Fred Manecke**

SHERLOCK HOLMES INN

5006 Main St. P.O. 7
Coulterville, CA 95311
Tel:1-800-354-5697
or 1-209-878-3915

COULTERVILLE 199

Rich with history, this inn offers guests beautifully decorated rooms with an unpretentious ambiance. Famous for her delicious breakfasts, your host offers homemade breads and Welsh-goldminers' pasties, an unusual treat. After breakfast browse in the antique shop downstairs.

3 ROOMS, 1 pb

$75-90   **OPEN: ALL YEAR**   **HOST: Mary Sherlock**

200 FISH CAMP

HOSTS: Vivien & Gerry Smith

APPLE TREE INN
1110 Highway 41
Fish Camp, CA 93623
Tel:1-209-683-5111

This inn boasts lovely cottages on seven wooded acres dotted with fir trees and wildflowers. Guests may enjoy a wagon ride in the summer and a sleigh ride in the winter. Relax with breakfast in bed. Close to Yosemite.

6 COTTAGE, 6 pb

OPEN: ALL YEAR ☕ 🔥   **$80-100**

201 FISH CAMP

HOSTS: Karen Bergh & Lee Morse

KAREN'S B&B YOSEMITE INN
1144 Railroad Ave. P.O. Box 8
Fish Camp, CA 93623
Tel: U.S. & Canada 1-800-346-1443
or 1-209-683-4550   ®

Nestled amid towering pines and whispering cedars at 5,000 feet, this inn offers a unique blend of contemporary and country living. Enjoy a bountiful country breakfast served family style. Your hostess will offer helpful touring information.

3 ROOMS, 3 pb

OPEN: ALL YEAR 🍴   **$80-85**

202 GROVELAND

HOSTS: Dody, Carl & Chris Yates

BERKSHIRE INN
P.O. BOX 207
19950 Highway 120
Groveland, CA 95321
Tel: CA 1-209-962-6744

Located in a secluded area with beautiful forest views, this grand inn boasts an English country ambiance. Guests will enjoy the quiet and privacy of rooms with french doors leading to a private deck. Close to shops, restaurants, skiing, and white-water rafting.

6 ROOMS, 6 pb

OPEN: ALL YEAR ☕ 🔥 SPA   **$69-180**

THE GROVELAND HOTEL

GROVELAND `203`

18767 Main St. P.O. 289
Groveland, CA 95321
Tel:CA 1-800-273-3314
or 1-209-962-4000

This historic inn invites you to sample southern hospitality in the heart of the Sierra. Rooms are furnished with European antiques, and the restaurant is a gourmet's delight, with daily specials. The conference room is ideal for business meetings and weddings.

14 ROOMS, 14 pb   3 SUITES, 3 pb

$75-155   SPA   OPEN: ALL YEAR   HOSTS: Peggy & Grover Mosley

THE NEIL HOUSE

KERNVILLE `204`

P.O. 1018
100 Tobias St.
Kernville, CA 93238
Tel:1-619-376-2771

Celebrate the past in a completely restored 1890s Victorian home, where you can enjoy quiet comfort and luxury in a peaceful mountain setting. Attention to detail and personalized service are hallmarks. Optional high tea service. Near skiing, river rafting, fishing, and other activities.

4 ROOMS, 2 pb

$95-135   OPEN: FEB - DEC   HOSTS: Dawn Jordan & Melissa Hetricle

MONTECITO-SEQUOIA LODGE

KINGS CANYON NAT'L PARK `205`

8000 Generals Highway   P.O. Box 858
Kings Canyon National Park, CA 93633
Tel:1-800-227-9900
or 1-209-565-3388

R

Located in the center of Sequoia and Kings Canyon National Parks, this charming mountain lodge at 7,500 feet offers stunning views of the 13,000-foot Western Divide. Enjoy swimming, canoeing and hiking. Tasty award-winning California cuisine. Rates include breakfast and dinner.

25 ROOMS, 25 pb   POOL

$126-198   SPA   OPEN: ALL YEAR   HOSTS: Scott Stowers & Ole Tustin

206 MAMMOTH LAKES

HOSTS: Lanie & Sean Somers

MAMMOTH COUNTRY INN

75 Joaquin Rd.
Mammoth Lakes, CA 93546

Tel:U.S. 1-800-358-2710
1-619-934-2710

R

Conveniently located in the heart of Mammoth Lakes, this cozy, secluded mountain retreat features an entertainment lounge, a fully equipped kitchen, and cheerful rooms with down comforters, television, and ski racks. Near shopping, restaurants, and ski shuttle. Perfect for small group celebrations.

7 ROOMS, 3 pb

OPEN: ALL YEAR 🍴☕ 🔥 **SPA**   **$40-85**

207 MAMMOTH LAKES

HOSTS: Carol & Bob Roster

SNOW GOOSE INN

57 Forest Trail
Mammoth Lakes, CA 93546

Tel:U.S. 1-800-874-7368
or 1-619-934-2660

R

Discover the Eastern High Sierra while you relax in your home away from home with a warm, European atmosphere. Winter visitors revel in world-renowned skiing. During other seasons, guests enjoy nearby hiking, fishing, biking, and sight-seeing.

15 ROOMS, 15 pb   4 SUITES, 4 pb

OPEN: ALL YEAR 🍴☕ 🔥 **SPA**   **$58-168**

208 MAMMOTH LAKES

HOSTS: Jonathan & Ramona Simmons

WHITE HORSE INN

P.O. 2326
2180 Old Mammoth Rd.
Mammoth Lakes, CA 93546

Tel:1-619-924-3656

R

This exclusive mountain residence provides a friendly and homey atmosphere complete with a billiard room, stone fireplace, bar, and kitchen for common use. Each guest room is carefully furnished with unique artifacts and antiques that represent a historical theme.

5 SUITES, 5 pb

OPEN: ALL YEAR 🍴☕ 🔥 **SPA**   **$95-200**

BOULDER CREEK
4572 Ben Hur Rd.
Mariposa, CA 95338
Tel:1-209-742-7729

MARIPOSA | 209

Located in the gateway to Yosemite National Park, with all its scenic splendor, this European chalet-style inn offers guests cozy and comfortable accommodations. Just two miles from the Gold Rush town of Mariposa, the area boasts museums, shops, and fine restaurants.

3 ROOMS, 3 pb

$70-75 **SPA** OPEN: ALL YEAR HOSTS: Nancy & Michael Habermann

CANYON VIEW
7117 Snyder Ridge Rd.
Mariposa, CA 95338
Tel:1-800-344-2696
or 1-209-742-6268

MARIPOSA | 210

Perched on a ridge with impressive canyon views, this cozy inn offers first-rate accommodations and a variety of activities. Winter brings plenty of snow for cross-country skiing and snowmobiling, while spring and summer bring warm air and lush green meadows.

3 ROOMS, 3 pb

$77-105 **SPA** OPEN: ALL YEAR HOSTS: Andrea & Kevin Hall

DUBORDS RESTFUL NEST
4274 Buckeye Creek Rd.
Mariposa, CA 95338
Tel:1-209-742-7127

MARIPOSA | 211

Eleven acres of resort accommodations await you in a tranquil country atmosphere. Swim in the pool. Fish and enjoy several other outdoor activities on the parklike grounds. Private entrances, televisions, refrigerators, and microwaves are available. Savor the delicious French-Canadian breakfast.

2 ROOMS, 2 pb   1 COTTAGE, pb   **POOL**

$75-85 OPEN: ALL YEAR HOSTS: Huguette & Armand Dubord

212 MARIPOSA

HOSTS: Lyn & Mac MacCarone

MARIPOSA HOTEL

P.O. 745
5029 Highway 140
Mariposa, CA 95338
Tel:1-209-966-4676

This historic inn offers the charm of yesteryear with deluxe conveniences and amenities. Each carefully appointed guest room has cable television, a radio/tape player, and in-room coffee and tea. In center of Mariposa near unique shops and restaurants. Garden veranda.

6 ROOMS, 6 pb

OPEN: ALL YEAR ☕ $68-80

213 MARIPOSA

HOSTS: Carol & Bob Shockley

MEADOW CREEK RANCH

2669 Triangle Rd.
Mariposa, CA 95338
Tel:1-209-966-3843   R

The famous Yosemite National Park lies just beyond this historical inn, where guests can relax in the beautiful country setting of the Old West. Enjoy a family-style breakfast with guests from all over the world surrounded by forest and meadows.

4 ROOMS, 1 pb

OPEN: ALL YEAR $75-95

214 MARIPOSA

HOSTS: Mary Ellen & Tom Kim

POPPY HILL

5218 Crystal Aire Dr.
Mariposa, CA 95338
Tel:1-209-742-6273

Country comfort surrounds you in this beautifully restored home that offers spacious guest rooms with American and European antiques, down comforters, and sitting areas. A hearty country breakfast features sourdough specialties. Enjoy complimentary hors d'oeuvres and beverages.

3 ROOMS, 1 pb

OPEN: ALL YEAR   POOL
                        SPA $75-85

SCHLAGETER HOUSE

P.O. 1202
5038 Bullion St.
Mariposa, CA 95338
Tel: 1-209-966-2471

Enhance your tour of the Gold Country and Yosemite with a stay in the quiet comfort of the Schlageter house. This home presents Victorian charm blended with the interesting history of the surrounding area. Furnishings are a relaxed combination of antiques, handmade quilts, four-poster beds, ceiling fans and modern amenities. The hospitable innkeepers are sixth generation Mariposa-Yosemite residents and will be happy to share their knowledge of the area.

HOSTS: Lee & Roger McElligott

3 ROOMS, 3 pb

$70-80

OPEN: ALL YEAR

VILLA MONTI

P.O. 1888
4990 Eighth St.
Mariposa, CA 95338
Tel:1-209-966-2439

Surrounded by hand-built stone walls, a swimming pool, a lanai, and trees, coupled with the warm southern hospitality of your hosts, this inn offers country ambiance in the heart of town. Villa Monti consists of the elegant Ellingham House and the Annex , a private suite overlooking the Mariposa Valley. Both are wheelchair accessible. Downtown Mariposa offers unique shops and excellent restaurants.

HOSTS: Susan Renna & Eugene Lawrence

2 ROOMS, 1 pb   1 SUITE, 1pb

$60-80

POOL

SPA   OPEN: ALL YEAR

217 OAKHURST

CHATEAU DU SUREAU

P.O. 577
48688 Victoria Lane
Oakhurst, CA 93644
Tel:1-209-683-6860

The warm reception that guests receive at this elegant castle instantly makes them feel at home. Relax in the Grand Salon with its well-stocked library, where you are invited to curl up with a good book while enchanting melodies emanate from the music tower and a fire crackles in the massive brick hearth. Guest rooms are furnished with selected antiques, toile fabrics, and precious art pieces from the owner's private collection.

HOSTS: Erna & Kathryn

9 ROOMS, 9 pb

OPEN: ALL YEAR

POOL

$250-350

218 SOUTH LAKE TAHOE

LITTLE TAHOE CABIN

2487 Elwood Ave.
South Lake Tahoe, CA 95731
Tel:1-415-331-3000
or 1-415-387-5595

You will be wrapped in Bavarian romance in Tahoe's coziest cabin. This quiet little cottage offers a rustic flair that's perfect for its mountain backdrop. A well-equipped kitchen is stocked with breakfast favorites, which guests may prepare at their leisure. The area is secluded yet close to Heavenly Valley ski resort, Lake Tahoe and its beaches, fine restaurants, quaint shops, and casinos. This cabin is intimate for two and sleeps four comfortably.

HOST: Christa Kerl-Konig

1 COTTAGE, pb

OPEN: ALL YEAR

$75

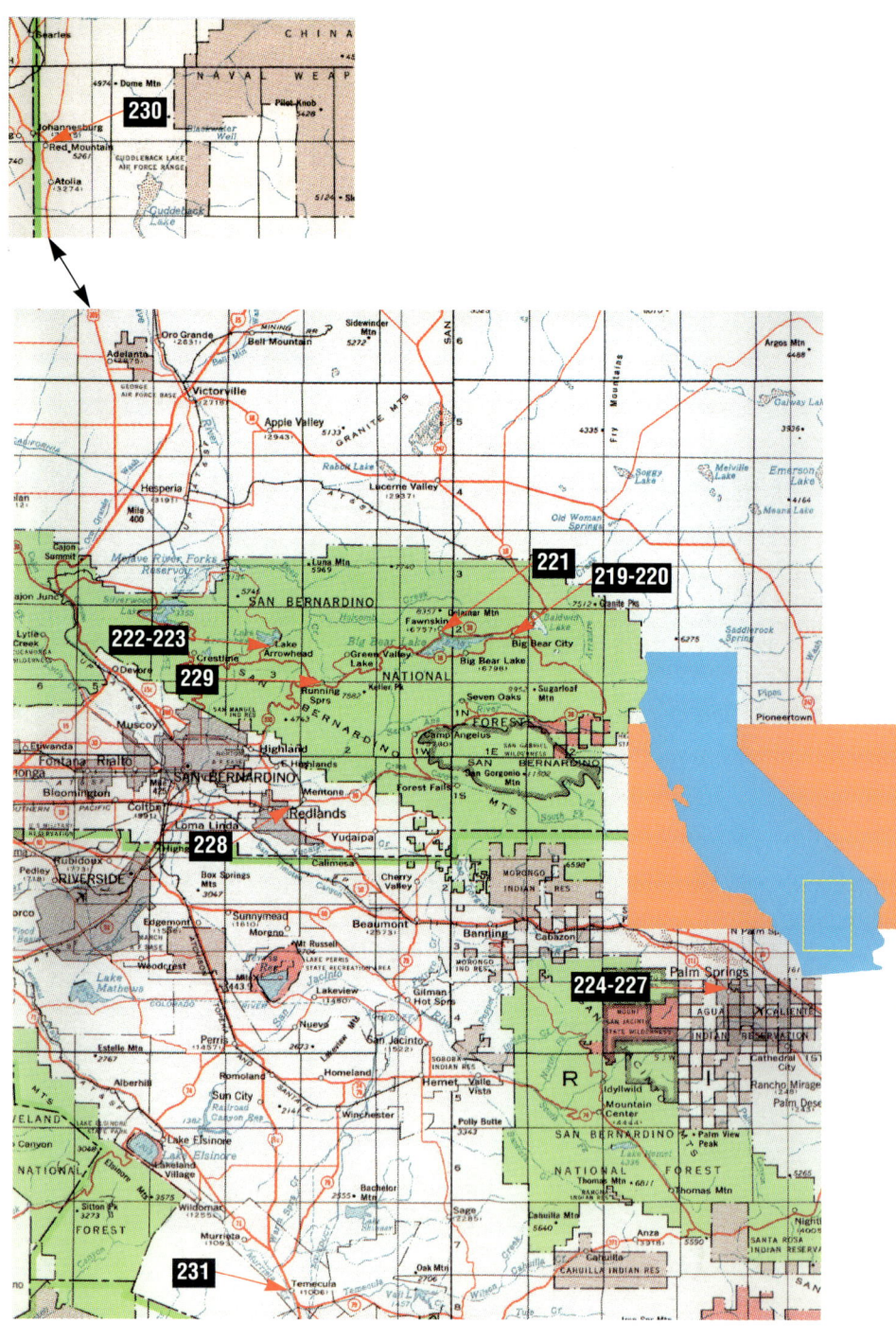

PALM SPRINGS

& THE DESERT COUNTIES

Travellers who want to escape the hustle and bustle of the city are in for a pleasant surprise. The desert counties offer an abundance of activities, scenic routes, and yes, even snow. **Inyo, San Bernardino,** and **Riverside** counties present their visitors with the rich, warm, earthy hues of the desert, majestic mountain ranges, and lush oases surrounded by hot sandy expanse. The beauty of this area is in its diversity and accessibility. A few hours will take you from the warmest desert valley to the chilliest mountain peak.

Your tour begins with a region known for its extreme conditions, where blasting temperatures contrast with grand snow-capped mountains. **Inyo County,** which contains both the high desert and the **Owens Valley,** boasts impressive mountain scenery, hiking trails, fishing, and ghost towns. Watch for hang gliders overhead; this area is popular with cross-country pilots. Highway 396 takes you through the valley towns of **Bishop** and Independence, where you will find a variety of hotels and restaurants, along with beautiful scenery.

Off Highway 395, east of Owens Valley, after you pass through **Lone Pine,** you will come to Inyo County's infamous **Death Valley,** with its views of the surrounding snow-capped mountains. Fantastic stories are told about its baking hot temperatures—this valley is definitely not for the faint of heart! The valley was formed by mighty earth movements, and sculpted over millions of years by wind and water. Daytime skies are an unbelievably clear, deep blue, and sunsets are spectacular. The earthy desert hues turn to shadows as the sun sets, creating a chiaroscuro backdrop. At night, a litany of stars pierce the black velvet sky.

Because of its extreme temperatures (the record is 134°F, or 57°C), visitors to Death Valley are encouraged to carry plenty of water and to take all necessary precautions to avoid being stranded, even for a few hours. Still, with caution, visitors can enjoy the magic and intrigue of the desert by hiking, mountain biking, and camping

In sharp contrast to the earthy palette of colors that paint the hot California desert, the lush green surroundings of the **San Bernardino County** mountain range make a refreshing change. Peaks here top 10,000 feet (3,050 meters). Visitors enjoy the crisp cool air and deep blue lakes. In the winter, the entire area is covered with a blanket of bright shimmering snow. Take I-10 east to State Highway 18 or Highway 330, then continue up the windy pass to several mountain communities. Highway 330 brings you to **Redlands,** a large town surrounded by orange groves. A forty-minute drive takes you to Lake Arrowhead, with its large, impressive mountain cabins—and some mansions. The lake is ideal for boating and water-skiing. In the summer, the sun is hot enough to let you tan (burn) on the docks. You can also hike and mountain bike on the many mountain trails. Snow skiing is popular in winter. **Lake Arrowhead village** offers many shops, restaurants, and even water-ski instruction. Nearby smaller resorts such as **Crestline, Lake Gregory,** and **Blue Jay** offer scenic beauty and cozy mountain hideaways.

Farther up the mountain, drive through the charming towns of **Running Springs, Arrowbear** and **Fawnskin.** The next big town is **Big Bear,** complete with a crystal-clear lake, year-round activities, a large ski resort, and an old-fashioned mountain village. To experience the essence of the surrounding woods, follow Moonridge Road from town as it climbs up to the **Moonridge Animal Park,** tucked away in the mountains. The park offers an authentic wilderness zoo in a picturesque mountain setting. Guests can view animals in their natural habitat—deer, wolves, bobcats, coyotes, eagles, hawks, raccoons, and bears, to name just a few.

Visitors can enjoy water-skiing on the glassy water of **Big Bear Lake.** In the summer, find a sandy beach and treat yourself to an afternoon of rest and relaxation, complete with sun bathing and a picnic lunch. For a pleasant side trip, visit the old mining town of **Red Mountain** on Highway 395, 75 miles north of the San Bernadino Mountains.

Can you take the heat? In **Palm Springs,** you may have to. But in spite of its hot, dry climate, this amazing city has lured the rich, the famous, and the curious from all over the world since it was established in 1938. Located in **Riverside County,** Palm Springs is easily accessible from Los Angeles. Take I-10 to State Highway 111, which becomes Palm Canyon Drive, the city's main street.

The initial attraction to this exclusive resort was the soothing power of its warm mineral waters. Later it became a respite for movie stars who sought privacy and relaxation from their hectic schedules. The presence of these Hollywood icons is still felt. In the city where Sonny Bono (ex-partner of the singing duo Sonny and Cher) is mayor, streets, public buildings, and sports events bear the names of the stars, and tour buses purport to provide an inside look at how those stars enjoy life in Palm Springs. Be sure to see Bob Hope's impressive copper-top estate. On a hot sunny day, the sun reflects blindingly off of its smooth metal dome.

Nestled beneath towering **Mount San Jacinto,** Palm Springs combines the best of a sophisticated resort and a casual, Mediterranean-style village. Visitors feel rejuvenated by the fantastic weather and clear blue skies. The warm air embraces you as you admire the billowy white clouds overhead. The area is surrounded by lush canyons, native palm trees, and grand mountains.

To be sure, Palm Springs is not all rest and relaxation; it is also a sports-lover's paradise. This may come as a surprise to those who think of the desert as having nothing more to offer than barren stretches of sand dotted with lonely cacti. Year-round activities include golf, tennis, bicycling, and horseback riding. Spring break in Palm Springs may provide all the excitement you need—the warm sunshine and nightlife attract college students from all

over. A word of caution: Squirt guns are not allowed. Other local activities include the Villagefest every Thursday evening and the **Palm Springs Desert Museum,** which presents special exhibits and lively arts performances from mid-September to mid-May.

The desert invites visitors to explore old mining towns. You can rock hunt in hidden valleys and dirt bike in nearby desolate canyons. The **Palm Springs Aerial Tramway** will take you up the mountain, where you can enjoy a picnic lunch and admire the vista. Or sunbathe by a pool and take a dip to refresh yourself when the sun gets too hot. Arrange to be pampered at any resort with a full massage.

The nearby towns of **Palm Desert** and **Desert Hot Springs** host many activities and offer chic resorts and first-class accommodations. The Desert Town Center (State 111 at Monterey Avenue) has department stores, more than a hundred shops, and a year-round indoor ice-skating rink. The attraction of Desert Hot Springs is its mineral spas. The springs, for both therapeutic and recreational use, are cooled to under 110°F (43°C) from the scalding temperature of 207°F (97°C) at which they emerge from the earth.

The final major attraction on your tour of the desert counties is the amazing **Joshua Tree National Monument,** just northeast of Palm Springs. The area is unique because of its yucca trees, without a doubt the most spectacular vegetation of the Mojave desert. From a distance the yuccas resemble giant desert flares. Up close they are an intimidating sight, covered with sharp green needles that project in a wild bunch at their apex. In bloom, the soft white flowers are a contradiction to the sharp spikes. Joshua Tree offers more than 850 square miles (2,200 sq km) in which you can drive, hike, picnic, and camp. In the spring, the desert floor is covered with flowers; year-round, the area boasts dramatic desert plants and wildlife.

Before you leave the sun-baked desert communities en route to San Diego, be sure to quench your thirst in the wine-growing region of **Temecula,** on the southern border of Riverside County.

ATTRACTIONS

Aerial Tramway, take State 111 north from Palm Springs and follow the signs, (619) 325-1391, open Mon.-Fri. 10-7:30, weekends 8-7:30, summer open until 9, $14.95 roundtrip for adults, $9.95 children 5-12. **Death Valley National Monument,** Death Valley, (619) 786-2331, $5 per vehicle. **Greater Palm Springs Convention and Visitors Bureau,** Airport Park Plaza, Suite 315, 255 N. El Cielo Rd., Palm Springs, (619) 327-8411. **Joshua Tree National Monument,** main entrance is from the north off State 62 at Twentynine Palms, about 50 miles northeast of Palm Springs, (619) 367-7511. **Moonridge Animal Park,** Big Bear, open daily 8:30-4, admission free. **Palm Springs Desert Museum,** 101 Museum Dr., open Tues.-Fri. 10-4, weekends until 5, closed in summer.

BIG BEAR AREA

Iron Squirrel
646 Pine Knot
(714) 866-9121
Country French cuisine $$

The Blue Whale
350 Alden Rd.
(714) 866-5771
Seafood, jazz on weekends $$

Mandarin Gardens
501 Valley Blvd.
(714) 585-1818
Chinese cuisine $$

The Vines
625 Pine Knot Blvd.
(714) 866-3033
Steaks, vegetarian, veal,
seafood $$

Queen of Siam
40271 Big Bear Blvd.
(714) 866-2863
Thai cuisine $

LAKE ARROWHEAD AREA

San Moritz
24640 San Moritz Dr.
Crestline
(714) 338-7791
Classic gourmet cuisine $$

Chef's Inn
29020 Oak Terrace
Cedar Glen
(714) 336-4487
Continental-German cuisine $$

Casual Elegance
26848 State Highway 189
Agua Fria
(714) 337-8932
Steaks, fish, poultry, varied menu
$$-$$$

Saddleback
300 S. State Highway 173
Lake Arrowhead
(714) 336-2017
American steakhouse, seafood,
pasta $$-$$$

PALM SPRINGS

Le Vallauris
385 W. Tahuquitz
(619) 325-5059
French cuisine $$$

Paul Di Amico
500 E. Palm Canyon Dr.
(619) 325-9191
Italian cuisine $$

Blue Coyote
445 N. Palm Canyon Dr.
(619) 327-1196
Mexican-Southwestern fare $

WINERIES

Callaway Vineyard and Winery
   32720 Rancho California Road
   Temecula, CA 92589
   (714) 676-4001
   Open: daily 10-5

Maurice Carrie Winery
   34255 Rancho California Road
   Temecula, CA 92591
   (714) 676-1711
   Open: daily 10-5

Clos Du Muriel
   40620 Calle Contento
   Temecula, CA 92591
   (714) 676-2938
   Open: daily 10-5

Culbertson Winery
   32575 Rancho California Road
   Temecula, CA 92390
   (714) 699-0099
   Open: Sun. thru Thurs. 10-5,
   Fri.+ Sat. 10-6

Mount Palomar Winery
   33820 Rancho California Road
   Temecula, CA 92591
   (714) 676-5047
   Open: daily 9-5

EAGLES NEST
P.O. 1003
41675 Big Bear Blvd.
Big Bear, CA 92315
Tel:1-909-866-6465

BIG BEAR 219

R

This lodge offers rustic western-style comfort in a mountain and pine setting. Guest rooms feature goose-down comforters. Relax in the spacious main room, surrounded by rustic logs and antiques. Close to ski and sports facilities and quaint alpine villages.

5 ROOMS, 5 pb

$75-100

OPEN: ALL YEAR   HOSTS: Jack Draper & James Joyce

KNICKERBOCKER MANSION
P.O. 3661
869 South Knickerbocker St.
Big Bear, CA 92315
Tel:1-909-866-8221

BIG BEAR 220

This unique 1920s rustic inn is situated on 2.5 acres of rolling lawns surrounded by the privacy of a heavily wooded national forest. Pine paneling, native stone fireplaces, antiques, forest views, a redwood deck, and a whirlpool-spa set a romantic mood.

8 ROOMS, 4 pb   2 SUITES, 2 pb

$85-165   **SPA** OPEN: ALL YEAR   HOST: Phyllis Knight

WINDY POINT
P.O. Box 375
39263 North Shore Dr.
Fawnskin, CA 92333
Tel:1-909-866-2746

FAWNSKIN 221

Revel in the romantic spirit of this luxurious inn set amid pine trees on a private peninsula..The only lakefront bed and breakfast on Big Bear Lake, it offers deluxe rooms with fireplaces, wet bars, private decks, and whirlpool-spas.

4 ROOMS, 4 pb

$90-255   **SPA** OPEN: ALL YEAR   HOSTS: Val & Kent Kessler

222 LAKE ARROWHEAD

HOSTS: Laverne & Tom Prophet Jr.

PROPHET'S PARADISE
P.O. Box 2116
26845 Modoc Lane
Lake Arrowhead, CA 92352
Tel:1-909-336-1969

You will appreciate the secluded wooded paradise of this Tudor mountain home. Antiques, stained glass, beautiful gardens, and a peaceful walking path enhance the romantic setting. The chill of winter invites you to snuggle inside around the fireplace. In the summer, you can enjoy a myriad of summer flowers from your own private deck. There is a game room with a pool table; or you can work off your breakfast in the gym.

R

1 ROOM, 1 pb   2 SUITES, 2 pb

OPEN: ALL YEAR   SPA   **$90-160**

223 LAKE ARROWHEAD

HOST: Mary Ann Hudson

WILLOW CREEK INN
P.O. Box 479
1176 Highway 173
Lake Arrowhead, CA 92352
Tel:1-909-336-2008

Quilts, heirloom antiques, assorted memorabilia, books, games, and exercise equipment create an atmosphere of charm and entertainment in this Cape Cod-style inn. Set amid pine and oak trees, the guest rooms offer forest views and comfortable Country French decor. Specialty gourmet breakfasts are served on china, crystal, and silver with heirloom linens. Guests may enjoy gourmet coffees, teas, and homemade cookies from the "open jar" any time.

3 ROOMS, 3 pb   1 SUITES, pb

OPEN: ALL YEAR   SPA   **$105-185**

CASA CODY COUNTRY INN
175 Cahuilla Rd.
Palm Springs, CA 92262
Tel:1-619-320-9346

PALM SPRINGS | 224

R

This romantic hideaway is nestled against the spectacular San Jacinto Mountains in the heart of Palm Springs village. Beautifully restored in Santa Fe decor. Studios and suites have private patios and fireplaces. Kitchens are available. Relax by the pool or in the whirlpool-spa.

10 ROOMS, 10 pb   6 SUITES, 6 pb   1 COTTAGE, pb

$45-160 ☕🔥 **SPA POOL** OPEN: ALL YEAR   HOSTS: Therese Hayes & Frank Tysen

KORAKIA PENSIONE
257 South Patencio Rd.
Palm Springs, CA 92262
Tel:1-619-320-0708

PALM SPRINGS | 225

Artistic archways, fountains, and tiles greet guests in this elegant 1920 Moorish villa. Relax, as Sir Winston Churchill once did, in Mediterranean elegance. Guest rooms are furnished with antiques and fine handmade furniture. Enjoy European-style service near galleries, theaters, and restaurants.

5 ROOMS, 5 pb   6 SUITES, 6 pb   POOL

$59-115   ☕🔥   OPEN: ALL YEAR   HOST: Douglas Smith

RAFFLES PALM SPRINGS HOTEL
280 East Mel Ave.
Palm Springs, CA 92262
Tel:1-619-320-3949

PALM SPRINGS | 226

Bathing suits are optional at this sophisticated desert hideaway. This accommodating inn offers an oasis of peace and tranquillity where comfort and relaxation are the prime concern. An Australian breakfast is a healthy and enjoyable high point of the day.

11 SUITES, 11 pb   POOL

$125-165 ☕🔥 **SPA** OPEN: ALL YEAR   HOSTS: Barry Rushton & Peter Whawell

227 PALM SPRINGS

VILLA ROSA INN
1577 South Indian Trail
Palm Springs, CA 92264
Tel:1-619-327-5915

This small and intimate Southwestern-style villa offers accommodations with private entrances that surround a heated pool in the center of a lovely garden courtyard. Some accommodations have private rear patios. Saltilio tiles and fountains add charm, while therapy jets and pool floats complete the atmosphere of total relaxation. Guests receive the daily newspaper, compliments of the host. The inn is within walking distance of many fine restaurants.

HOSTS: Darrell Goff & Steve Hill

R

2 ROOMS, 2 pb   4 SUITES, 4 pb   **POOL**

OPEN: SEPT - JULY   **$65-125**

228 REDLANDS

MOREY MANSION
190 Terracina Blvd.
Redlands, CA 92373
Tel:1-909-793-7970

An original carved wood staircase, beveled windows from Belgium, leaded Tiffany-like stained glass from France, and a claw-footed Roman tub in the master bath grace the interior of this exquisitely detailed 1890 Victorian home. Turn-of-the-century antiques accent the guest rooms. Standing among thousands of orange trees, this historical landmark inn has been featured in movies and books and is open for weddings.

HOSTS: Leona Connelly

4 ROOMS, 3 pb   1 SUITE, pb

OPEN: ALL YEAR   **$109-185**

SPRING OAKS
P.O. 2918
2465 Springoak Dr.
Running Springs, CA 92382
Tel:1-909-867-9636

RUNNING SPRINGS 229

R

Oak and pine trees surround this country-style home, with breathtaking views of the forest and valley. Close to Los Angeles and San Diego pine furniture, antiques, and a large stone fireplace provide a warm, inviting atmosphere. Hiking tours and skiing are available nearby.

3 ROOMS, 1 pb

$95-130 **SPA** OPEN: ALL YEAR HOSTS: Laura & William Florian

OLD OWL INN
P.O. 755
701 Highway 395
Red Mountain, CA 93558
Tel:1-619-374-2235

RED MOUNTAIN 230

This inn offers the nostalgic atmosphere of the turn of the century. It used to be a gambling hall, bar, and brothel. Play the piano or shoot pool in the game room. Repose by the fireplace or enjoy the lovely garden with its extensive shade and fruit trees, roses, barbecue picnic area, and spa.

1 ROOMS, 1 pb

$60 **SPA** OPEN: ALL YEAR HOSTS: Lynn & Jeanie Walker

LOMA VISTA
33350 La Serena Way
Temecula, CA 92591
Tel:1-909-676-7047

TEMECULA 231

R

These guest rooms capture the tranquillity of the Temecula Valley. Surrounded by lush citrus groves and premium vineyards, the inn offers an unparalleled view of the encircling mountains. Distinctive furnishings in each room add personality and charm. Hot air ballooning is available.

6 ROOMS, 6 pb

$95-125 OPEN: ALL YEAR HOSTS: Betty & Dick Ryan

SAN DIEGO
C O U N T Y

Sharing a border with Mexico, **San Diego County** offers deserts, forested mountains, lakes, rivers, farmlands, and a coastline of great beaches that lure visitors from all over.

The city of **San Diego,** the oldest Spanish settlement in California, was founded in 1542 by Juan Rodriguez Cabrillo, a Portuguese explorer. Father Junipero Serra built the first of twenty-one California missions here in 1769. San Diego, which was the center for the coastal hide trade,

became a city in 1850. It was a lively town, largely occupied by Mexicans who held bullfights, cockfights, and spectacular balls. In 1885, the Santa Fe Railroad brought the train to San Diego, and with it American entrepreneurs and their diverse industries.

Today San Diego is a bustling port city and a popular tourist destination, offering many recreational and cultural attractions in a very relaxed atmosphere. It is the second largest city in California, and benefits from a beautiful location and a spectacular harbor. With an average daily temperature of 70°F (21°C), San Diego's ideal climate makes it a popular year-round resort.

San Diego today is the home of the largest naval air station on the West Coast. The harbor is shared by the U.S. Navy, a large fishing fleet, cruise ships, and sport fishing boats. It is an ideal destination for water sports enthusiasts.

San Diego's **Sea World** is the largest aquarium in the country. The spacious and attractive **Balboa Park** is located close to the downtown shopping areas and contains the world-famous **San Diego Zoo,** home to over 3,000 animals of more than 800 species. Also located in this 1,158-acre (469 ha) park and cultural center are the **San Diego Aerospace Museum** and **International Aerospace Hall of Fame,** honoring the heroes of aviation and space, the **Botanical Building,** housing tropical and subtropical plants, the **San Diego Automotive Museum,** the **San Diego Museum of Art,** the **San Diego Model Railroad Museum,** the **Museum of Photographic Arts,** and the **Natural History Museum.**

San Diego is an exciting city with several charming neighborhoods offering excellent restaurants, colorful shops, and interesting historical attractions. Old Town's **San Diego State Historic Park** captures the atmosphere of the early Mexican-American settlers. The 12-acre (5 ha) park is surrounded by a variety of delightful contemporary shops and restaurants. The **Gaslamp Quarter** is a sixteen-block downtown neighborhood that has been restored and is now designated as a National Historic District. In the evenings it is a lively area that offers many clubs and restaurants for wining, dining, and dancing.

For an interesting side trip inland, visit the pioneer mountain-farming community of **Dulzura,** 30 miles (48 km) southeast of San Diego. Returning to San Diego and travelling north along Highway 1 for a few miles brings you to **La Jolla,** a popular resort town built along a rocky coastline. It features an elegant downtown shopping area, and the surrounding hills have an interesting variety of custom-built homes overlooking the ocean. Check out the **La Jolla Caves** and the **Scripps Aquarium-Museum,** located at the **Scripps Institute of Oceanography.**

Two miles due west of San Diego is the charming island of **Coronado,** only accessible by a bridge. Famous for the Hotel del Coronado, Coronado is an exclusive residential community with lovely beaches, restaurants, and shops.

Continuing north along the San Diego County coastline takes you through many small, charming resort towns such as **Del Mar,** where you can bet on horses at the race track, **Solano Beach, Cardiff-by-the-Sea, Encinitas,** and **Carlsbad.** Thirty miles (48 km) east you will find rural charm in **Escondido,** a pleasant wine-growing region. For a taste of African and Asian wildlife, visit the **San Diego Wild Animal Park.** More than 2,500 animals representing 240 species roam the 1,800 acres (729 ha) of land that resemble African and Asian plains.

From Escondido, drive east through the farming town of **Ramona** on your way to the quaint old mining town of **Julian.** Pick apples in the many orchards and enjoy the wonderful mountain air 4,300 feet (1,300 m) above sea level. Wherever you travel in San Diego County, you will enjoy the warm hospitality and mild, sunny climate.

International Visitor Information Center, in Horton Plaza, 1st Ave. and F St., San Diego, (619) 236-1212, open daily 8:30-5:30. **La Jolla Caves,** La Jolla Cave and Shell Shop at 1325 Coast Blvd., (619) 454-6080, open Mon.-Sat. 10-5, Sun. 11-5, $1.25 adults, $.50 children 3-11. In **Balboa Park:**[call (619) 239-0512 for more park information] Botanical Building, open Tues.-Sun. 10-4:30, free admission; **Museum of Photographic Arts,** in the Casa de Balboa, (619) 239-5262, open daily 10-5, Thurs. 10-9, $2.50 admission; **Natural History Museum,** opposite park's main fountain, (619) 232-3821, open daily 10-4:30, $5 adults, $1 children 6-18; **San Diego Aerospace Museum and International Aerospace Hall of Fame,** near Pan American Plaza, (619) 234-8291, open daily 10-4:30, $4 adults, $1 children 6-17; **San Diego Automotive Museum,** (619) 231-2886, open daily 10-4:30, $3.50 adults, $1 children 6-16; **San Diego Model Railroad Museum,** in the basement of Casa de Balboa, (619) 696-0199, open Wed.-Fri. 11-4, weekends 11-5, $1 adults, $.50 children; **San Diego Museum of Art,** faces the central parking lot, (619) 232-7931, open Tues.-Sun. 10-4:30, $5 adults, $4 seniors, $2 children 6-17; **San Diego Zoo,** (619) 234-3153, open daily 9-4, open July-Labor Day 9-5, $12 adults, $4 children 3-11. **San Diego Convention and Visitors Bureau and International Visitors Information Center,** 11 Horton Plaza, (619) 236-1212. **San Diego Wild Animal Park,** from San Diego, take Interstate 15 north and Via Rancho Parkway exit east onto San Pasqual Valley Road and follow signs, (619) 234-6541, open daily 9-4, summer hours may vary, $15.95 adults, $8.95 children 3-11. **Scripps Institute of Oceanography,** 8602 La Jolla Shores Dr., La Jolla, (619) 534-6933, open daily 9-5, suggested admission by donation, $3 adults, $2 children 12-18, $1 children 3-11. **Sea World,** Sea World Dr. at western end of Interstate 8, Mission Bay, (619) 226-3901, open daily 10-5, later in summer, $25.95 adults, $19.95 children 3-11.

JULIAN

Julian Grille
224 Main St.
(619) 765-0172
Continental cuisine $-$$

Romano's Dodgehouse
2718 B St.
(619) 765-1003
Sicilian cuisine $-$$

Rong Branch
2722 Washington St.
(619) 765-2265
Barbeque/gift shop $-$$

LA JOLLA

Avanti
857 Prospect Ave.
(619) 454-4288
Northern Italian/dancing $$

George's at the Cove
1250 Prospect St.
(619) 454-4244
Steaks, seafood, pasta $$-$$$

SAN DIEGO

Cafe Pacifica
2414 San Diego Ave.
(619) 291-6666
Seafood $-$$

Dobson's
956 Broadway Circle
(619) 231-6771
American with French flair $$-$$$

Ocean Beach
4996 W. Pt. Loma Blvd.
(619) 224-2884
French continental $-$$

Truly Yours
2304 San Diego Ave.
(619) 291-4966
Continental cuisine $-$$

WINERIES

Thomas Jaeger Winery
    13455 San Pasqual Road
    Escondido, CA 92025
    (619) 745-3553
    Open: daily 10-6

CARDIFF-BY-THE-SEA LODGE
CARDIFF-BY-THE-SEA `232`

142 Chesterfield
Cardiff-By-The-Sea, CA 92007

Tel:1-619-944-6474

The lodge's graceful curves, gray stone walls, flagstone walkways, and shimmering fountain beckon your arrival. Luxuriate in richly appointed one-of-a-kind guest rooms. Unwind in the natural beauty of Cardiff-by-the-Sea. Linger over breakfast on the ocean-view terrace a few steps from the blue Pacific, and savor sunsets around an open-pit fire ring on the rooftop garden. Some rooms boast fireplaces, ocean views, and whirlpool-spas.

R **HOSTS: Jeanette & James Statser**

17 ROOMS, 17 pb

$105-250 SPA OPEN: ALL YEAR

CORONADO VICTORIAN HOUSE
CORONADO `233`

1000 8th St.
Coronada, CA 92118

Tel:1-619-435-2200

Featured in magazines and television shows, this award-winning Coronado establishment is a haven for those who are looking for a uniquely pampering experience. The friendly hostess offers gourmet health and Armenian/Lebanese food, along with professional instruction on fitness and dance. Built in 1894, this lovingly restored Victorian is an ideal setting to rejuvenate and relax. Secluded balconies and private whirlpool-spas are available. Inquire about holiday and VIP packages.

R **HOST: Bonnie Marie Kinosian**

8 ROOMS, 6 pb

$150-350 SPA OPEN: ALL YEAR

SAN DIEGO

234 DULZURA

HOSTS: Sally & Edd Guishard

BROOKSIDE FARM
1373 Marron Valley Rd.
Dulzura, CA 91917
Tel:1-619-468-3043

This 1927 farm house is surrounded by five acres of beautiful gardens, fountains, and terraces. Grounds include a stream, a spa, and farm animals. Many rooms have fireplaces and private porches. Each room is uniquely decorated with antiques, quilts, paintings, and flowers. The common room contains a library and a game area. A delicious country breakfast is prepared by your host, who also happens to be a professional chef.

8 ROOMS, 6 pb   2 COTTAGE, 2 pb

OPEN: ALL YEAR   SPA   **$45-85**

235 ENCINITAS

HOST: Kirsten Cline

INNCLINE
121 North Vulcan Ave.
Encinitas, CA 92024
Tel:1-619-944-0318

Beautiful ocean views surround this southwest-style contemporary home. Within walking distance of Moonlight Beach and many restaurants, it is also an easy drive to Sea World, Mexico, and Del Mar Race Track. Enjoy a continental breakfast featuring "Marvelous Muffins," fresh fruit, yogurt, and juice. Afternoon wine and cheese are served compliments of the host. This beach-side inn is perfect for quiet getaways, romantic weddings, and family reunions.

3 ROOMS, 3 pb   2 SUITES, 2 pb

OPEN: ALL YEAR   SPA   **$75-150**

ZOSA RANCH
9381 West Lilac Rd.
Escondido, CA 92026
Tel:1-619-723-9093

ESCONDIDO 236

This elegant 22-acre country ranch estate is perched atop a high plateau in the Monserate Mountains. Guest rooms are beautifully furnished, and the grounds include a luxurious pool and sports court for your enjoyment. The estate is available for parties and business meetings.

9 ROOMS, 6 pb   1 SUITE, pb   1 COTTAGE, pb

$90-250 ☕ **POOL SPA** OPEN: ALL YEAR   HOSTS: Nena & Noli Zosa

BUTTERFIELD
P.O. Box 1115
2284 Sunset Dr.
Julian, CA 92036
Tel:1-619-765-2179

JULIAN 237

Nestled under pine and oak trees on a gentle hillside, this mountain retreat features country collectibles, antiques, and special holiday decorations. The owners delight in arranging and catering intimate weddings, anniversaries, and holiday festivities. Country carriage rides are available.

5 ROOMS, 5 pb   1 COTTAGE, pb

$89-119   OPEN: ALL YEAR   HOSTS: Mary & Ray Trimmins

THE HOMESTEAD
P.O. 1208
4924 Highway 79
Julian, CA 92036
Tel:1-619-765-1536

JULIAN 238

Enjoy the tranquility of this comfortable family-run mountain retreat that offers a 270-degree forest view at 4,600 feet. Hike on the nearby trails, relax by a cozy fire, or visit quaint downtown Julian. A gourmet breakfast is served.

4 ROOMS, 2 pb

$85-95   OPEN: ALL YEAR   HOSTS: Mary Ellen & Dick Thilken

SAN DIEGO

239 JULIAN

HOSTS: Gig & Steve Ballinger

THE JULIAN HOTEL
P.O. Box 1856
2032 Main St.
Julian, CA 92036
Tel:1-619-765-0201

R

This 1897 Victorian hotel, built by a freed slave and his wife, is listed in the National Register. The inn once provided lodging and food for gold miners. Long-forgotten stories seem to linger in the antique-filled rooms. Walk to shops and restaurants.

17 ROOMS, 3 pb   1 SUITE, pb   1 COTTAGE, pb

OPEN: ALL YEAR   **$38-145**

240 JULIAN

HOSTS: Linda & Jim Huie

JULIAN LODGE
P.O. Box 1930
2720 C Street
Julian, CA 92036
Tel:1-800-542-1420

R

Enjoy the beauty and freshness of the mountains. Designed after the Washington Hotel and built in 1885, the lodge is just steps away from rustic shops and historic sites. The rooms combine beautiful antiques with a comfortable setting. Walk to shops and restaurants.

23 ROOMS, 23 pb

OPEN: ALL YEAR   **$72-92**

241 JULIAN

HOSTS: Carol & Mirko

MOUNTAIN HIGH
P.O. Box 268
4110 Deerlake Park Rd.
Julian, CA 92036
Tel:1-619-765-1083

Trees and meadows surround you on three acres of beautiful park-like grounds. Enjoy the Woods Room with its stone fireplace, original art, and family antiques, or stay in a country cottage set among Ponderosa pines. A wonderful breakfast is brought to your room.

1 ROOMS, 1 pb   1 COTTAGE, pb

OPEN: ALL YEAR   **$95-105**

THE BED & BREAKFAST INN AT LA JOLLA

7753 Draper Ave.
La Jolla, CA 92037
Tel:1-707-976-0263

Inhabited by the John Philip Sousa family in the 1920s, this historic landmark built by Irving Gill is now a deluxe inn that offers charmingly appointed rooms, some with ocean views and fireplaces. A Parisian hostess heads the young, delightfully sophisticated staff.

15 ROOMS, 14 pb   1 SUITE, pb

$85-225   OPEN: ALL YEAR   HOST: Pierrette Timmerman

SCRIPPS INN

555 Coast Blvd. S.
La Jolla, CA 92037
Tel:1-619-454-3391

This inn offers the perfect ambiance for enjoying La Jolla. Only a small grassy knoll comes between the inn and the waves, and only a short walk separates guests from the shops, parks, and restaurants that make La Jolla famous.

13 ROOMS, 13 pb

$80-165   SPA   OPEN: ALL YEAR   HOST: Charlene Browne

LUCY'S ATTIC

760 Cedar St.
Ramona, CA 92065
Tel:1-619-788-9543

R

This cozy house overlooks four acres of avocado, citrus, and apple orchards. Relax by the pool, play croquet on the lawn, and walk or cycle to town. Lucy's Attic is close to the Wild Animal Park, and forty-five minutes from San Diego.

2 ROOMS, 1 pb

POOL

$65-85   OPEN: ALL YEAR   HOST: Luanne Corea

SAN DIEGO

245 SAN DIEGO

HOSTS: Carol & Robert Emerick

THE COTTAGE
3829 Albatross St.
San Diego, CA 92103
Tel:1-619-299-1564

Located between the zoo, Sea World, and downtown, the Cottage is a quiet retreat in the heart of a residential neighborhood. Enjoy the gardens and relax in a home filled with turn-of-the-century furnishings. Each morning you will be served a freshly prepared breakfast.

1 ROOMS, 1 pb   1 COTTAGE, pb

OPEN: ALL YEAR   ☕   **$49-85**

246 SAN DIEGO

HOSTS: Katie & Phil Elsbree

THE ELSBREE HOUSE
5054 -5058 Narragansett Ave.
San Diego, CA 92107
Tel:1-619-226-4133

This adorable Cape Cod-style home features elegant bedrooms with private patios. Located in a quiet residential neighborhood, just half a block from the beach, it is also a short walk to shops and restaurants.

2 ROOMS, 2 pb

OPEN: ALL YEAR   ☕   **$75**

247 SAN DIEGO

HOST: D.A. Milbourn

HARBOR HILL GUEST HOUSE
2330 Albatross St.
San Diego, CA 92101
Tel:1-619-233-0638

Enjoy fantastic views of the San Diego Harbor at this 1920s inn. Perfect for business, weekend getaways, honeymoons and anniversaries. The Carriage House is a separate hideaway for two. Within easy reach of all that San Diego has to offer.

5 ROOMS, 5 pb   1 SUITE, pb

OPEN: ALL YEAR   ☕   **$65-85**

SAN DIEGO

HERITAGE PARK INN

2470 Heritage Park Row
San Diego, CA 92110

Tel:1-800-995-2470
or 1-619-299-6832

Nestled on a quiet eight-acre Victorian park in the heart of San Diego's historic Old Town, this beautiful Queen Anne mansion has been restored to its original 1889 splendor. The nostalgic interior features authentic antiques, documented Victorian wall coverings, oriental rugs, and handmade quilts. A tantalizing breakfast buffet is enjoyed on the veranda. The adjacent residence houses the ballroom and bridal suite. Near Sea World and the zoo.

R HOSTS: Nancy & Charles Helsper

8 ROOMS, 4 pb
$65-120

OPEN: ALL YEAR

HILL HOUSE

2504 A Street
San Diego, CA 92102

Tel:1-619-239-4738

Centrally located in historic Golden Hill, old-world charm and warm hospitality await you at this stately 1904 home. Enjoy a delicious communal breakfast in the formal dining room. Later, relax in the beautifully appointed parlour, with its romantic fireplace, or in the serenity of the lathe-house garden, where there is always something blooming. The inn is close to the zoo, museums, downtown, convention center, and Sea World.

R HOSTS: Russell Atwater & Ron Oster

4 ROOMS, 0 pb   2 SUITES, 2 pb
$45-85

OPEN: ALL YEAR

250 SAN DIEGO

PLUM TREE COTTAGE
4220 St. James Place
San Diego, CA 92103
Tel:1-619-291-2930

Light and airy with lovely views of treetops and gardens, this private second-story guest cottage has kitchen and sitting areas, providing a quiet and comfortable retreat. Charmingly decorated, the cottage was built in the 1930s and is located in a peaceful, older residential neighborhood. You can walk to restaurants and shops in the village-like community. By car, San Diego's finest attractions are only minutes away.

HOST: Lee Eisenberg

1 COTTAGE, pb

OPEN: ALL YEAR $75

251 SAN DIEGO

QUINCE STREET TROLLEY
P.O. Box 7654
3022 Quince St.
San Diego, CA 92167
Tel:1-619-226-8454

This cottage is as cozy and private as a summer hideaway in the woods, yet it's just a few minutes from all of San Diego's major attractions. The century-old, board-and-batten bungalow has an original 1907 trolley car and a central garden featuring topiary sculptures and an antique platform swing. Decks overlook the wooded canyon below. Antiques, collectibles, and comfortable family pieces create a warm and welcoming interior.

HOSTS: George Pearn & Jason Price

3 SUITES, 3 pb

OPEN: ALL YEAR $75-80

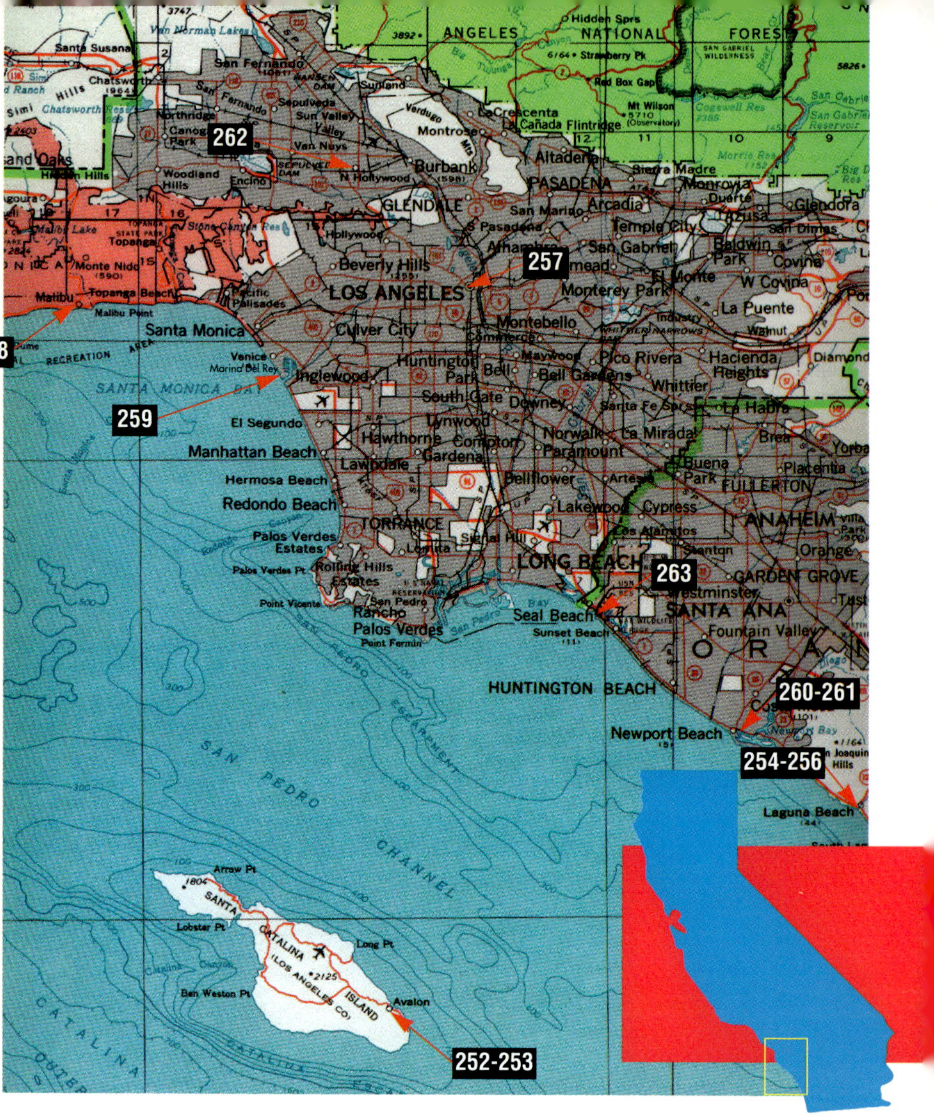

ANGELES NATIONAL FOREST

Van Norman Lakes

Santa Susana

Chatsworth

Simi Chatsworth Res.

Hidden Hills

Agoura

Malibu Lake

Topanga

Monte Nido

Malibu

Topanga Beach

Pacific Palisades

San Fernando

Northridge

Canoga Park

Woodland Hills

Encino

Sun Valley

Verdugo

Crescenta

Cañada Flintridge

Mt Wilson (Observatory)

Red Box Gap

Strawberry Pk

SAN GABRIEL WILDERNESS

Cogswell Res

San Gabriel Reservoir

Morris Res

262

Burbank

N Hollywood

Sepulveda

Van Nuys

Montrose

Altadena

PASADENA

Sierra Madre

Monrovia

Duarte

Azusa

Glendora

San Dimas

GLENDALE

Hollywood

Pasadena

San Marino

Arcadia

Temple City

San Gabriel

Baldwin Park

W Covina

Covina

Beverly Hills

257

Alhambra

mead

El Monte

La Puente

Walnut

LOS ANGELES

Monterey Park

Culver City

Montebello

Commerce

Pico Rivera

Hacienda Heights

Diamond

Santa Monica

Bell

Bell Gardens

Whittier

La Habra

Brea

Yorba

258

RECREATION AREA

SANTA MONICA BAY

Venice

Marina Del Rey

Inglewood

Huntington Park

Maywood

South Gate

Downey

Santa Fe Springs

La Mirada

Buena Park

Placentia

FULLERTON

259

El Segundo

Manhattan Beach

Hermosa Beach

Redondo Beach

Palos Verdes Estates

Palos Verdes Pt.

Rolling Hills Estates

San Pedro

Rancho Palos Verdes

Point Vicente

Point Fermin

Hawthorne

Lawndale

Gardena

Lynwood

Compton

Paramount

Bellflower

Norwalk

Artesia

Cypress

Los Alamitos

Santn

Buena Park

Anaheim

Orange

263

GARDEN GROVE

SANTA ANA

TORRANCE

Lomita

Signal Hill

LONG BEACH

Westminster

Seal Beach

Sunset Beach

Fountain Valley

O R A N

HUNTINGTON BEACH

260-261

Newport Beach

254-256

San Joaquin Hills

Laguna Beach

SAN PEDRO CHANNEL

Arrow Pt

SANTA CATALINA

Lobster Pt

Long Pt

Ben Weston Pt

LOS ANGELES CO.

ISLAND

Avalon

CATALINA

252-253

186

LOS ANGLELES
& ORANGE COUNTIES

Los Angeles—La La Land—Hollywood, hunks, beaches and babes, freeways and freaks. L.A. is like something that only exists in a movie—so much larger and louder than life. L.A. is not so much one city as it is lots of small cities tied together with an attitude. Although it's virtually impossible to "do" L.A. and its popular surrounding vicinities in a few short days, don't be discouraged. Just remember that most natives still haven't seen half of what their city has to offer.

The main areas to see on your first visit are Disneyland in Orange County, downtown L.A. (for the experience and the museums), Beverly Hills, West and North Hollywood, Bel Air, where you can drive down Sunset Boulevard to the sea, Santa Monica, and Venice. You'll also want to visit Griffith Park and see the classic L.A. view at night from the observatory, the L.A. County Museum on Wilshire Boulevard, the Norton Simon Museum in Pasadena, and the Huntington Museum and Library in San Marino, to name just a few attractions.

Let's hop in the car and begin our tour in **Anaheim** with the magical dreamscape for all ages: **Disneyland,** where Mickey Mouse, Donald Duck, and the rest of the goofy crew will keep you entertained for hours. Over twelve million visitors each year indulge in the pleasures of the nation's most popular theme park, which spans a constantly changing 76 acres (31 ha) of surreal landscape, fantasy rides, musical performances, parades, fireworks at night, theme restaurants, and souvenir shops.

In neighboring Buena Park is **Knott's Berry Farm,** which originally got its start as a 10-acre (4 ha) fruit patch, re-created ghost town, and a spot to sample Mrs. Knott's famous fried chicken and boysenberry pies. Today you can get a taste of the Old West and go for a thrill on a variety of rides both in and out of river-like rapids.

The next stop in Orange County is **Laguna Beach,** with its beautiful blue water and white sand. The downtown area is conveniently located near the beach, with easy access to the movie house, shops, and cafes. The town prides itself on its mix of artists, bohemians, business people, and beach bums who mingle with an air of carefree sophistication that is typically Southern California.

Nearby **Balboa Island,** with its million-dollar waterfront cottages, offers a great boardwalk surrounded by harbor views. Continuing north on the Pacific Coast Highway, stop in ritzy **Newport Beach,** where you will find the true blue bloods of Southern California. The boardwalk provides entertainment for bicyclists, joggers, roller bladers,

and people watchers. This is a town where the surf is frothy, the restaurants divine, and the houses expensive—a must-see for anyone new to Southern California.

The quaint, unspoiled coastal town of **Seal Beach,** on the border between L.A. and Orange counties, is complete with a fishing pier at the end of Main Street and a beautiful swimming and surfing beach. The downtown area offers charming souvenir shops and restaurants.

Still farther north are **Los Angeles Harbor** and **Long Beach,** a city that features new downtown highrises and is home to the majestic oceanliner called the **Queen Mary,** which is open to the public. The village next to downtown and the harbor offers shops, restaurants, and a merry-go-round.

Offshore is **Santa Catalina Island,** accessible by ferry, plane, or helicopter. Boats from Long Beach and San Pedro take passengers to and from Avalon; flights from L.A. and Orange county take less than twenty minutes. The area beckons visitors to explore and have fun. Half-day bus tours and glass-bottom boat rides allow visitors to sample the pleasures of this island resort.

Next on the agenda are the typically laid-back coastal towns of **Redondo Beach, Hermosa Beach,** and **Manhattan Beach.** Then travel north to lovely **Marina del Rey,** which boasts the world's largest manmade recreational boat harbor.

For some real excitement, check out the shores of **Venice Beach.** Built in 1904 by Abbot Kinney as a mecca for art and enlightenment, the area was designed with isthmuses and canals, true to the spirit of the original Venice. Today, although the canals have been filled in, the unique air still lingers. The famous **Venice Boardwalk** beginning at Washington Street is host to a variety of activities. Poets recite their work while jugglers toss whirring chainsaws and roller-blade competitors provide thrills and chills to a rapt audience with their daredevil antics. The walkway is lined with vendors selling their wares, including the best funnel cake in California. Bicycles and roller skates can be rented anywhere along the walk. Bicycle or skate from the **Venice Pavilion** at Windward Avenue to the Santa Monica pier—it's great exercise, and the path along the beach allows you to watch the waves and enjoy the ocean breeze.

Just north of Venice is **Santa Monica,** the busiest beach town in the Los Angeles area. Santa Monica offers both rent-controlled apartments and upscale beachfront properties, a combination that attracts a diverse group. The **Third Street Promenade,** just one block from the beach, is a collection of cafes, galleries, music stores, and clothing boutiques in a lively outdoor setting. Also worth visiting is **Main Street,** which offers a wonderfully funky array of the latest trends. Inland you will find a collection of shopping centers, including the **Santa Monica Place mall,** towering office buildings, and residential neighborhoods. Visitors will enjoy the town's youthful, enthusiastic atmosphere throughout the year.

A gathering place for residents and visitors alike is the ever-popular **Santa Monica Pier.** Complete with arcades, photo booths, and cotton-candy ven-

dors, the pier at the foot of Colorado on Santa Monica State Beach offers fun in the sun. Children and adults alike will enjoy a spin on the Victorian-era merry-go-round.

Several miles east of Santa Monica and northeast of Wilshire Boulevard and Gayley Avenue is Westwood Village, originally a quaint Mediterranean-style village, which features an ever-changing variety of movie theaters, trendy shops, and restaurants. Catering mainly to a college crowd, the Village is adjacent to the world-famous University of California at Los Angeles (UCLA). Also in Westwood is the Armand Hammer Museum of Art and Cultural Center, which houses Hammer's personal collection of Western European art.

Coming up next is 90210—Beverly Hills, that is, home of Rodeo Drive, countless celebrities, chic restaurants, exclusive hotels, and an indulgent population. This city, where property taxes are among the highest in the country, can provide a day of elegant, fund-depleting entertainment. Although Beverly Hills is surrounded by Los Angeles, it is a fiercely independent municipality. The main areas in this posh city are bordered by Wilshire Boulevard, which also extends from downtown to the ocean, Canon Drive, and Little Santa Monica Boulevard.

Several miles from Beverly Hills before you reach downtown via Wilshire Boulevard is the George C. Page Museum and Rancho La Brea Tar Pits, where you can see skeletons and re-creations of mammoths and other prehistoric animals trapped in the tar pits during the Ice Age. Nearby is the Los Angeles County Museum of Art (LACMA), with its stunning collection of works that range from pre-Columbian art to twentieth-century sculpture and a Japanese Art Pavilion.

With its wealth of sleek skyscrapers, museums, and cultural centers, downtown L.A. offers quite a bit more than just smog and traffic. You can spend an afternoon in the Museum of Contemporary Art, participate in hands-on science demonstrations and watch a film on a huge IMAX screen at the California Museum of Science and Industry, visit the California Afro-American Museum, see Egyptian mummies and reconstructed dinosaurs at the Natural History Museum, and view Native American art and artifacts at the Southwest Museum. The Music Center, the heart of L.A. culture, is home to the Los Angeles Philharmonic and the Joffrey Ballet. Within the center is the elegant Dorothy Chandler Pavilion, where you can star-gaze during the Oscar Awards ceremony, the Mark Taper Forum, and the Ahmanson Theater. The Los Angeles Civic Center is one of the largest government complexes in the nation. For a taste of the orient, dine and shop in bustling Chinatown, Little Tokyo, and Koreatown. Mexico is just around the corner on Olvera Street, a block-long marketplace where you can buy handicrafts, tasty churros, and other treats. The Los Angeles Memorial Coliseum offers tours of the site of the 1932 and 1984 Olympics.

In south-central L.A., admire the spectacular Watts Towers, built by Simon Rodia, an immigrant Italian tilesetter, who spent thirty-three years creating these ninety-nine foot towers from cement, broken tiles, bottles, seashells, and steel rods.

In and around Pasadena are two museums that shouldn't be missed. The

Norton Simon Museum of Art has a highly regarded collection of artwork from around the world. See sculpture from India and Southeast Asia and works by Rubens, Rembrandt, Rousseau, Matisse, Picasso, Monet, and Van Gogh. Also featured are American impressionist and modern paintings as well as medieval tapestries.

If you could visit only one museum in the Los Angeles area, it should be the impressive **Huntington Library, Art Collections, and Botanical Gardens** in San Marino. Formerly the estate of rail tycoon Henry E. Huntington, this gorgeous 207 acre (84 ha) property is now an educational and cultural center that houses rare books and manuscripts such as a Gutenberg Bible and Benjamin Franklin's handwritten autobiography. The mansion also contains one of the best collections of eighteenth-century French and British art in the United States, including Thomas Gainsborough's Blue Boy and Thomas Lawrence's Pinkie. The lush gardens feature an incredible variety of desert plants, a palm garden, Japanese-style ponds, and an avocado grove. There is also an elegant restaurant on the premises that serves high tea, for which you should make reservations in advance.

Let's jump back in the car and continue the tour where L.A. began: **Hollywood.** The movie capital of the world was originally a campground for the Cahuenga Indians. Hollywood took its name from a summer home in the area that appealed to the wife of a realtor from Chicago named Harvey Wilcox. Hollywood soon became popular with film makers, and studios such as Paramount and Metro-Goldwyn-Mayer bought up acres of real estate in the 1920s. Today, Tinsel Town is still the mecca of movie-making glamour. You can take studio tours, watch live filming, and be part of the studio audience on your favorite TV show. Compare your nose print with that of Bob Hope at **Mann's Chinese Theater,** stroll the **Walk of Fame,** admire your favorite star immortalized at **The Hollywood Wax Museum,** check out the now ill-reputed corner of Hollywood and Vine, and then drive by your favorite movie star's home hidden away in some exclusive corner of town. In the summer, catch an outdoor show at the **Hollywood Bowl.** At night, cruise **Sunset Boulevard** from downtown out toward star-studded **Spago's** and the **Roxy** nightclub, where The Doors got their start, past the exclusive **Beverly Hills Hotel,** until you reach the **Pacific Ocean.** Watch the Hollywood crowd parade around in the latest threads. Wherever you go, you can't escape the neon bustle of Hollywood magic.

Near West Hollywood, check out the hip and trendy people-watching scene on colorful **Melrose Avenue** between Fairfax and La Brea Avenues, where you can find items such as evening gowns (or lack thereof) formerly worn by Cher, funky grunge and Euro-fashions, gourmet delicacies, and even antique gumball machines.

Northeast of Hollywood is the second-largest city-owned park in the world, the 4,253- acre (1,722 ha) **Griffith Park.** In it you will find the **Los Angeles Zoo,** with over 2,000 mammals, birds, and reptiles; the **Griffith Park Observatory and Planetarium,** where you can learn about earthquakes, galaxies, meteorites, and other cosmic disciplines; the **Greek Theater;** and **Travel Town Transportation Museum,** where the kids and kids-at-heart can play on old rail cars and airplanes. At night admire the panorama of L.A. from the top of the Park.

Universal City Studios, just off the Hollywood Freeway at the Lankershim Boulevard exit in Burbank, is the largest movie studio in the world. It was the site for such blockbusters as *Jaws, E.T.,* and *Conan the Barbarian,* and for popular television series such as "Dragnet" and "The Incredible Hulk." The 2 1/2-hour guided tour of the 420-acre (170 ha) lot will leave you wanting to experience the exciting live shows, like the incredible simulated earthquake (for those who haven't had the opportunity to experience the real thing).

Heading back toward the coast, our last stop is **Malibu,** one of the most impressive and beautiful beaches near L.A. Visitors will find serenity and luxury in the town's waterfront restaurants and accommodations. Despite treacherous storms in the winter and threatening mud slides, the rich and famous continue to flock to Malibu for its crystal blue waters, warm sunshine, and relaxed lifestyle. Home of **Pepperdine University,** Malibu offers a variety of attractions, including the **J. Paul Getty Museum,** which sits atop a bluff between Sunset and Topanga Canyon boulevards and offers beautiful views of the ocean. This exquisite museum, created for the donated collection of the wealthy industrialist, includes Greek and Roman antiquities, Renaissance and Baroque paintings, and European decorative arts. The grounds are meticulously kept. Guides here offer a comprehensive and impressive tour of the gardens and building.

ATTRACTIONS

DOWNTOWN L.A. AND ENVIRONS

California Afro-American Museum, Exposition Park at 600 State Dr., (213) 744-7432, open daily 10-5. **California Museum of Science and Industry,** Exposition Park at 700 State Dr., (213) 744-2014 or 2015, open daily 10-5, admission free, IMAX Theater programs $5.50 adults, $4 children and seniors. **Downtown Visitor Information Center,** 695 S. Figueroa St., (213) 689-8822. Farmers Market, 3rd St. and Fairfax Ave., (213) 993-9211, Mon.-Sat. 9-6, Sun. 10-5, open an hour later in summer. **George C. Page Museum and the Rancho La Brea Tar Pits,** 5801 Wilshire Blvd., (213) 936-2230, observatory open weekends 10-5, free, museum admission $5 adults, $2.50 students and seniors, $1 children 6-12, free second Tues. of each month. **Los Angeles County Museum of Art,** 5905 Wilshire Blvd., (213) 857-6111, open Tues.-Thurs. 10-5, Fri. 10-9, weekends 11-6, $6 adults, $4 students and seniors, free for everyone second Tues. of each month. **Museum of Contemporary Art,** 250 S. Grand Ave., another facility at 152 N. Central Ave., (213) 621-2766, open Tues.-Sun. 11-5, Thurs. until 8, $4 adults, $2 students and seniors, free for children under 12 and for all visitors after 5. **Natural History Museum,** Exposition Park at 900 Exposition Blvd., (213) 744-3466, open Tues.-Sun. 10-5, $5 adults, $3.50 students and seniors, $2 children 5-12, free first Tues. of each month. **Southwest Museum,** 234 Museum Dr., Highland Park, (213) 221-2163, open Tues.-Sun. 11-5, $5 adults, $3 seniors and students, $2 children 7-18. **Watts Tower,** 1765 E. 107th St., (213) 569-8181, open weekdays 9-5, Sat. 10-2, can always be seen from outside.

HOLLYWOOD AND ENVIRONS

In Griffith Park: Griffith Observatory and Planetarium, (213) 664-1181, open Tues.-Fri. 2-10, weekends noon-10, free admission for observatory, Planetarium fees $3.50 adults, $2.50 seniors, $2.50 children 5-12, under five not admitted; The Los Angeles Zoo, (213) 666-4090, open daily 10-5, $7 adults, $5 seniors, $3 children; Travel Town Transportation Museum, (213) 662-9678, open 10-4 weekdays, until 5 weekends and holidays. Hollywood Visitor Information Center, The Janes House, 6541 Hollywood Blvd., (213) 461-4213. The Hollywood Wax Museum, 6767 Hollywood Blvd., (213) 462-8860, open Sun.-Thurs. 10-midnight,   Fri.-Sat. 10 A.M.-2 A.M., $8 adults, $6.50 seniors, $5 children, under 6 free with adult. Mann's Chinese Theatre (formerly Grauman's), 6925 Hollywood Blvd., (213) 464-8111. Universal Studios, off the Hollywood Freeway at the Lankershim Blvd. exit, Universal City, (818) 508-9600, tours daily 9-5 in summer, 10-3:30 rest of year, 9:30-3:30 on weekends, $27 over 12, $21 seniors, $21 children 3-11.

ORANGE COUNTY

Disneyland, 1313 Harbor Blvd., Anaheim, (714) 999-4565, open weekdays 10-6 , weekends 9-midnight, extended hours for summer and some holidays, one-day passports $28.75 adults, $23.00 children 3-11. Knott's Berry Farm, 8039 Beach Blvd., Buena Park, (714) 220-5200, winter weekdays 10-6, later on weekends, summer Sun.-Fri. 10-midnight, Sat. until 1 A.M., $25.95 adults, $17.95 seniors, $15.95 children under 54 inches.

PASADENA

Huntington Library, Art Collections, and Botanical Gardens, 1151 Oxford Rd., San Marino, (818) 405-2100, open Tues.-Sun. 1-4:30, Sun. visitors must have advanced reservations, donation of $2 per adult suggested. The Norton Simon Museum of Art, Colorado Blvd. and Orange Grove, Pasadena, (818) 449-6840, open Thurs.-Sun. noon-6, $4 adults, $2 students and seniors, free under 12 years accompanied by an adult, $4 admission for everyone on Sun.

WEST SIDE AND BEYOND

Armand Hammer Museum of Art and Cultural Center, 10889 Wilshire Blvd., Westwood, (310) 208-8800, open Tues.-Sun. 10-6, $4.50 adults, $3 seniors and students. Beverly Hills Visitors Bureau, 239 S. Beverly Dr., Beverly Hills, (310) 271-8174. J. Paul Getty Museum, 1798 Pacific Coast Hwy., Malibu, (310) 458-2003, open Tues.-Sun. 10-5, free, parking reservations are necessary and should be made one week in advance by phone or in writing to the museum's Reservation Office. The Queen Mary, Pier J, Long Beach, (310) 435-3511, call for schedules and fees. Santa Catalina Island Visitors Center, on corner of Crescent and Catalina Aves., Avalon, Santa Catalina Island, (310) 510-2000. University of California at Los Angeles (UCLA), main entrance is at Westwood Blvd. and LeConte Ave., tours at 10945 LeConte St., room 1417, on south edge of campus, weekdays 10:30 and 1:30.

AVALON, SANTA CATALINA ISLAND
Armstrong's
306 Crescent Ave.
(310) 510-0113
Seafood $$
El Galleon
321 Crescent Ave.
(310) 510-1188
Steaks, seafood, pasta $$

BEVERLY HILLS
The Bistro Garden
176 N. Cañon Dr.
(310) 550-3900
Continental cuisine $$-$$$
The Cheesecake Factory
364 N. Beverly Dr.
(310) 278-7270
American fare $-$$
Lawry's the Prime Rib
55 N. La Cienaga Blvd.
(310) 652-2827
Steaks, American $$-$$$

HOLLYWOOD
Chan Dara
1511 N. Cahuenga Blvd.
(213) 464-8585
Thai cuisine $-$$
Dar Maghreb
7651 W. Sunset Blvd.
(213) 876-7651
Moroccan cuisine $$$

LAGUNA BEACH
Cedar Creek Inn
384 Forest Ave.
(714) 497-8696
Continental cuisine $$
Dizz's As Is
2794 South Coast Hwy.
(714) 494-5250
Continental cuisine $$-$$$

NEWPORT BEACH
Cano's
2241 W. Coast Hwy.
(714) 631-1381
Spanish seafood $$-$$$
Twenty One Ocean Front
(base of Newport Beach pier)
(714) 673-2100
Seafood $$$

PACIFIC PALISADES
Gladstone's 4 Fish
17300 W. Pacific Coast Highway
(310) GL-4-FISH
Seafood $$-$$$

MALIBU
The Whale Watch Inn
6800 Westward Beach Rd.
(310) 457-5571
Seafood $$-$$$

SANTA MONICA
Warwzawa
1414 Lincoln Blvd.
(310) 393-8831
Polish cuisine $$-$$$

VENICE BEACH
West Beach Café
60 N. Venice Blvd.
(310) 399-9246
Ameican fare $$-$$$

WEST HOLLYWOOD
Angeli Caffé
7274 Melrose Ave.
(213) 936-9086
Rustic Italian cuisine $-$$
L'Orangerie
903 N. La Cienaga Blvd.
(213) 652-9770
Classic French cuisine $$$

The Source
8301 Sunset Blvd.
(213) 656-6388
California health food $-$$
Spago
8795 Sunset Blvd.
(213) 652-4025
California cuisine $$$

WEST L.A.
Bombay Cafe
12113 Santa Monica Blvd.
(310) 820-2070
Indian cuisine $-$$
La Grange
2005 Westwood Blvd.
(310) 279-1060
Country-French cuisine $$
Ramayani of Westwood
1777 Westwood Blvd.
(310) 477-3315
Indonesian cuisine $-$$
Shamshiri
1916 Westwood Blvd.
(310) 474-1410
Persian cuisine $
U-ZEN
11951 Santa Monica Blvd.
(310) 477-1390
Japanese cuisine/sushi bar $-$$

GARDEN HOUSE INN

P.O. Box 1881
125 Clarissa
Avalon, CA 90704
Tel:1-310-510-0356

R

This elegant 1923 historic home is just steps away from the beach. A delightful breakfast buffet is served on the impressive garden patio. Antiques and elegant touches enhance the romantic atmosphere. Wine and appetizers are served compliments of your host.

9 COTTAGE, 9 pb

$90-250 OPEN: APR - OCT HOSTS: Candy (Innkeeper) & Jon Olsen

GULL HOUSE

P.O. Box 1381
344 Whittley Ave.
Avalon, CA 90704
Tel:1-310-510-2547

R

Discover the romance of Santa Catalina Island. Its distinct Mediterranean flavor makes the Gull House a feast for the senses. Breakfast at leisure on the patio by the pool and spa. The warm hospitality at this inn adds an extra dimension of comfort to your visit.

3 ROOMS, 2 pb   2 SUITES, 2 pb   **POOL**

$110-145 **SPA** OPEN: APR-OCT HOSTS: Hattie & Bob Michalis

CASA LAGUNA INN

2510 South Coast Hwy.
Laguna Beach, CA 92651
Tel:1-800-233-0449

R

Casa Laguna combines the beauty of Spanish Mission architecture with magnificent ocean views. Arches, patios, courtyards, and palm-filled gardens create a peaceful, cloistered atmosphere. Guest rooms are furnished with antiques and exotic art. Relax by the pool.

16 ROOMS, 16 pb 4 SUITES, 4 pb 2 COTTAGE, 2 pb

$90-205 OPEN: ALL YEAR HOSTS: Louise & Ted Gould

LOS ANGELES

255 LAGUNA BEACH

HOSTS: Dee, Vernon & Tom Taylor

THE CARRIAGE HOUSE
1322 Catalina St.
Laguna Beach, CA 92651
Tel:1-714-494-8945

This charming New Orleans-style inn is just a few steps from the beach, and it's a pleasant walk to the village shops and galleries. Each suite has a sitting room and separate bedroom. Wine and cheese await your arrival.

6 SUITES, 6 pb

OPEN: ALL YEAR 🍵🍽️ **$95-150**

256 LAGUNA BEACH

HOSTS: Annette & Henk Wirtz

EILER'S INN
741 South Coast Hwy.
Laguna Beach, CA 92651
Tel:1-714-494-3004

Eiler's European hosts provide guests with hospitality in the old-world tradition. Each suite is uniquely furnished with handsome antiques and colorful linens. Special touches include fresh flowers, fruit, and candies. A gourmet breakfast welcomes guests each morning.

12 ROOMS, 12 pb

OPEN: ALL YEAR ☕ **$100-175**

257 LOS ANGELES

HOST: Patsy Carter

THE INN AT 657
657 West Twenty-Third Street
Los Angeles, CA 90007
Tel: U.S. 1-800-347-7512
or 1-213-741-2200

A hidden treasure in the heart of the city, the Inn at 657 is a renovated 1930s apartment house that was conceived by its proprietor as a haven for people who want to be cradled in gracious hospitality. Guest suites are roomy and beautifully decorated.

5 SUITES, 5 pb

OPEN: ALL YEAR 🍽️ **SPA** **$75-95**

MALIBU BEACH INN

22878 Pacific Coast Hwy.
Malibu, CA 90265

Tel:U.S. 1-800-4-MALIBU
or Canada 1-800-255-1007

Malibu, a tiny and exclusive strip of coast just north of Los Angeles, is world famous for its sandy beaches, natural beauty, and casual but elegant lifestyle. This California Mission-style inn offers lovely ocean-view rooms with private balconies and hand-painted tile baths and fireplaces, creating the feeling of being in your own beach-front cottage. Come experience real California dreamin'—we're saving a sunset for you!

HOST: Dan Ferrante

44 ROOMS, 44 pb   3 SUITES, 3 pb

$125 and up    **OPEN: ALL YEAR**

THE MANSION INN

327 Washington Blvd.
Marina Del Rey, CA 90291

Tel:U.S. & Canada 1-800-828-0688
or 1-310-821-2557

Accommodations at this stately inn were designed to give guests the feel of a private mansion near the beach. The inn's two-level suites were designed with comfort in mind. Accommodations are luxurious and the grounds offer a respite for visitors who wish to relax and take in the beauty of the marina. Breakfast is served in the Cobblestone Cafe—the perfect place to delight in the fresh morning air.

R   **HOST: Richard Hunnicutt**

43 ROOMS, 43 pb

$59-125   **OPEN: ALL YEAR**

260 NEWPORT BEACH

DORYMAN'S INN
2102 West Ocean Front
Newport Beach, CA 92663

Tel:1-800-634-3303
or 1-714-675-7300

This inn offers romance, luxury, and a resounding elegance reminiscent of a by-gone era. Each classic Victorian guest room is furnished with fine French and American antiques. Rise at your own leisurely pace and find yourself drawn to the parlor for a delicious breakfast of pastries, brown eggs, and fresh fruit. Then explore the cobblestone walkways and browse through the shops of nearby Lido Marine Village and the Cannery Village

HOST: Michael Palitz

1.6k 0.2k 32k 3k 0k 0k 13k

6 ROOMS, 6 pb   4 SUITES, 4 pb

OPEN: ALL YEAR   SPA $135-275

261 NEWPORT BEACH

LITTLE INN ON THE BAY
617 Lido Park Dr.
Newport Beach, CA 92663

Tel:1-800-438-4466

This contemporary inn overlooks the fishing harbor, where private pleasure boats dock in front of the terrace and provide a romantic yachting atmosphere. A short walk takes you to the cobblestone street in the Lido Marina village, where you will find a historical cannery restaurant. Relax by the pool or stroll along the waterfront to the town center, where you can enjoy delightful shops and restaurants.

HOSTS: Lisa Williams & Kari Yee

5k 0k 32k 3k 0.5k 0.5k 13k

17 ROOMS, 17 pb   12 SUITES,12 pb   POOL

OPEN: ALL YEAR $100-150

198

LA MAIDA HOUSE
11159 La Maida St.
North Hollywood, CA 91601
Tel:1-818-769-3857

This gracious old-world villa boasts rich mahogany, tile, marble, and stained glass. Luxurious rooms appointed with art and antiques offer guests the utmost in comfort and elegance. Amenities include fresh flowers, aperitifs, and turn-down service. Early risers may enjoy tea or coffee and a newspaper delivered to their room. Lunch and dinner prepared by gourmet chef available upon request. Gymnasium on premise. Dining rooms accommodate banquets and parties. Centrally located.

HOST: Megan Timothy

7 ROOMS, 7 pb   **4 SUITES, 4 pb**   **POOL**

$85-210   SPA   **OPEN: ALL YEAR**

THE SEAL BEACH INN & GARDEN
212 Fifth Street
Seal Beach, CA 90740
Tel:1-310-493-2416

Set in the seaside village of Seal Beach, this peaceful French-Mediterranean country inn is conveniently located near beaches, shopping, Disneyland, Universal Studios, and other attractions. Filigreed gates and balustrades, ornate street lights, and a brick courtyard provide the perfect setting for the inn's exquisite rooms. Guest accommodations are appointed with handsome antiques, beautiful rugs, stained glass windows, original art, and Victorian prints. This is one of California's most acclaimed inns.

R   HOSTS: Margorie Bettenhausen & Harry Schmaehl

23 ROOMS, 23 pb   **POOL**

$108-175   SPA   **OPEN: ALL YEAR**

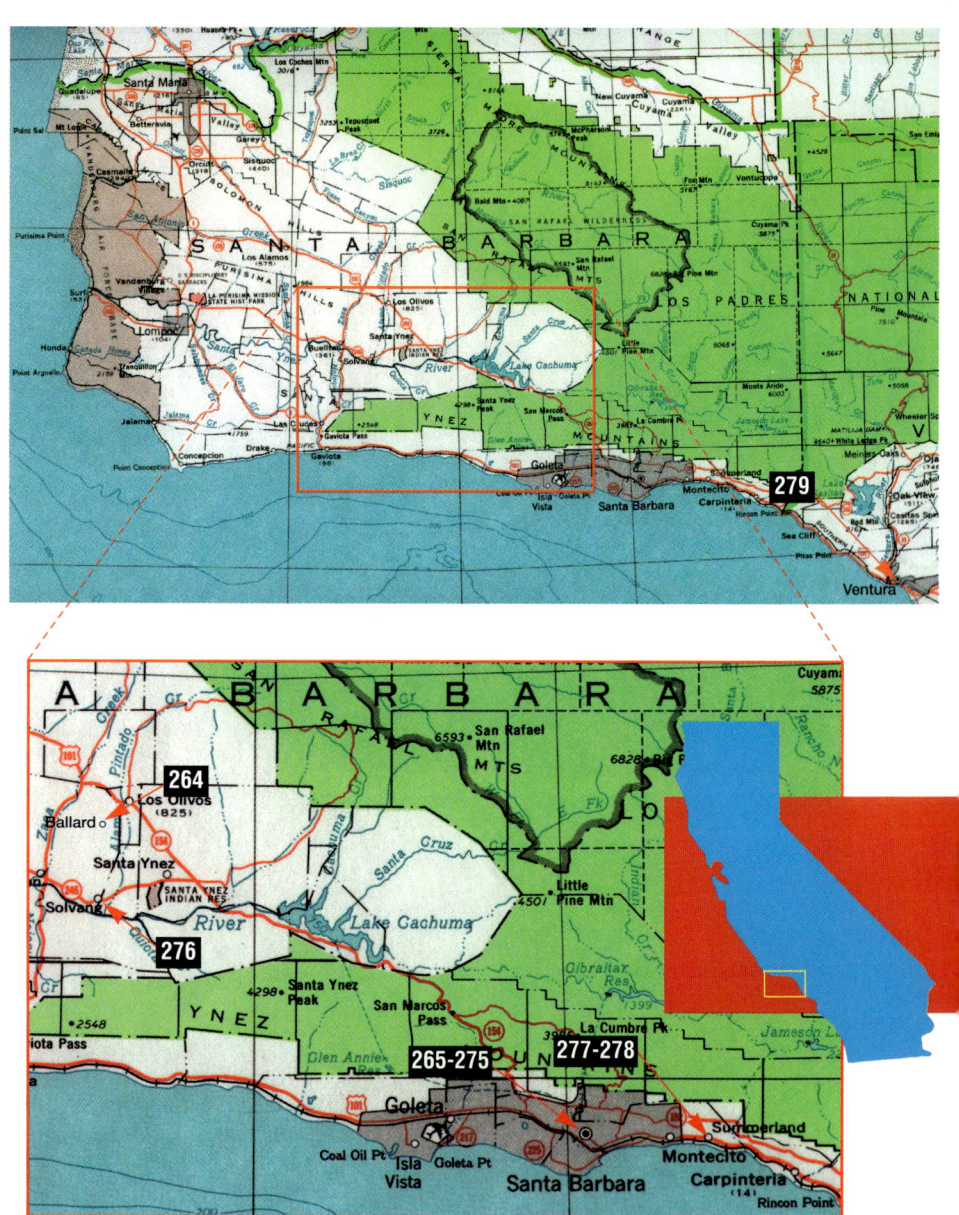

SANTA BARBARA
& VENTURA COUNTIES

The Southern California cliché of beaches crammed with blond hunks and babes, surfers, and palm trees reveals itself to be true in the beachside resort towns of Santa Barbara and Ventura counties. But let's be fair. Blessed with mild weather and rugged natural beauty, these two counties also offer unlimited outdoor activities, cultural events, and an interesting historical past.

Miles of wide beaches, a nice fishing pier, and a developed harbor in **Ventura** provide swimming, fishing, surfing, and boating. The harbor here is the point of embarkation for cruises to the Channel Islands.

For a pleasant lake and mountain detour between Ventura and Santa Barbara, drive on State Highways 33 and 150 to **Ojai.** Pronounced "O-high," this rural resort town is tucked away among hillsides covered with citrus and avocado groves. Here you can go hiking, biking, and horseback riding on miles of trails that lead to **Los Padres National Forest. Lake Casitas,** just west of town off Highway 1, hosted the rowing competition of the 1984 Olympics and is great for camping, boating, fishing, and picnicking. Driving north on Highway 33 takes you through miles of rugged mountains with creeks, campsites, and pleasant picnicking spots. Visit the natural mineral oasis of **Wheeler Hot Springs,** 7 miles (11 km) north of Ojai off Highway 33, where you can relax in the pool and hot tubs, get a massage, and dine on the premises.

You may want to stop in the quiet, charming towns of Summerland and Montecito on your way to Santa Barbara. **Summerland** offers antique stores, arts and crafts shows, shops, restaurants, lovely beaches, and of course, the cozy Clinton hideaway. Just north is the exclusive **Montecito** district, where Charlie Chaplin built a house for visiting guests while he was making movies in Santa Barbara. Nearby is the elegant neighborhood of **Hope Ranch.**

Continuing on Highway 150 to Highway 101, you soon reach **Santa Barbara**—a city where the rich and famous find refuge, spiritualists learn the truth, surfers ride the waves, and soap operas gain inspiration. It was not by accident that the Spanish priest Fray Lasuén in 1786 chose Santa Barbara as the site of one of the first missions. Just 90 miles (144 km) north of Los Angeles, Santa Barbara boasts the Pacific coast on one side and the rugged Santa Ynez mountains on the other.

The city of Santa Barbara was named in 1602 by Sebastian Vizcaino, after the saint who held the birthdate of the Spanish conquistador's arrival. Characterized by a warm climate, a relaxed atmosphere, an interesting Chumash Indian and Spanish heritage, and stunning natural beauty, this lovely beachside resort town soothes the nerves. For a nice change from urban chaos, there are no buildings in town over three stories high, thanks to a city building restriction. The Spanish and mission-style architecture, with its red-tiled roofs, adobe construction, bell towers, and lush landscaping, creates a refreshing Mediterranean quality that also permeates the Santa Barbara lifestyle.

Begin your tour at **State Street,** the city's palm-tree-lined main boulevard, which offers unique boutiques, cafes, and restaurants. At the end of this street **Stearns Wharf** gives a nice view of palm-fringed beaches, which offer swimming, roller skating/blading, surfing, picnicking, scuba diving, grunion runs, and Olympic-class volleyball. This area also offers hiking paths and horseback-riding trails, as well as twenty-eight municipal tennis courts. The picturesque 92-acre (37 ha) yacht harbor is perfect for strolling, fishing, motorboating, and sailboating.

The center of downtown features the **Courthouse,** which resembles a Moorish palace. Admire the hand-painted tiles and fine architecture. **El Presidio State Historic Park,** built in 1782, was one of four military strongholds established by the Spanish along the California coast. A short distance from downtown is one of the best-preserved missions in California; the **Santa Barbara Mission** is still used as a Catholic church. Every Sunday the **Santa Barbara Arts and Crafts Show** gives local artists half a mile of Cabrillo Boulevard to exhibit their works.

Goleta, just northwest of Santa Barbara, has some of the best beaches around—Goleta, El Capitan, and farther away, Refugio, and Gaviota beaches. Goleta is a thriving university town catering to the **University of California at Santa Barbara.** You will notice that there are more bicycles per square meter here than anywhere else in the United States. Conform. Rent a bicycle and follow the bike trails around town and on the beach.

Continuing north brings you to **Solvang** in the Santa Ynez Valley. Windmill structures, thatched roofs, cobblestone walkways, and horse-drawn trolleys are constant reminders of the town's Scandinavian heritage. Roughly sixty-five percent of the 3,500 residents are of Danish decent. In 1911 the area was chosen as the site for a folk school by Danish educators from Minnesota. Though extremely touristy, this quaint town offers a taste of Denmark's finest in its bakeries, restaurants, delicatessens, and import shops, which provide an enormous selection of food from all over Europe. Be sure to try the scrumptious puffy Danish pancakes called *aebleskiver*. Colorful Danish celebrations take place in summer and mid-September. Stop at the Visitor's Bureau for more information. Before you leave town, visit the beautifully restored **Mission Santa Ines.** Founded in 1805, it is still in use and has a chapel, museum, and cemetery.

Picturesque little towns are sprinkled around the **Santa Ynez Valley.** **Santa Ynez** will remind you of the Old West, with its carriage house and quaint museum that displays relics from nineteenth-century life. **Los Olivos** offers a tavern, galleries, and wine tasting rooms. Established in 1880, nearby **Ballard** was the first settlement in the valley. Its classic little red schoolhouse is now a Registered Historic Landmark.

ATTRACTIONS

SANTA BARBARA

El Presidio State Historic Park, 123 E. Cañon Perdido St., (805) 966-9719, open daily 10:30-4:30. Santa Barbara County Courthouse, 1100 block of Anacapa St., (805) 962-6464, open weekdays 8-5, weekends 9-5, free admission. Santa Barbara Mission, Laguna and Los Olivos Sts., (805) 682-4149, open daily 9-5, $2 adults, under 16 free. Santa Barbara Visitor Information Center, 1 Santa Barbara St., (805) 965-3021.

SOLVANG

Mission Santa Ines, 1760 Mission Dr., (805) 688-4815, open Mon.-Sat. 9:30-4:30, Sun. 12-4:30, $1 adults, under 16 free. Solvang Visitors Bureau, 1593 Mission Dr., (805) 688-6144, (800) 468-6765.

BALLARD AREA
The Ballard Store:
Restaurant and Wine Bar
2449 Baseline Ave.
(805) 688-5319
Continental cuisine $$
The Hitching Post
Highway 246
Beullton
(805) 688-0676
Steakhouse $$$

SANTA BARBARA
Brophey Brothers
At the Breakwater
(805) 966-4418
Seafood $$
El Encanto Dining Room
1900 Lasuen Rd.
(805) 687-5000
California cuisine with French
flair $$-$$$

Emilio's
324 W. Cabrillo Blvd.
(805) 966-4426
Italian cuisine $$
Louie's in the Upham Hotel
1404 De la Vina
(805) 963-7003
California cuisine $$
Montecito Cafe
1295 Coast Village Rd.
(805) 969-3392
Continental-California cuisine $-$$
The Palace Cafe
8 E. Cota St.
(805) 966-3133
Cajun-Caribbean cuisine $$-$$$

SOLVANG
Danish Inn
1547 Mission Dr.
(805) 688-4813
Danish cuisine $$

Paoli's
478 Fourth Place
(805) 688-9966
Italian cuisine $$
Taj Palace
In the Tivoli Inn
1564 Copenhagen Dr.
(805) 686-5853
Indian cuisine $$

WINERIES

Austin Cellars
2923 Grand Ave
Los Olivos, CA 93441
(805) 688-9665
Open: daily 11-5

Babcock Vineyards
5175 Highway 246
Lompoc, CA 93436
(805) 736-1455
Open: Sat.+ Sun. 10:30-4

Buttonwood Farm Winery
1500 Alamo Pintado Road
Solvang, CA 93463
(805) 688-3032
Open: Fri. thru Mon. 10-5

Byron Vineyard & Winery
5230 Tepusquet Road
Santa Maria, CA 93454
(805) 937-7288
Open: daily 10-4

Firestone Vineyard
5017 Zaca Station Road
Los Olivos, CA 93441-0244
(805) 688-3940
Open: daily 10-4

The Gainey Vineyard
3950 E. Highway 246
Santa Ynez, CA 93460
(805) 688-0558
Open: daily 10-5

Mosby Winery at Vega
Vineyards
9496 Santa Rosa Road
Buellton, CA 93427
(805) 688-2415
Open: daily 10-4

Santa Barbara Winery
202 Anacapa St.
Santa Barbara, CA 93101
(805) 963-3633
Open: daily 10-5

THE BALLARD INN
BALLARD 264

2436 Baseline Ave.
Ballard, CA 93463
Tel:1-800-638-2466

Enjoy elegant accommodations in the heart of Santa Barbara's wine country. Guests are treated to quality local wines and specialty hors d'oeuvres each evening in a country setting. Worlds away, yet close to everything Santa Barbara County has to offer.

15 ROOMS, 15 pb

$155-185    **OPEN: ALL YEAR**   **HOST:** Kelly Robinson

BATH STREET INN
SANTA BARBARA 265

1720 Bath St.
Santa Barbara, CA 93101
Tel:1-805-682-9680

R

The friendly host will pamper you with gracious service in this 1890 Queen Anne Victorian inn. Within walking distance of downtown, the inn offers elegant balconies with mountain views. A hearty breakfast is served in the dining room or in the garden.

8 ROOMS, 8 pb   2 SUITES, pb   1 COTTAGE, pb

$65-115   **OPEN: ALL YEAR**   **HOST:** Susan Brown

THE BAYBERRY INN
SANTA BARBARA 266

111 West Valerio St.
Santa Barbara, CA 93101
Tel:1-805-682-3199

R

This charming post-Victorian inn is decorated with beautiful silk wall coverings, imported antiques, crystal, and beveled mirrors. Guest rooms feature canopied beds. Some have fireplaces. Play croquet or badminton, and walk to downtown, the Spanish mission, and other historical sites.

8 ROOMS, 8 pb   2 SUITES, pb   1 COTTAGE, pb

$85-135   **SPA** **OPEN: ALL YEAR**   **HOST:** Keith Pomeroy

267 SANTA BARBARA

HOST: Jeanise Suding Eaton

BLUE QUAIL INN
1908 Bath St.
Santa Barbara, CA 93101
Tel:USA 1-800-676-1622 CA 1-800-549-1622
or 1-805-687-2300

This inn offers cottages and suites in a quiet country garden setting close to town and beaches. Guests enjoy a wonderful breakfast on the patio, afternoon wine and hors d'oeuvres, and evening sweets and hot spiced apple cider. Bicycles, picnic lunches, and gift certificates are available.

5 ROOMS, 5 pb   3 SUITES, 3 pb   1 COTTAGE, pb

OPEN: ALL YEAR   **$74-165**

268 SANTA BARBARA

HOSTS: Michael, Steve, Jim & Ken

GLENBOROUGH INN
1327 Bath St.
Santa Barbara, CA 93101
Tel:1-800-962-0589
or 1-805-966-0589

This inn boasts three turn-of-the-century Craftsman-style homes close to shops and attractions. Enjoy breakfast in your room, in the lush garden, or in the elegant dining room, and indulge in the privacy of the enclosed garden hot tub.

8 ROOMS, 2 pb   3 SUITES, 3 pb

OPEN: ALL YEAR   **SPA**   **$55-160**

269 SANTA BARBARA

HOST: Mary Robinson

THE IVANHOE INN
1406 Castillo St.
Santa Barbara, CA 93101
Tel:1-805-963-8832

Built by a retired Danish sea captain, this 19th-century home filled with country antiques features private sitting rooms and lovely gardens. Nestled between the mountains and the ocean, it's a short walk to shops, fine restaurants, and other attractions.

5 SUITES, 3 pb

OPEN: ALL YEAR   **$85-150**

THE OLD YACHT CLUB INN
SANTA BARBARA 270

431 Corona Del Mar Dr.
Santa Barbara, CA 93103
Tel:1-800-786-6422
or 1-805-962-4902

Santa Barbara's first bed and breakfast is known for its hospitality, beach location, and gourmet cuisine. It is decorated with antiques, period pieces, and oriental rugs. A delicious five-course dinner is served on Saturdays. Amenities include bicycles, beach chairs, and towels.

9 ROOMS, 9 pb

$60-140   SPA   OPEN: ALL YEAR   HOSTS: Lu, Sandy, & Nancy

THE OLIVE HOUSE
SANTA BARBARA 271

1604 Olive St.
Santa Barbara, CA 93101
Tel:1-800-786-6422
or 1-805-962-4902

This 1904 California Craftsman home offers peaceful elegance and warm hospitality. In a quiet area near the Santa Barbara Mission and downtown, guests may relax on the sun deck or on the terraced gardens. Enjoy picturesque views of the ocean, city, and mountains.

6 ROOMS, 6 pb

$125-175   OPEN: ALL YEAR   HOST: Lois Gregg

THE PARSONAGE
SANTA BARBARA 272

1600 Olive St.
Santa Barbara, CA 93101
Tel:1-805-962-9336

Originally built as a parsonage for the Trinity Episcopal Church, this beautiful Queen Anne Victorian inn offers rooms filled with period pieces and oriental rugs. Enjoy sumptuous breakfasts, and city and harbor views. Walk to the Santa Barbara Mission, restaurants, and boutiques.

6 ROOMS, 6 pb

$65-185   OPEN: ALL YEAR   HOSTS: Holli, Terry, Audrey, & Dick Harmon

273 | SANTA BARBARA

HOSTS: Linda & Glyn Davies

SIMPSON HOUSE INN
121 East Arrellaga St.
Santa Barbara, CA 93101

Tel:1-800-676-1280
or 1-805-963-7067

This beautifully restored Victorian estate is secluded on an acre of English gardens. The rooms are elegantly decorated with English lace, antiques, oriental carpets, and fine art. All guest rooms feature private baths, and many have fireplaces and private decks overlooking the gardens. Rates include full gourmet breakfast, local Santa Barbara wines, hors d'oeuvres, and use of bicycles. Walk five minutes to historic downtown restaurants, shops, museums, and theaters.

7 ROOMS, 7 pb **4 SUITES, 4 pb** **3 COTTAGE, 3pb**

OPEN: ALL YEAR **$80-185**

274 | SANTA BARBARA

HOSTS: Carol & Larry MacDonald

TIFFANY INN
1323 De La Vina
Santa Barbara, CA 93101

Tel:1-800-273-3778
or 1-805-963-2283

Relaxation begins the moment you arrive. Leave your car and stroll to exclusive shops, restaurants, galleries, clubs, and museums. Your hosts will make your visit unforgettable. Breakfast at Tiffany's is a sumptuous affair, served in the formal dining room or on the veranda overlooking the garden. Enjoy evening refreshments. Classic antiques, period furnishings, and fireplaces welcome you throughout this lovingly restored 1898 Victorian.

7 ROOMS, 5 pb

OPEN: ALL YEAR **SPA** **$60-175**

UPHAM HOTEL
SANTA BARBARA 275

1404 De La Vina
Santa Barbara, CA 93101

Tel:1-800-727-0876
or 1-805-962-0058

Established in 1871, this beautifully restored Victorian Hotel is situated on an acre of gardens in the historic downtown area of Santa Barbara. The cozy cottage rooms, some with fireplaces, afford garden views. Louie's Restaurant serves excellent California cuisine for lunch and dinner.

47 ROOMS, 47 pb   2 SUITES, 2 pb

$95-295   OPEN: ALL YEAR   HOST: Jan Martin Winn

THE TIVOLI INN
SOLVANG 276

1564 Copenhagen Dr.
Solvang, CA 93463

Tel:1-800-688-0559
or 1-805-688-0559

World-class flair is the hallmark of this luxurious European inn. Order breakfast in bed. Enjoy a cocktail in the Pacific Coast Pub or dine in the acclaimed Pacific Coast Cafe. Special touches include champagne, a fruit basket, and arranged flowers.

29 ROOMS, 29 pb   **POOL**

$65-195   OPEN: ALL YEAR   HOST: Robert Remak

SUMMERLAND INN
SUMMERLAND 277

P.O. 1209
2161 Ortega Hill Rd.
Summerland, CA 93067

Tel:1-805-969-5225

This New England Colonial-style inn is ideal for a romantic interlude or a private business meeting. Rooms are decorated with unique folk art, antiques, and handmade quilts. Some rooms have fireplaces and ocean views. Special touches include fresh flowers and breakfast in bed.

11 ROOMS, 11 pb

$55-140   OPEN: ALL YEAR   HOSTS: Farah K. Unwalla & James R. Farned

278 SUMMERLAND

HOST: Verlinda Richardson

INN ON SUMMER HILL
P.O. 376
2520 Lillie Ave.
Summerland, CA 93067
Tel:1-800-845-5566

Captivating English country decor is the highlight of this award-winning California Craftsman-style inn. Set in the seaside village of Summerland, this three-year-old inn has a spectacular ocean view. Guests may enjoy the minisuites, each with a private balcony or patio, whirlpool-spa, fireplace, canopied bed, stereo, original art, and antiques. Your host offers a sumptuous breakfast. Hor d'oeuvres and dessert add to the consistent warmth and charm.

16 ROOMS, 16 pb   1 SUITES, 1 pb

OPEN: ALL YEAR   SPA $155-275

279 VENTURA

HOST: Gisela Flender Baida

R

LA MER GÄSTEHAUS
411 Poli St.
Ventura, CA 93001
Tel:1-805-643-3600

This Victorian Cape Cod-style home, built in 1890, is a historic landmark nestled on a green hillside with a beautiful view of the California coastline. Each distinctive guest room features the privacy of a separate entrance. The accommodations are an artistic adventure; furnished with European antiques, each room captures the atmosphere of a different country. Bavarian breakfast, midweek specials, and carriage rides are just a few of the special touches.

5 ROOMS, 5 pb

OPEN: ALL YEAR   SPA $80-155

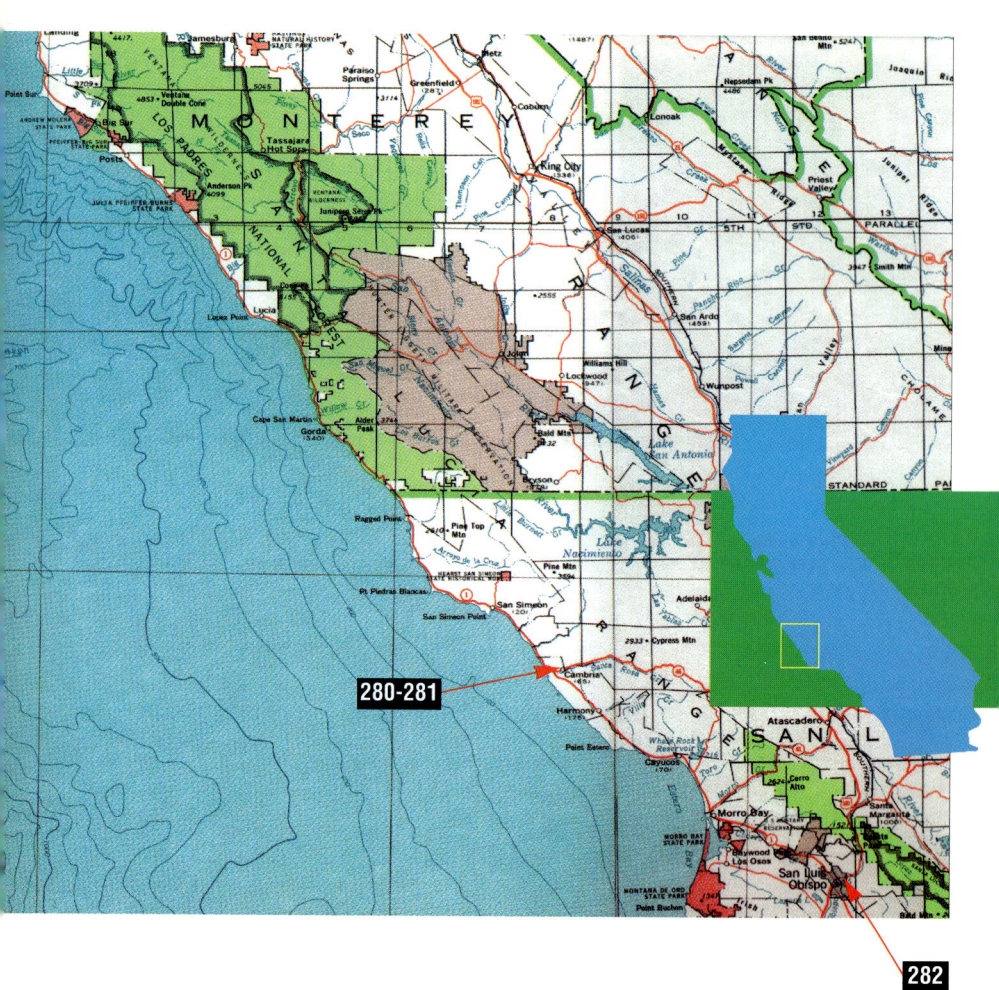

280-281

282

CENTRAL COAST
& B I G S U R

The stretch of Highway 1 between Pismo Beach and Big Sur reveals some of the most spectacular coastline in California. You will see gorgeous scenery as you travel north, but don't expect many bathers on the beaches. The striking rock cliffs and wave-formed coves have inspired many artists and photographers, including Ansel Adams.

Pismo Dunes State Vehicular Recreation Area is an exciting place for off-road vehicles to explore miles of dunes. You can also drive your regular car on the hard-packed beaches. A few miles north, in the town of **Avila Beach,** fishing and boating enthusiasts can enjoy the sheltered harbor, while sun bathers can relax on the fine sandy beach with its excellent swimming.

Thirteen miles (21 km) northeast lies **San Luis Obispo,** founded in 1772 around the **Mission San Luis Obispo de Tolosa.** San Luis Obispo grew into a town in 1894, when the Southern

Pacific Railroad brought trains into the area. Today it is a bustling city with a charming downtown shopping and business district. The old adobe mission occupies a place of honor in the center of town, surrounded by a verdant plaza and bordered by San Luis Creek, which is lined with many delightful restaurants, shops, and galleries. Visit the **San Luis Obispo County Historical Museum** containing local history and American Indian exhibits. The town is bordered by the **Coast Range mountains** and is only a few miles from the coast, with its excellent beaches, sand dunes, and secluded coves.

Twelve miles (19 km) northwest of San Luis Obispo, the resort town of **Morro Bay** is named after the bay on which it is located. A conical rock 578 feet (177 m) tall and resembling the Rock of Gibraltar guards the bay; for centuries it has served as a landmark for mariners. In the 1870s Morro Bay was a bustling port that supplied the ranching and dairy industries. Today fishing and tourism are the main industries. Visit the **Morro Bay State Park Museum of Natural History** and learn about the sea life that abounds in this area.

The picturesque town of **Cambria** is located 33 miles (53 km) northwest of San Luis Obispo. It is surrounded by majestic Monterey pines and affords a spectacular view of the ocean. Cambria was founded in 1866 as a trading center for whaling, mercury mining, and lumber. Today you can enjoy the Victorian-style architecture, ocean-view restaurants, cozy inns, and art galleries. Walk along the expansive state beaches, explore the tidepools, and watch for otters and whales.

Before you leave Cambria, be sure to visit the **Bric-a-Brac Mansion** on **Nitt Witt Ridge.** The owner, Art Beal, is known locally as "Captain Nitt Witt." Built out of everything from beer bottles to bicycle parts, this unique mansion has been evolving since 1928. This entertaining example of eccentric folk art house design is listed in the National Register of Historic Landmarks.

Eight miles (13 km) north of Cambria on Highway 1 is the village of **San Simeon,** built and occupied by Portuguese whalers from 1865 to 1890. It is now home to the opulent **Hearst Castle,** which became a major tourist attraction in 1957 when the William Randolph Hearst Corporation deeded the property to the state of California. William Randolph Hearst began construction of the castle in 1919 and continued to create an eclectic masterpiece until his death in 1951. Built on 137 acres (55 ha) atop a 1,600-foot (489 m) mountain, the estate is truly exotic, featuring marble terraces, Greco-Roman pools, fountains, marble statuary, mosaic floors, and a priceless art collection. The main house contains twenty-four bedrooms and has provided elegant accommodations to a host of international celebrities.

After you leave this palatial estate, head north and begin a thrilling journey along the legendary **Big Sur** coast, which begins above Cambria and extends northward for approximately 80 miles (128 km). Don't forget to keep your eyes on the narrow ribbon of winding highway that clings precariously to the side of the Santa Lucia mountains as you are led on a breathtaking coastal journey. Marvel at the remote beaches, secluded canyons, spectacular state parks, and grassy promontories with grazing cattle, and enjoy the delightful inns and restaurants that are perched hundreds of meters above the

Pacific Ocean. Twenty-six miles (42 km) south of Carmel, stop at **Pfeiffer Big Sur State Park,** which features 821 acres (333 ha) of redwood forest on the **Big Sur River.** Enjoy camping, hiking on wilderness trails, and swimming and fishing in the rivers and at the ocean beaches.

ATTRACTIONS

Hearst San Simeon Historical Monument (Hearst Castle), 750 Hearst Castle Rd., San Simeon, (619) 452-1950, (800) 444-7275, tours daily 8:20-3 (later in summer), $14 adults, $8 children, advance reservations recommended. **Mission San Luis Obispo de Tolosa,** 782 Monterey St., San Luis Obispo, (805) 543-6850, open daily 9-5, donation suggested. **Morro Bay Museum of Natural History,** Morro Bay State Park, State Park Rd., Morro Bay, (805) 772-2694, open daily 10-5. Pfeiffer Big Sur State Park, (408) 667-2315. **Pismo Dunes State Vehicular Recreation Area,** 3 miles south of Pismo Beach, (805) 473-7220.

RESTAURANTS $=under $10, $$=$10 to $20, $$$=over $20

CAMBRIA

Brambles
4005 Burton Dr.
(805) 927-4716
Steaks, seafood $$-$$$

Hamlet at Moonstone Gardens
Highway 1, five miles S.
of Hearst Castle
(805) 927-3535
American-Continental cuisine $$

Sea Chest Oyster Bar
6216 Moonstone Beach Dr.
(805) 927-4514
Seafood $$

Sow's Ear
2248 Main St.
(805) 927-4865
American specialties $$

MORRO BAY

Hoppe's at 901
901 Embarcadero
(805) 772-9012
French gourmet $$$

Inn at Morro Bay
Dining Room
Morro Bay State Park
(805) 772-5651
California-French cuisine $$

MOSS BEACH

Moss Beach Distillery
Beach and Ocean
(415) 728-5595
Steaks, seafood, pasta $$

SAN LUIS OBISPO

Benvenuti
450 Marsh St.
(805) 541-5393
Italian cuisine $$

Cafe Roma
1819 Osos St.
(805) 541-6800
Northern Italian cuisine $$

Rhythm Cafe
1040 Broad
(805) 541-4048
Thai cuisine $$

Sebastian's
Mission Plaza
Chorro and Monterey
(805) 544-5550
Continental cuisine $$

Tavola
1037 Monterey
(805) 545-8000
Italian cuisine $$

Arciero Winery
5625 Highway 46 E.
Paso Robles, CA 93447
(805) 239-2562
Open: daily 10-5

Baron Vineyards
1985 Penman Springs Road
Paso Robles, CA 93446
(805) 239-3313
Open: daily 11-5

Castoro Cellars
1480 N. Bethel Road
Templeton, CA 93465
(805) 238-0725
Open: daily 11-5

Corbett Canyon Vineyards
2195 Corbett Canyon Road
Arroyo Grande, CA 93420
(805) 544-5800
Open: Mon. thru Fri. 10-4:30,
Sat.+ Sun. 10-5

Eberle Winery
Highway 46 East
Paso Robles, CA 93446
(805) 238-9607
Open: summer, daily 10-6,
winter, daily 10-5

Edna Valley Vineyard
2585 Biddle Ranch Road
San Luis Obispo, CA 93401
(805) 544-9594
Open: daily 10-4

Harmony Cellars
#10 Old Creamery Road
Harmony, CA 93435
(805) 927-1625
Open: daily 10-5

Maison Deutz Winery
453 Deutz Drive
Arroyo Grande, CA 93003
(805) 481-1763
Open: Wed. thru Mon. 11-5

Meridian Vineyards
7000 Highway 46 E.
Paso Robles, CA 93446
(805) 237-6000
Open: Thurs. thru Mon. 10-5

Mission View Vineyards & Winery
13350 N. River Road
San Miguel, CA 93451
(805) 467-3104
Open: daily 11-5

Pesenti Winery
2900 Vineyard Drive
Templeton, CA 93465
(805) 434-1030
Open: Mon. thru Sat. 8-5:30,
Sun. 9-5:30

Talley Vineyards
3031 Lopez Drive
Arroyo Grande, CA 93420
(805) 489-0446
Open: daily 11-5

York Mountain Winery
York Mountain Road West
Templeton, CA 93465
(805) 238-3925
Open: daily 10-5

Zaca Mesa Winery
6905 Foxen Canyon Road
Los Olivos, CA 93441
(805) 688-3310
Open: daily 10-4

THE BEACH HOUSE
CAMBRIA 280

6360 Moonstone Beach Dr.
Cambria, CA 93428
Tel:1-805-927-3136

A home away from home, this beautiful inn is located in a quaint artists' colony. A full breakfast and wine tasting are served in a large comfortable living room with walls of glass and a deck that offer stunning ocean views.

5 ROOMS, 5 pb   2 COTTAGES, 2 pb

$120-150   OPEN: ALL YEAR   HOSTS: Penny Hitch & Kernn MacKinnon

THE BLUE WHALE INN
CAMBRIA 281

6736 Moonstone Beach Dr.
Cambria, CA 93428
Tel:1-805-927-4647

This inn is located six miles south of Hearst Castle on scenic Moonstone Beach Drive. Exquisite minisuites feature custom wall coverings, cozy fireplaces, private entrances, and canopied beds draped with a collection of French and English country fabrics.

6 ROOMS, 6 pb

$135-165   OPEN: ALL YEAR   HOSTS: Fred, Nancy & John

GARDEN STREET INN
SAN LUIS OBISPO 282

1212 Garden St.
San Luis Obispo, CA 93401
Tel:1-805-545-9802

The grace and simplicity of yesteryear prevail at this 1887 Italianate/Queen Anne home, restored and filled with antiques by your hosts. The inn is located one block from a 1772 mission and the old-fashioned downtown of one of California's most picturesque communities.

9 ROOMS, 9 pb   4 SUITES, 4 pb

$90-160   SPA   OPEN: ALL YEAR   HOSTS: Kathy & Dan Smith

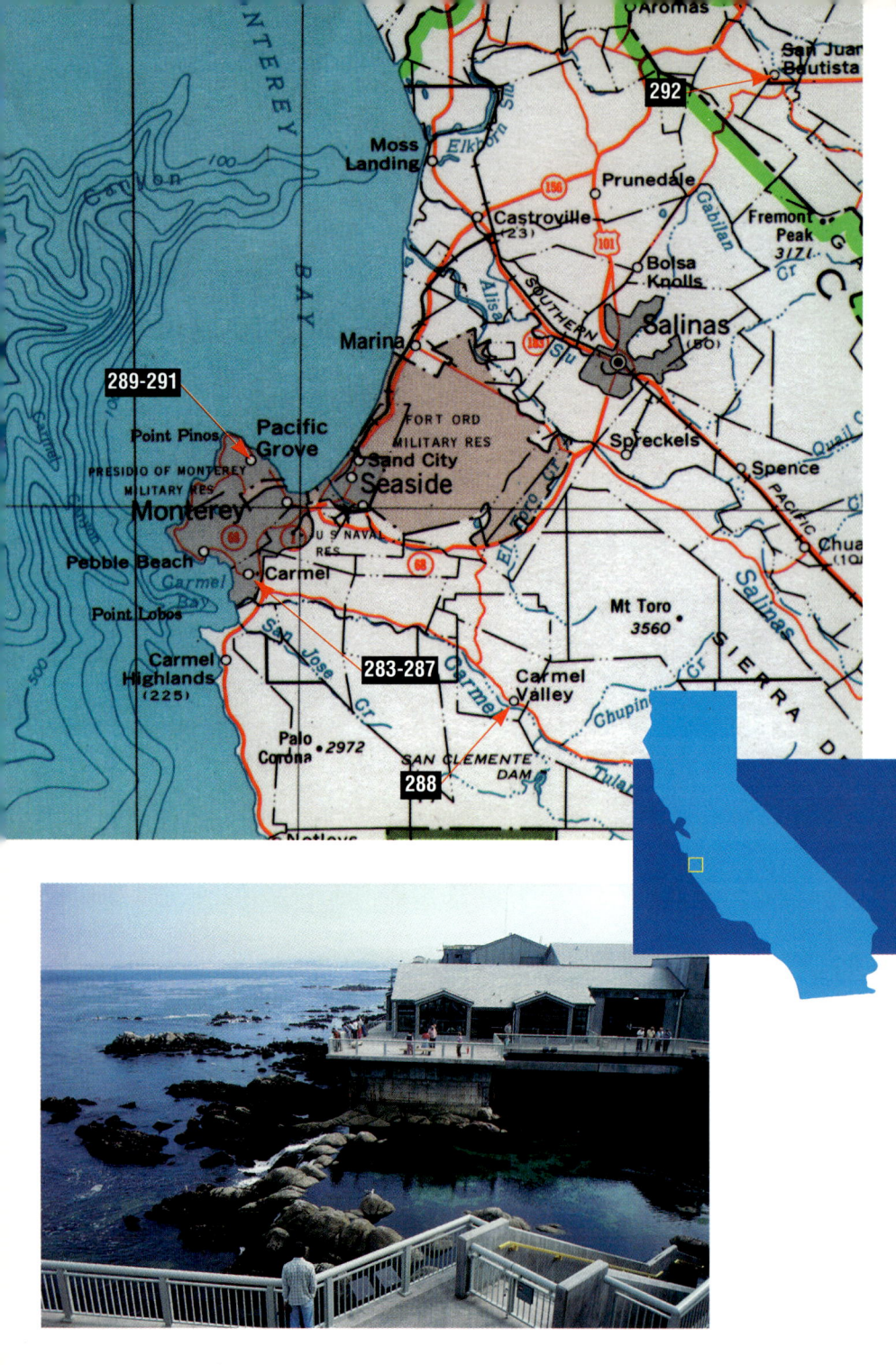

MONTEREY
PENINSULA & CARMEL

Eerily warped cypresses, surf crashing against the jagged rock formations, pristine beaches, uniquely exquisite mansions, old adobe homes, and acres of inspirational golf courses attract over three million visitors to the **Monterey Peninsula** each year. Even the early morning and late afternoon fog casts an inviting spell over the waters. These elements, combined with the historically rich sites that dot the region, have been celebrated by writers and artists for more than a century. Robert Louis Stevenson in 1879 called the peninsula "a spectacle of ocean greatness." He had his reasons.

Begin your journey at the **Point Lobos State Reserve,** located at the southern end of the Monterey Peninsula on Carmel Bay. Hike on the trails that wind through 1,276 acres (517 ha) of cypress trees, in some parts sheltering hidden emerald coves, perfect for scuba diving.

Go ahead—make your day...by

visiting the quaint village of **Carmel,** just north of the state reserve. With over seventy art galleries, numerous boutiques, and a smorgasbord of restaurants, the town hosts swarms of visitors each year. Despite the crowds, Carmel still exudes a charm (albeit attached to a dollar sign) that is well worth a visit. Whether you're good, bad, or ugly, be sure to eat at the **Hog's Breath Inn** (San Carlos St. and 5th Ave., 408/624-0444), owned by former Carmel mayor and movie star Clint Eastwood.

At the edge of town stands a beautifully restored reminder of California's Spanish heritage: **Mission San Carlos Borremeo del Rio.** Founded in 1770, the mission was headed by Father Junipero Serra and served as the headquarters for all twenty-one of the missions in California. In 1987 Pope John Paul II made a special visit to this mission.

Just north of Carmel, the **17-Mile Drive** is the next highlight of your tour. Though many people question the $6 per car charge to enter, just pay it. You won't regret it as you marvel at some of the most spectacular seascapes in the world. Distractions include six world-class golf courses, luxurious Pebble Beach resorts, splendid estates, towering pine trees, and gnarled cypresses, including the intriguing and dramatic **Lone Cypress,** which grows on a rocky outcropping above the crashing waves.

The northern gate of this scenic drive brings you to **Pacific Grove,** otherwise known as "Butterfly Town USA," thanks to the yearly mass migration of orange and black monarch butterflies from Canada and the Pacific Northwest. Bordered by a gorgeous 3-mile stretch of tidepools and rocky beaches, Pacific Grove was originally founded as a religious retreat in 1875. It now proudly features elaborate Victorian homes and lovely parks.

Monterey, on the northern end of the peninsula, is next on the itinerary. Settled thousands of years ago by the Esselen and Ohlone Indians, **Monterey Bay** was first sighted by a European in 1542. This man was Juan Rodriguez Cabrillo, a Portuguese explorer representing Spain. In 1602, the bay was named by Sebastian Vizcaino after the Viceroy of Mexico. But it was not until the Fransiscan friar Junipero Serra and Captain Gaspar de Portola arrived from Mexico in 1769 that Monterey was finally settled by Spain. Monterey became one of California's first and most successful settlements, and was the Spanish capital of upper California until the American flag was raised in 1846.

Monterey's Mexican past is apparent in its dozen or so wonderfully preserved adobe houses. For a complete look at these historic structures, which include the Stevenson House and the Custom House, enter the **Monterey State Historic Park.** The **Custom House,** located across from the entrance of Fisherman's Wharf, is perhaps the best of these structures, and also makes a good embarkation point for your city tour. The oldest government building in California, it was built under Mexican rule. This is the site where Commodore John Drake Sloat officially raised the United States Flag in 1846, putting California under the rule of the American government.

Our next stop is bustling **Fisherman's Wharf,** which has been the center of activity since Monterey's beginnings. Originally the wharf was the focal point for the whaling, sardine, and trading industries. Today seafood restaurants, specialty shops, and of course fish markets line the pier. If you follow your ears, you will often find playful sea lions frolicking and raising a ruckus in the water.

Made famous by author John Steinbeck, **Cannery Row** once supported a booming sardine industry. Between 1921 and 1948, sixteen canneries packed a quarter of a million tons of sardines a year. The boom stopped suddenly in 1948, when the sardines disappeared for reasons that are still unclear. These days the "Row" has replaced its sardines with tourists, and is a hatching ground for souvenir and specialty shops, restaurants, and art galleries. Perhaps the most exciting attraction in this area is the 216,000-square-foot (20,164 sq m) **Monterey Bay Aquarium,** which explores the fascinating sea life of one of the richest marine resources in the world: the Monterey Bay. Twice as deep as the Grand Canyon, the bay provides the aquarium with over 6,500 sea creatures, big and small, common and bizarre.

John Steinbeck fans should visit **Salinas,** half an hour inland from Monterey off Highway 68. Paying tribute to the literary legend who was born in this Victorian frame home, the **Steinbeck House,** run by volunteers from the Valley Guild, is now a great lunch spot featuring fresh regional fare. You may also want to visit the **Steinbeck Library,** which displays, astonishingly enough, Steinbeck relics and memorabilia.

ATTRACTIONS

The Custom House, 1 Custom House Plaza, Monterey, (408) 649-7118, open daily 10-4, Mar.-Oct. 10-5, free admission. **Fisherman's Wharf,** 885 Abrego St., Monterey, (408) 373-3720. **Mission San Carlos Borremeo del Rio** (Carmel Mission), Rio Rd. and Lasuen Dr., Carmel, (408) 624-3600, open Mon.-Sat. 9:30-4:30, Sun. 10:30-4:30, donations suggested. **Monterey Bay Aquarium,** 886 Cannery Row, Monterey, (408) 649-6466, open daily 10-6, $10.50 adults, $7.75 seniors, $4.75 children 3-12. **Monterey Peninsula Chamber of Commerce and Visitors and Convention Bureau,** 380 Alvarado St., Monterey, (408) 649-1770, open 8:30-5. **Monterey State Historic Park,** 525 Polk St., Monterey, (408) 649-7118, hours and days open vary. **Point Lobos State Reserve,** Highway 1, Carmel, (408) 624-4909, or (800) 444-7275 for scuba diving, open daily May-Sept. 9-7; Oct.-Apr. 9-5, $6 per car, seniors $5 per car. **Steinbeck House** (restaurant), 132 Central Ave., Salinas, (408) 424-2735, open weekdays for two sittings at 11:45 A.M. and 1:15 P.M., reservations required. **Steinbeck Library,** 110 W. San Luis, Salinas, (408) 758-7311, open Mon.-Thurs. 10-9, Fri.-Sat. 10-6, admission free. **17-Mile Drive,** off Lighthouse Ave. in Pacific Grove, and off Hwy. 1 and North San Antonio Ave. in Carmel, open 8:30-4, $6 per car.

CARMEL

Anton & Michel
Mission between Ocean
and Seventh Aves.
(408) 624-2406
Continental cuisine $$$

Bon Apetit
7 Delfino Place
(408) 659-3559
Seafood $$-$$$

Giuliano's Ristorante
at Mission and Fifth Sts.
(408) 625-5231
Northern Italian cuisine $$

The Ridge Restaurant
200 Puenta Del Monte
(408) 659-0170
California cuisine $$$

Thai Bistro
55 West Carmel Valley Rd.
(408) 659-5900
Thai cuisine, French pastries $-$$

MONTEREY

Café Fina
In Fisherman's Wharf
(408) 372-5200
Seafood, pasta $$$

Fresh Cream
In Heritage Harbor
99 Pacific St.
(408) 375-9798
French cuisine $$$

PACIFIC GROVE

The Old Bath House
620 Ocean View Blvd.
(408) 375-5195
French-Continental cuisine $$-$$$

WINERIES

Chateau Julien Winery
8940 Carmel Valley Road
Carmel, CA 93923
(408) 624-2600
Open: Sat.+ Sun. 11-5
Mon. thru Fri. 8:30-5

Jekel Vineyards
40155 Walnut Ave.
Greenfield, CA 93927
(408) 674-5522
Open: daily 10-5

Monterey Peninsula Winery
786 Wave St.
Monterey, CA 93940
(408) 372-4949
Open: daily 12-5

The Monterey Vineyard
800 S. Alta St.
Gonzales, CA 93926
(408) 675-2316
Open: daily 10-5

Smith and Hook
37700 Foothill Road
Soledad, CA 93960
(408) 678-2132
Open: daily 11-4

MONTE VERDE INN

P.O. Box 394
Monte Verde & Ocean Ave.
Carmel, CA 93921
Tel:1-408-624-6046

R

What was once a charming residence is now a beautiful inn. When you're not enjoying the balconies and gardens, take a walk to Carmel's shops or white sandy beach. The friendly staff will help you in any way they can.

7 ROOMS, 6 pb   3 SUITES, 3 pb

$95-155   OPEN: ALL YEAR   HOSTS: Wendy & Peter Aylaian

SANDPIPER INN-AT-THE-BEACH

Bayview Ave. at Martin Way
Carmel, CA 93923
Tel:1-408-624-6433

R

Listen to the surf and enjoy the view of Carmel's magnificent white beach. This inn features delightful guest rooms and cottages, individually furnished with country antiques and fresh flowers. Quiet comfort and luxury make the Sandpiper Inn a great place for anniversaries and special occasions.

16 ROOMS, 16 pb

$95-185   OPEN: ALL YEAR   HOSTS: Irene & Graeme MacKenzie

THE STONEHOUSE INN

8th Street below Monte Verde
Carmel, CA 93921
Tel:1-408-624-4569

A complete stone exterior surrounds this luxurious country house. Lounge by the living room's large stone fireplace or on the glass-enclosed front porch. Carmel's beach is within walking distance, and Point Lobos State Park is only two miles away.

6 ROOMS, 0 pb

$95-125   OPEN: ALL YEAR   HOST: Barbara Cooke

286 CARMEL

SEAVIEW INN
P.O. Box 4138
Camino Real bet. 11th & 12th
Carmel, CA 93921
Tel:1-408-624-8778

This 1905 country Victorian is one of Carmel's oldest and finest inns. Guests enjoy breakfast and sherry by the fire in the cozy living and dining rooms. The friendly and knowledgeable hosts offer the utmost in personal attention and comfort. Guest rooms are beautifully decorated with antiques and country furnishings, featuring canopied and four-poster beds. The quaint shops and restaurants of downtown are within easy walking distance.

HOSTS: Diane & Marshall Hydorn

8 ROOMS, 6 pb

OPEN: ALL YEAR

$80-120

287 CARMEL

SUNSET HOUSE
P.O. Box 1925
Camino Real & Ocean
Carmel, CA 93921
Tel:1-408-624-4884

This romantic inn on a quiet residential street in the heart of Carmel is close to shops, restaurants, galleries, and the beach. Each room is uniquely decorated and has a wood-burning fireplace and a scenic view. Listen to the sound of the surf from your room. Wake up to a delicious breakfast, brought to your room, so that you may enjoy the glow of the fire and the beauty of the view.

HOSTS: Camille & Dennis Fike

3 ROOMS, 3 pb

OPEN: ALL YEAR

$110-135

THE VALLEY LODGE
8 Ford Rd., P.O. Box 93
Carmel Valley, CA 93924

Tel:1-800-641-4646
or 1-408-659-2261

This quiet country inn is located on three beautifully land-scaped acres in picturesque Carmel Valley, the sunbelt of the Monterey Peninsula. Relax in a garden patio room, a fire-place suite, or a cozy one- or two-bedroom fireplace cottage with kitchen. Enjoy the heated pool, hot spa, sauna, and fitness and game area. Walk to fine restaurants and quaint shops in the Carmel Valley Village, or just sit and "listen to your beard grow."

HOSTS: Sherry & Peter Coakley

POOL

14 ROOMS, 14 pb   5 SUITES, 5 pb   12 COTTAGE, 12 pb

$95-250   SPA   OPEN: ALL YEAR

MARTINE INN
255 Ocean View Blvd.
Pacific Grove, CA 93950

Tel:1-800-852-5588

You can watch whales, sea otters, sailboat races, and the fishing fleet from the two sitting rooms of this Pacific Grove inn, whose nineteen rooms are elegantly furnished with antiques. Some rooms have views of the ocean; some have wood-burning fireplaces. When twilight falls, enjoy wine and hors d'oeuvres in the parlor with your hosts. The inn is conveniently located four blocks from the Monterey Bay Aquarium and Cannery Row.

HOSTS: Tracy, Theresa and Tom

19 ROOMS, 19 pb   3 SUITES, 3 pb

$115-225   SPA   OPEN: ALL YEAR

289 | PACIFIC GROVE

HOSTS: Barbara & Don Foster

OLD ST. ANGELA INN
321 Central
Pacific Grove, CA 93950
Tel:1-408-372-3246

Originally a convent, this Cape Cod-style inn is decorated with country pine furniture. Enjoy breakfast in the glass and redwood solarium and share afternoon wine, tea, or sherry with the other guests by the fireplace. Walk to beaches, parks, and museums.

9 ROOMS, 6 pb

OPEN: ALL YEAR $90-150

291 | PACIFIC GROVE

HOSTS: The Flatley Family & Staff

SEVEN GABLES INN
555 Ocean View Blvd.
Pacific Grove, CA 93950
Tel:1-408-372-4341   **R**

A spectacular rocky-point setting offers unsurpassed views of Monterey Bay and coastal mountains from every room. This landmark Victorian mansion is elegantly furnished with fine European antiques. Your hosts will endeavor to make your holiday a memorable one.

13 ROOMS, 13 pb   1 COTTAGE, pb

OPEN: ALL YEAR $95-185

292 | SAN JUAN BATISTA

HOSTS: Jeanne & Todd Cleave

B&B SAN JUAN
P.O. Box 613
315 The Alameda
San Juan Batista, CA 95045
Tel:1-408-623-4101

This charming 125-year-old Gothic Revival house on the National Register of Historic Places features cheerful and tastefully restored rooms. Enjoy friendly hospitality and Paraguayan harp music. Near Luis Valdez Teatro Campesino, San Juan Bautista State Park, and Mission San Juan Bautista.

5 ROOMS, 0 pb

OPEN: ALL YEAR $65-70

PETER RABBIT
& FRIENDS

THE
VIENNESE
SHOP
handmade dresses

AUGUSTINA

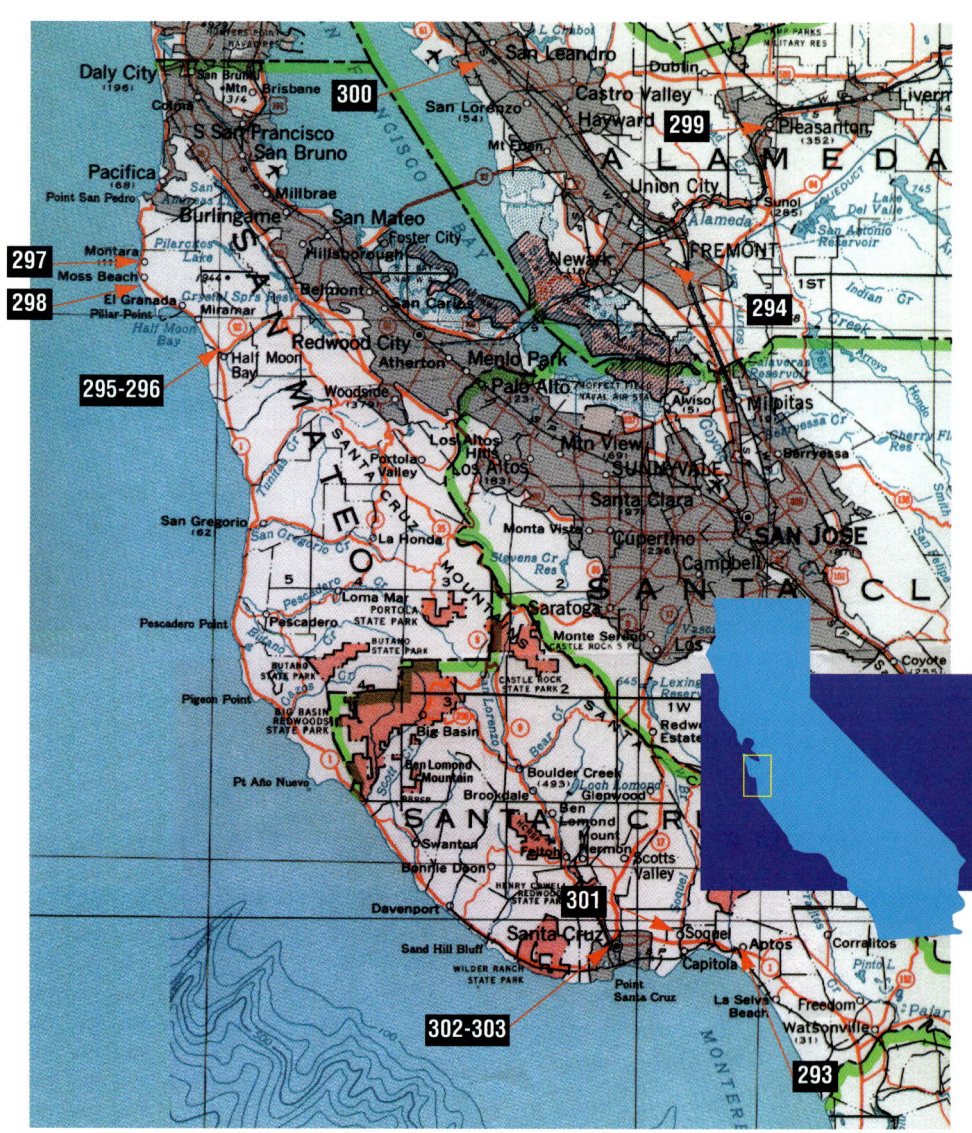

SANTA CRUZ
& SOUTH BAY COUNTIES

Rugged natural beauty, cultural and outdoor activities for everyone, and Hispanic history in Santa Cruz and South Bay counties offer nonstop entertainment for even the most energetic traveller.

Off Highway 1 just south of Santa Cruz, a few miles inland from the coast, is **Watsonville.** This farming community was founded in 1852 by Judge John H. Watson, who purchased the land from the Rodriguez family, owners of a large ranch that occupied most of the area. The **Pajaro River** runs through the town and the surrounding farmlands, supporting apples, strawberries, and colorful flowers.

Seven miles (11 km) north of Watsonville you will find the charming little resort towns of **Aptos** and **Capitola.** At the end of the last century they were part of a large rancho owned by Don Rafael Castro. The rancho was purchased by Claus Spreckels, founder of California's first sugar industry, who built a magnificent mansion that included a private race track. Today Aptos and Capitola offer a variety of shops, art galleries, and restaurants adjacent to a beautiful beach. As you drive north to Santa Cruz, you will pass through peaceful residential communities with elegant homes overlooking the ocean.

Santa Cruz was founded by the Franciscan monks when they built one of their twenty-one California missions there in 1791. This particular mission was named Mission la Exaltacion de la Santa Cruz. Santa Cruz is a large, bustling business center as well as a festive resort town that attracts all types of people, from the tie-dye clad to the business-tie crowd. As in many beach towns, "relaxed" is the first word that comes to mind here. Averaging 300 sunny days a year, Santa Cruz has a colorful boardwalk complete with an amusement park that features a Ferris wheel and a roller coaster. There is also a fishing pier with excellent seafood restaurants. Enjoy a window seat and watch the boats go by, or sit on the boardwalk and watch the people go by. Unfortunately the historical downtown area was almost completely destroyed in 1989 by the Loma Prieta earthquake and is slowly being rebuilt. However, you can still find excellent shops and restaurants.

Santa Cruz is home to the **University of California at Santa Cruz,** located on a spectacular 2,000-acre (810 ha) forested hilltop overlooking the town of Santa Cruz and Monterey Bay. If you have a chance, visit the student union building, which resembles a giant treehouse.

If you like tidepools, be sure to visit the **Natural Bridges State Park.** During the winter months you will see abundant marine life as well as the world's largest habitat for migrating monarch butterflies.

Visit the town of **Felton** and ride an old steam train owned by the **Roaring Camp and Big Trees Railroad.** It will take you on a 6-mile (10 km) journey through the forests of the Santa Cruz mountains. **Big Basin Redwoods State Park** occupies almost 16,000 acres (6,480 ha) and has some redwood trees that have grown to the impressive height of over 300 feet (92 m).

The 70-mile (113 km) drive along Highway 1 from Santa Cruz to San Francisco is one of the most beautiful coastal journeys in California. This scenic drive takes you past colorful vegetable stands on your right and imposing cliffs and beautiful state beaches on your left. You probably won't find bikinis or beach volleyball here as you would on the beaches of Southern California—you might not even find the sun. Fog often settles on the coast in the morning; sometimes it clears up by the afternoon and sometimes it doesn't. Although the fog makes the water very cold, it redeems itself by bringing a beautifully mystical quality to these beaches. Twenty miles (32 km) north of Santa Cruz is the **Ano Nuevo State Reserve,** the breeding area for several thousand elephant seals between December and April of each year.

As you head north along Highway 1 you will pass several delightful small sandy beaches. Many offer great surfing opportunities, as well as numerous picnic and viewing areas. Then pass through **Davenport,** which was founded in the 1850s by Captain John P. Davenport, a whaling man. There are fine accommodations, dining, and an art gallery.

A fifteen-minute drive north brings

you into sight of **Pigeon Point Lighthouse** built in 1872. It is adjacent to the charming old fishing village of Pescadero, once known as the whitest town in the state due to a shipwrecked cargo of white paint that washed ashore near Pigeon Point and was lavishly used by the inhabitants.

A thirty-minute drive north brings you to the town of **Half Moon Bay.** This picturesque little town boasts several inns, restaurants, and art galleries, and is surrounded by farmlands planted with artichokes, brussels sprouts, and world-class pumpkins. In late October the town hosts a pumpkin festival. Half Moon Bay itself has many excellent swimming beaches and is also popular for fishing and whale-watching cruises. Several villages and artists' colonies are located around this long, gently curving bay, including **Miramar, El Granada, Princeton-by-the-Sea,** and **Moss Beach,** each of which offers its own unique flavor. Be sure to visit **Montara,** which has one of the prettiest beaches in the area.

A small mountain range that runs parallel to Highway 1 all the way from Santa Cruz to San Francisco separates the coastal region from the interior counties and towns known as the **Peninsula.** This long finger of land is bounded on the eastern side by the South Bay, an extension of the San Francisco Bay; the northern tip of this peninsula is the city of San Francisco. The Peninsula encompasses some of the wealthiest towns in the San Francisco Bay Area. **Stanford University** is located here in the city of **Palo Alto,** near **Silicon Valley,** computer capital of the world. **Los Gatos** and **Los Altos** are pleasant, affluent towns that are well worth visiting. Nearby **Woodside** is the home of the **Filoli Estate.** This forty-five-room mansion with spectacular gardens, designed by Willis Polk and built in 1916, is open to the public. Everyone can enjoy a tour of this beautiful residence, but "Dynasty" fans will enjoy it the most—the estate was used as the home of the Carrington family in the once-popular TV series. While you are in Woodside, be sure to explore the forested **Huddart Park** and take advantage of the numerous hiking trails.

North of Woodside, and 15 miles (24 km) south of San Francisco on Highway 280, is the **Crystal Springs Reservoir,** which provides water to the Bay Area. To get a closer look, leave the freeway at Black Mountain Road and take Skyline Drive (Route 35) south. One of the most beautiful sights on the Peninsula is the evening fog creeping over the hills west of the reservoir. You can't get close to the water for sanitation reasons, but you can walk, jog, or bike on the paved, 12-mile (19 km) **Sawyer Camp Trail,** which runs beside the reservoir.

Taking Highway 101 on the east side of the Peninsula to San Francisco is not as scenic as Route 1 or Interstate 280, but it is quicker. Close to San Francisco International Airport is **Coyote Point Park,** which features an environmental museum and a live animal exhibit that includes birds, reptiles, and mammals native to the Bay Area. After you have communed with the bobcats and badgers, enjoy the park's hiking and cycling trails, picnic grounds, and public golf course. The bayside park also features swimming, fishing, windsurfing, and jet-skiing areas.

Continuing on Highway 101 south brings you to **Great America** theme park in Santa Clara. This 100-acre (41 ha) park that brings back the spirit of old America features thirty-one rides, shows, special attractions, a cinema with the world's largest motion-picture screen, arcades, games and lots more to keep you amused for hours.

If you want to get away from the fog, travel east across one of the three bay bridges to the East Bay. There you can explore a variety of towns such as **San Leandro, Fremont,** and **Pleasanton.**

ATTRACTIONS

SANTA CRUZ

Natural Bridges State Beach, on West Cliff Dr. on Highway 1, (408) 423-4609. **Santa Cruz Beach Boardwalk,** 400 Beach St., off Hwys. 17 and 1, (408) 423-5590, open daily in summer, weekends in spring and fall 11-9, free admission, unlimited rides $16.95. **Santa Cruz Mission,** 126 High St., (408) 426-5686, open daily 9-5, donations requested. **University of California at Santa Cruz,** to reach main entrance, take Hwy. 1 to Bay St., (408) 459-0111.

SOUTH BAY

Ano Nuevo State Reserve, 20 miles north of Santa Cruz border, (415) 879-0227 or (415) 879-0595. **Big Basin Redwoods State Park,** 20 miles north of Santa Cruz via Hwys. 9 and 236, (408) 338-6132. **Coyote Point Park,** Coyote Point, San Mateo, (415) 342-7755, open Tues.-Sat. 10-5, Sun. 12-5, $3 adults, $2 seniors, $1 children 6-17, children under 6 free, $4 car fee at recreation area. **Filoli Estate,** Cañada Rd., Woodside, (415) 366-4640, open Tues.-Sat., call for tour schedule, $8 admission. **Great America Theme Park,** 45 miles south of San Francisco off Hwy. 101 at Great America exit, Santa Clara, (408) 988-1800, open during Easter week vacation and daily in summer 10-9, open weekends during spring and fall 10-9, $23.95 adults, $16.95 seniors, $11.95 children 3-6. **Roaring Camp/Big Trees Narrow-Gauge Railroad,** 70 miles south of San Francisco in the Santa Cruz Mountains, Felton, (408) 335-4484, trains leave Wed.-Sun. from noon, trains leave daily in summer, call for departure schedule, $11.50 adults, $8.50 children 3-15.

MOSS BEACH
The Moss Beach Distillery
Corner of Beach Way and Ocean
Blvd.
(415) 726-3425
Seafood, steaks, ribs $$-$$$
Pasta Moon
315 Main St.
(415) 726-5125
Italian cuisine $-$$
The San Benito House
356 Main St.
(415) 726-3425
Eclectic gourmet cuisine $-$$

SANTA CRUZ
Casa Blanca
101 Main St.
(408) 426-9063
California-Continental cuisine $$
The Crow's Nest
2218 E. Cliff Dr.
(at the yacht harbor)
(408) 476-4560
Seafood/Vegetarian $-$$$
India Joze
1001 Center St.
(408) 427-3554
Indian cuisine $$

CAPITOLA
Shadow Brook
1750 Wharf Rd.
(408) 475-1511
California-Continental cuisine
$$-$$$

Bargetto Winery
3535 N. Main St.
Soquel, CA 95073
(408) 475-2258
Open: Mon. thru Sat. 10-5

Bonny Doon Vineyard
10 Pine Flat Road
Santa Cruz, CA 95060
(408) 425-3625
Open: Wed. thru Mon. 12-5

Devlin Wine Cellars
3801 Park Ave.
Soquel, CA 95073
(408) 476-7288
Open: Sat.+ Sun. 12-5

Emilio Guglielmo Winery
1480 E. Main Ave.
Morgan Hill, CA 95037
(408) 779-2145
Open: Sat.+ Sun. 10-5
Mon. thru Fri. 9-5

Fortino Winery
4525 Hecker Pass Highway
Gilroy, CA 95020
(408) 842-3305
Open: daily 9-6

Hallcrest Vineyards
379 Felton Empire Road
Felton, CA 95018
(408) 335-4441
Open: daily 11-5:30

Thomas Kruse Winery
4390 Hecker Pass Road
Gilroy, CA 95020
(408) 842-7016
Open: daily 12-5

J. Lohr Winery
1000 Lenzen Ave.
San Jose, CA 95126
(408) 288-5057
Open: daily 10-5

Mirassou Champagne Cellars
300 College Ave.
Los Gatos, CA 95032
(408) 395-3790
Open: daily 12-5

Mirassou Winery
3000 Aborn Road
San Jose, CA 95135
(408) 274-4000
Open: Mon. thru Sat. 10-5,
Sun. 12-4

Obester Winery
12341 San Mateo Road
(Highway 92)
Half Moon Bay, CA 94019
(415) 726-9463
Open: daily 10-5

Ridge Vineyards
17100 Monte Bello Road
Cupertino, CA 95014
(408) 867-3233
Open: Sat.+ Sun. 11-3

Rapazzini Winery
4350 Highway 101
Gilroy, CA 95020
(408) 842-5649
Open: daily 9-6

Rapazzini Winery/Garlic Shoppe
4310 Highway 101
Gilroy, CA 95021
(408) 848-3646
Open: daily 9-7

Roudon-Smith Vineyards
2364 Bean Creek Road
Santa Cruz, CA 95066
(408) 438-1244
Open: Sat.+ Sun. 10-4

Storrs Winery
Old Sashmill, 303 Potrero St., #35
Santa Cruz, CA 95060
(408) 458-5030
Open: Fri. thru Mon. 12-5

Sunrise Winery
13100 Montebello Road
Cupertino, CA 95014
(408) 741-1310
Open: Fri. thru Sun. 11-3

Sycamore Creek Vineyards
12775 Uvas Road
Morgan Hill, CA 95037
(408) 779-4738
Open: Sat.+ Sun. 11:30-5

Windsor Vineyards
Tiburon Tasting Room
72 Main St., Tiburon, CA 94920
(415) 435-3113
Open: Fri.+ Sat. 10-7
Sun. thru Thurs. 10-6

MANGELS HOUSE
APTOS **293**

P.O. Box 302
570 Aptos Creek Rd.
Aptos, CA 95001
Tel:1-408-688-7982

R

Experience the beauty of a European country house. This Italianate Victorian is situated on four acres of lawn and orchard, less than a mile from the beach. Behind the inn is a 10,000-acre redwood park. Relax and forget the city.

6 ROOMS, 6 pb

$98-120

OPEN: ALL YEAR   HOST: Jacqueline Fisher

LORD BRADLEY'S INN
FREMONT **294**

43344 Mission Blvd.
Fremont, CA 94539
Tel:1-510-490-0520

R

All your needs are met in the tradition accorded royalty at Lord Bradley's Inn. The comfortable rooms feature Victorian-style furnishings. A common room and English garden patio offer relaxing retreats. See San Francisco, hike on Mission Peak, and visit Mission San Jose.

8 ROOMS, 8 pb

$65-75

OPEN: ALL YEAR   HOSTS: Anne & Keith Medeiros

CYPRESS INN
HALF MOON BAY **295**

407 Mirada Rd.
Half Moon Bay, CA 94019
CA only Tel:1-800-83-BEACH
1-415-726-6002

R

Enjoy ocean views, massages, great breakfasts, and personal attention in the Cypress Inn. Traditional Mexican folk art, terra cotta floors, and authentic Southwest furniture add atmosphere with an ethnic flavor. Each room has its own color scheme and character.

8 ROOMS, 8 pb

$129-275   SPA OPEN: ALL YEAR   HOST: Cindy Granados

296 HALF MOON BAY

HOST: Anne & Simon Lowings

ZABALLA HOUSE
324 Main St.
Half Moon Bay, CA 94019
Tel:1-415-726-9123

Built in 1859, the Zaballa House is the oldest house in Half Moon Bay. Rooms have garden views and fireplaces, and some have double whirlpool-spas. Walk to shops, fine restaurants, and the beach. Easy drive to San Francisco International Airport and Elephant Seal Reserve.

9 ROOMS, 9 pb

OPEN: ALL YEAR $65-150

297 MONTARA

HOSTS: Emily & Raymond Hoche-Mong

GOOSE & TURRETS
P.O. Box 937
835 George St.
Montara, CA 94037-0937
Tel:1-415-728-5451

R

In a quiet garden half a mile from the beach, the Goose and Turrets offers comfortable beds, pretty rooms, four-course breakfasts, and afternoon tea with tasty treats. There is also a hammock and reading nook in which one can do nothing companionably. Nous parlons Français!

5 ROOMS, 5 pb

OPEN: ALL YEAR $90-105

298 MOSS BEACH

HOSTS: Karen & Richard Herbert

SEAL COVE INN
221 Cypress Ave.
Moss Beach, CA 94038
Tel:1-415-728-7325

Built to resemble an English country home, the Seal Cove Inn is very rich and traditional in its decor. Each of the guest rooms creates its own romantic haven, complete with wood-burning fireplaces. Rooms overlook wildflowers, cypress trees, and the ocean.

10 ROOMS, 10 pb

OPEN: ALL YEAR   SPA $170-250

PLUM TREE INN
262 West Angela St.
Pleasanton, CA 94566
Tel:1-510-426-9588

PLEASANTON 299

R

This impressive 1890s Victorian inn has cozy suites, each uniquely decorated with pine and oak furnishings, accented with antiques. One suite has a four-poster bed and french doors opening onto a veranda. Near beautiful picnic areas and wineries.

6 SUITES, 6 pb

$65-75

OPEN: ALL YEAR   HOSTS: Joan & Bob Cordtz

BEST HOUSE INN
1315 Clarke St.
San Leandro, CA 94577
Tel:1-510-351-0911

SAN LEANDRO 300

Originally the townhouse for a popular civic leader, this stately Victorian has guest rooms to suit every taste. Some feature marble fireplace facades and canopied beds. Conveniently located near public transportation. Oakland, Silicon Valley and San Francisco are easily accessible.

6 ROOMS, 6 pb

$75-85   SPA OPEN: ALL YEAR   HOSTS: Lori Anderson

BLUE SPRUCE INN
2815 South Main St.
Soquel, CA 95073
Tel:1-800-559-1137
or 1-408-464-1137

SOQUEL 301

This 1857 farm house features whirlpool-spas, fireplaces, quiet gardens, and original local art. Located near the north coast of Monterey Bay, it blends the leisurely flavor of yesteryear with the luxurious comforts of today. Professional personal attention is their hallmark.

6 ROOMS, 6 pb

$70-125   SPA OPEN: ALL YEAR   HOSTS: Pat & Tom O'Brien

302 SANTA CRUZ

HOST: Helen King

THE BABBLING BROOK
1025 Laurel
Santa Cruz, CA 95060
Tel:1-800-866-1131
or 1-408-427-2437

Cascading waterfalls, a historic waterwheel, a creek, and a romantic gazebo grace an acre of gardens, pines, and redwoods surrounding this secluded inn, built in 1909. A French country motif decorates the rooms, some of which have fireplaces, high-beam ceilings, whirlpool-spas, and private decks overlooking the garden. Superbly located, this inn is within walking distance of the beach, wharf, boardwalk, shops, running path, tennis courts, and historic homes.

12 ROOMS, 12 pb

OPEN: ALL YEAR

$85-160

303 SANTA CRUZ

HOSTS: Alice June & Franz Benjamin

CHATEAU VICTORIAN
118 First St.
Santa Cruz, CA 95060
Tel:1-408-458-9458

Built around the turn of the century, this wonderful inn offers Victorian-style guest rooms, each with a cozy fireplace. Breakfast is a treat with fresh fruit, juices, and croissants, while afternoon refreshments make an excellent prelude to dinner at one of the area's many fine restaurants. The inn is one block from the beach and near the world-famous Boardwalk, with its many shops and attractions.

7 ROOMS, 7 pb

OPEN: ALL YEAR

$105-135

BED & BREAKFAST INDEX

BED & BREAKFAST INDEX

BED & BREAKFAST INDEX

BED & BREAKFAST INDEX

TOWN & ATTRACTION INDEX

ILLUSTRATION INDEX

BOOK ORDER FORM   *Please photocopy*

Please photocopy this order form if you would like additional copies of **The Definitive California Bed & Breakfast Touring Guide.**

Please send me_____ copies of **The Definitive California Bed & Breakfast Touring Guide** at $15.95, plus $1.95 for shipping and handling of each book.

SEND TO:

Name _____

Address _____

City _____ State _____ Zip _____

I enclose my check or money order for $_____.

Please charge $_____ to my credit card.

MASTERCARD OR VISA ONLY

Name _____

Type of card _____

Card # _____

Expiration Date _____

Signature _____

MAIL THIS COMPLETED ORDER FORM TO :

TRAVEL PRINT INTERNATIONAL
P.O. BOX 1117
POINT REYES, CA 94956
(415) 459-3320

Please photocopy

Please fill out this subscription form if you would like to receive our complimentary newsletter. **The International Association of Innkeepers Newsletter** will give you interesting information about new inns, discount offers, and special events. You will also be eligible for introductory discounts on our other publications.

Please send me_____ copies of **The International Association of Innkeepers Newsletter.**

SEND TO:

Name

Address

City   State   Zip

MAIL THIS COMPLETED FORM TO :

TRAVEL PRINT INTERNATIONAL
P.O. BOX 1117
POINT REYES, CA 94956
(415) 459-3320

Bed & Breakfast
P.O. Box 420009
San Francisco, CA 94142

Please fold along dotted line

RESERVATION FORM *CAREFULLY REMOVE OR PHOTOCOPY*

GUEST NAME & ADDRESS

NAME

ADDRESS

HOME PHONE #

WORK PHONE #   FAX #

CREDIT CARD INFORMATION *VISA OR MASTERCARD ONLY*

TYPE OF CARD

CARD #

EXPIRATION DATE

SIGNATURE

PLEASE LIST THREE (3) BED AND BREAKFAST INNS IN ORDER OF PREFERENCE *CODE IS LOCATED IN THE CORNER ABOVE EACH INN*

BED & BREAKFAST INN #1

NAME

CODE #

YOUR DESIRED PRICE RANGE:
FROM $ TO $

BED & BREAKFAST INN #2

NAME

CODE #

YOUR DESIRED PRICE RANGE:
FROM $ TO $

BED & BREAKFAST INN #3

NAME

CODE #

YOUR DESIRED PRICE RANGE:
FROM $ TO $

RESERVATION INFORMATION: *PLEASE INDICATE YOUR ACCOMMODATION REQUIREMENTS BELOW*

ARRIVAL DATE:

OF NIGHTS REQ'D

OF ROOMS REQ'D

OF BEDS REQ'D   #____ ☐ DOUBLE   #____ ☐ TWIN

DEPARTURE DATE:

OF ADULTS IN YOUR GROUP

OF CHILDREN IN YOUR GROUP

INDICATE APPROX. ARRIVAL TIME (2 HOUR SPAN)

PRIVATE BATH IS ESSENTIAL?   ☐ YES   ☐ NO

SHARED BATH IS ACCEPTABLE?   ☐ YES   ☐ NO

IF YOU HAVE ANY SPECIAL REQUIREMENTS PLEASE INDICATE:

CANCELLATION POLICY: EACH INN HAS ITS OWN CANCELLATION POLICY. ALL CANCELLATIONS MUST BE MADE DIRECTLY WITH EACH INN.

Bed & Breakfast
P.O. Box 420009
San Francisco, CA 94142

- -

Please fold along dotted line

RESERVATION FORM *CAREFULLY REMOVE OR PHOTOCOPY*

GUEST NAME & ADDRESS

NAME

ADDRESS

HOME PHONE #

WORK PHONE #

FAX #

CREDIT CARD INFORMATION *VISA OR MASTERCARD ONLY*

TYPE OF CARD

CARD #

EXPIRATION DATE

SIGNATURE

PLEASE LIST THREE (3) BED AND BREAKFAST INNS IN ORDER OF PREFERENCE *CODE # IS LOCATED IN THE CORNER ABOVE EACH INN*

BED & BREAKFAST INN #1

NAME

CODE #

YOUR DESIRED PRICE RANGE:
FROM $ TO $

BED & BREAKFAST INN #2

NAME

CODE #

YOUR DESIRED PRICE RANGE:
FROM $ TO $

BED & BREAKFAST INN #3

NAME

CODE #

YOUR DESIRED PRICE RANGE:
FROM $ TO $

RESERVATION INFORMATION: *PLEASE INDICATE YOUR ACCOMMODATION REQUIREMENTS BELOW*

ARRIVAL DATE:

DEPARTURE DATE:

INDICATE APPROX. ARRIVAL TIME (2 HOUR SPAN)

OF NIGHTS REQ'D

OF ADULTS IN YOUR GROUP

OF ROOMS REQ'D

OF CHILDREN IN YOUR GROUP

PRIVATE BATH IS ESSENTIAL? ☐ YES ☐ NO

OF BEDS REQ'D   # ____ ☐ DOUBLE   # ____ ☐ TWIN

SHARED BATH IS ACCEPTABLE? ☐ YES ☐ NO

IF YOU HAVE ANY SPECIAL REQUIREMENTS PLEASE INDICATE:

CANCELLATION POLICY: EACH INN HAS ITS OWN CANCELLATION POLICY. ALL CANCELLATIONS MUST BE MADE DIRECTLY WITH EACH INN.

Place
Stamp
Here

Bed & Breakfast
P.O. Box 420009
San Francisco, CA 94142

Please fold along dotted line

RESERVATION FORM *CAREFULLY REMOVE OR PHOTOCOPY*

GUEST NAME & ADDRESS

NAME

ADDRESS

HOME PHONE #

WORK PHONE #

FAX #

CREDIT CARD INFORMATION *VISA OR MASTERCARD ONLY*

TYPE OF CARD

CARD #

EXPIRATION DATE

SIGNATURE

PLEASE LIST THREE (3) BED AND BREAKFAST INNS IN ORDER OF PREFERENCE *CODE # IS LOCATED IN THE CORNER ABOVE EACH INN*

BED & BREAKFAST INN #1

NAME

CODE #

YOUR DESIRED PRICE RANGE:
FROM $ TO $

BED & BREAKFAST INN #2

NAME

CODE #

YOUR DESIRED PRICE RANGE:
FROM $ TO $

BED & BREAKFAST INN #3

NAME

CODE #

YOUR DESIRED PRICE RANGE:
FROM $ TO $

RESERVATION INFORMATION: *PLEASE INDICATE YOUR ACCOMMODATION REQUIREMENTS BELOW*

ARRIVAL DATE:	DEPARTURE DATE:
# OF NIGHTS REQ'D	# OF ADULTS IN YOUR GROUP
# OF ROOMS REQ'D	# OF CHILDREN IN YOUR GROUP
# OF BEDS REQ'D #____ ☐ DOUBLE #____ ☐ TWIN	

INDICATE APPROX. ARRIVAL TIME (2 HOUR SPAN)

PRIVATE BATH IS ESSENTIAL? ☐ YES ☐ NO

SHARED BATH IS ACCEPTABLE? ☐ YES ☐ NO

IF YOU HAVE ANY SPECIAL REQUIREMENTS PLEASE INDICATE:

CANCELLATION POLICY: EACH INN HAS ITS OWN CANCELLATION POLICY. ALL CANCELLATIONS MUST BE MADE DIRECTLY WITH EACH INN.

Bed & Breakfast
P.O. Box 420009
San Francisco, CA 94142

- -

Please fold along dotted line

RESERVATION FORM *CAREFULLY REMOVE OR PHOTOCOPY*

GUEST NAME & ADDRESS

NAME

ADDRESS

HOME PHONE #

WORK PHONE #   FAX #

CREDIT CARD INFORMATION *VISA OR MASTERCARD ONLY*

TYPE OF CARD

CARD #

EXPIRATION DATE

SIGNATURE

PLEASE LIST THREE (3) BED AND BREAKFAST INNS IN ORDER OF PREFERENCE CODE # IS LOCATED IN THE CORNER ABOVE EACH INN

BED & BREAKFAST INN #1

NAME

CODE #

YOUR DESIRED PRICE RANGE:
FROM $ TO $

BED & BREAKFAST INN #2

NAME

CODE #

YOUR DESIRED PRICE RANGE:
FROM $ TO $

BED & BREAKFAST INN #3

NAME

CODE #

YOUR DESIRED PRICE RANGE:
FROM $ TO $

RESERVATION INFORMATION: *PLEASE INDICATE YOUR ACCOMMODATION REQUIREMENTS BELOW*

ARRIVAL DATE:

OF NIGHTS REQ'D

OF ROOMS REQ'D

OF BEDS REQ'D   #____ ☐ DOUBLE   #____ ☐ TWIN

DEPARTURE DATE:

OF ADULTS IN YOUR GROUP

OF CHILDREN IN YOUR GROUP

INDICATE APPROX. ARRIVAL TIME (2 HOUR SPAN)

PRIVATE BATH IS ESSENTIAL?   ☐ YES   ☐ NO

SHARED BATH IS ACCEPTABLE?   ☐ YES   ☐ NO

IF YOU HAVE ANY SPECIAL REQUIREMENTS PLEASE INDICATE:

CANCELLATION POLICY: EACH INN HAS ITS OWN CANCELLATION POLICY. ALL CANCELLATIONS MUST BE MADE DIRECTLY WITH EACH INN.